DEMANDING RESPECT

DEMANDING RESPECT

THE EVOLUTION OF THE AMERICAN COMIC BOOK

Paul Lopes

TEMPLE UNIVERSITY PRESS
Philadelphia

TEMPLE UNIVERSITY PRESS
1601 North Broad Street
Philadelphia PA 19122
www.temple.edu/tempress

Text design by Kate Nichols

∞ The paper used in this publication meets the requirements of the American
National Standard for Information Sciences—Permanence of Paper for
Printed Library Materials, ANSI Z39.48–1992

Library of Congress Cataloging-in-Publication Data

Lopes, Paul Douglas.
Demanding respect : the evolution of the American comic book / Paul Lopes.
p. cm.
Includes bibliographical references and index.
ISBN 978-1-59213-442-7 (cloth : alk. paper) — ISBN 978-1-59213-443-4 (pbk. : alk. paper)
1. Comic books, strips, etc.—United States—History and criticism.   I. Title.
PN6725.L67 2009
741.5'973—dc22   2008043806

2 4 6 8 9 7 5 3 1

Contents

Acknowledgments

During the years leading to the publication of this book, Michelle Bigenho has been a pillar of support as I managed balancing my personal and professional lives in the world of an itinerate academic. She was always there when I most needed her. I would like to thank all my colleagues in the Sociology and Anthropology Department at Colgate University who eventually provided me a permanent home. Without their support this book would not have been possible. I would also like to thank Michelle and James Ennis for their insightful comments on my book manuscript. My project also was made possible with the hard work of my research assistants Kathryn Phillips and Katherine Martin. I deeply appreciate my editor Micah Kleit's patience and support in getting me through this book project. The production of this book also was made possible through a generous grant from the Research Council at Colgate University. Finally, I must thank all the wonderful fans and artists in the world of comic books whose work and words made this book possible; and whose efforts have made the American comic book the great art form that it is.

Introduction

The Evolution of the American Comic Book[1]

It is striking how over the last seven years comic book culture seems to have captured center stage in American popular entertainment. Hollywood seems addicted to this culture, churning out blockbuster film after blockbuster film based on a superhero or another comic book genre. The entertainment industry has also borrowed from comic book culture to create new prime-time television series. Children's television is not immune either, particularly with the huge popularity of Japanese animation, but including American superheroes as well. And let's not forget those nifty video games! Over the last few years, the San Diego Comic-Con, the largest comic book convention in North America, has become the premiere gathering for anyone interested in pushing the newest in electronic popular entertainment. Top Hollywood stars arrive at the convention to hawk the newest pulp Hollywood product. Meanwhile, journalists from newspapers and magazines swarm around the convention to discover why "geek" culture now defines the universe known as pop culture. It seems that popular culture has gone comic book crazy.

But what is most striking about the newfound interest in comic book culture is the decidedly minor presence of actual comic books. While comic book and science fiction fans at the San Diego Comic-Con now have a cachet as arbiters of the newest cool pop entertainment, the biggest entertainment industry players are promoting video games, television shows, and films. Fans, publishers, artists, and dealers at the convention are buying, selling, discussing, and celebrating comic books as they have since the convention began in 1970. But the mainstream of the culture industry seems less interested in the quaint old printed form of comic books. This makes sense. There is not a lot of money to be made selling comic books compared to the profits in other media. While comic books were one of the most popular forms of entertainment in the mid-twentieth century, they have since suffered a steady decline. By the late 1980s, many claimed the comic book no longer was a *mass medium* in the sense that it no longer enjoyed a mass market of readers. By this time, comic books had receded into a subculture of fans, specialty shops, and conventions. Comic books no longer filled the racks at newsstands or convenience stores like in the past. By the end of the last century, some feared the American comic book was on its way to extinction. And while the last seven years have seen better times for American comic books, most consumers of popular culture have little interest in reading them.

This lack of respect for the actual comic book medium is not new. Even during its heyday as a mass medium in the 1940s and 1950s its popularity was equally matched by a deep suspicion of its cultural value and social impact. Comic book artists were considered hacks compared to artists illustrating or writing for comic strips, illustrated books, or popular fiction. Virtually all comic book artists remained anonymous. Many preferred it that way. And the very popularity of comic books among children and adolescents proved to many the dangers of a popular entertainment they considered lowbrow and of extremely poor quality. Critics accused comic books of everything from damaging children's eyesight to promoting juvenile delinquency. Such fears led to an anti–comic book crusade in the late 1940s and early 1950s, sparking lists of unacceptable and acceptable comic books, government hearings on the comic book menace, and even a few comic book burnings.

This crusade forced the comic book industry into a retreat in the mid-1950s. It imposed a self-regulatory code that eliminated any comic book that might corrupt the mind of an innocent child or young teenager. While readers of all ages actually enjoyed comic books, the perception in the popular imagination of comic books as a children's medium won over this reality. And where once the comic book faced the stigma of being a danger to the youth of America, after the new code, it faced the stigma that it could not conceivably be anything but a medium suited only for children or readers suffering from arrested development. The idea that comic books had the potential to engage older teenagers and adults with serious stories and graphic art seemed preposterous. That comic books could be hip, socially relevant, or mature forms of popular fiction would probably elicit a raised eyebrow and a laugh. The idea that comic books could be as "literary" as the finest American literature would probably elicit an angry glare from a member of the cultural cognoscenti. For most of its history the American comic book could get no respect.

While official culture held the comic book and comic book artists in such low regard, certain individuals in the 1960s began demanding respect for this art form and its artists. Some comic book publishers began to target a new generation of older teen and twentysomething readers with new hip and socially relevant comic books. A comic book fandom appeared dedicated to celebrating past and contemporary comic books and their artists as worthy of adoration and respect. Out of the counterculture came underground "comix" artists who radically transformed comic books with adult material from the most profane to the most political. And over the next four decades, artists continued to expand the medium to rival the best in popular fiction and the best in literature. Over the same time period, comic book fandom also continued to grow.

Unfortunately, all the moves by publishers, artists, and fans to demand respect for comic books happened for the most part "under the radar" of official culture as this art form moved into a marginal subculture in the late 1980s. At first, articles about comic books would occasionally appear in the press. Some articles were respectful, while most were written with a bemused patronizing tone. But over time the efforts of publishers, artists, and fans did eventually find an increase in respectful press coverage. At the beginning of the twenty-first century, one could argue that the efforts in the comic book field to have comic books taken seriously had made tremendous gains compared to most of the twentieth century. Of course, one problem remained: catching the respectful attention of the press and official culture is not the same as convincing everyday readers who long ago abandoned comic books to pick them up once again. And even if they were interested, most would have to find one of those small comic book shops hidden away in a nondescript suburban strip mall.

This book is a social history of the modern American comic book. While my main interest is in the various ways individuals since the 1960s have engaged in taking comic books seriously as an art form, their story only makes sense if we understand the history of the American comic book, beginning with its commercial birth in the 1930s. Comic books started with the crassest of commercial interests. They were produced in sweatshop, assembly-line fashion. And eventually they were subject to one of the most successful crusades of censorship in the United States. But the modern comic book would eventually be reborn and become the center of a vibrant, creative field of art. How this came about will tell us a lot about art, commerce, and the politics of culture in America. As the legendary comic book artist Will Eisner once said, comic books came from a humble background, were forced into a cultural ghetto, but did eventually rise up and demand as equal a respect as any other art form in America.[2]

Themes

This social history of the modern American comic book stretches over seventy-five years and resembles more a roller-coaster ride than the smooth evolution of a new art form from infancy to maturity. Of course no art form develops in a clearly determined path without its conflicts, disappointments, unexpected turns, or periods of crisis. But the comic book suffered such a willful low regard for most of its history, and its industry struggled so long to find some semblance of stability after its boom market ended in the 1950s, that demanding respect for comic books has covered a rather broad array of meanings, practices, and actors. Given this long, turbulent, and diverse history, I decided to present the social history of comic books in a more or less chronological order. This means that critical themes in understanding this history will often appear more than once. So I thought it best to present these analytical themes from the outset. While these themes shape the basic structure of this social history, a chronological narrative allows me to focus in more detail on the evolution in the meanings and practices associated with the field of the modern American comic book.

Like my previous work on jazz, my method is to immerse myself in the discourse and practices surrounding a field of art to guide my analysis.[3] The core of my study of comic books, therefore, relies on analyzing the discourse on comic books over time. This analysis focuses on two basic cultural fields. Following the framework of John Fiske, I analyze the evolution of comic book discourse in both "official culture" and the "subculture" of comic book fandom.[4] "Official culture" refers to the discourse about comic books outside the field of comic books, that is, the reception of the American comic book over time in the press, trade books, and professional as well as academic journals. The discourse of the comic book subculture provides an alternative story of the modern American comic book developed by those committed to celebrating and transforming what they consider a great artistic medium. This discourse is in the large compendium of books, articles, interviews, and Web sites in comic book fandom. The power of this alternative story is that it emerges from a collective dialogue among fans, artists, and publishers in the comic book field. In many ways, the ultimate question in demanding respect for the comic book is to what extent this alternative story crossed over into the comic book discourse of official culture.

Fields of Art: Heroic and Industrial Ages

I refer to the period from the 1980s to the present as the "Heroic Age" of comic books. I borrow this term from the French scholar Pierre Bourdieu and his analysis of French literature in the mid and late nineteenth century.[5] Bourdieu called this period a "heroic age" because this is when writers generated "principles of autonomy" in the French literary field. These principles claimed independence from the "rules of art" governing this field at the time: the power of commercial markets and elite patronage to determine the economic and symbolic value of books and their authors. French writers and critics were able to revolt against these rules of art by forming their own "restricted subfield" of production where they could create independent criteria for determining the best in French literature. The first rumblings of this rebellion began during the bohemian revolt against bourgeois culture and art in the mid-nineteenth century by artists like the French writer Charles Baudelaire. This bohemian revolt while charismatic was unfortunately less than systematic. Bourdieu argued, however, that over time an artistic subfield governed by the principles of autonomy first articulated in the bohemian revolt did gain a coherency that made it a permanent part of the literary field. So by the late nineteenth century, staking claim to artistic autonomy became a recurring theme in French literature.

In the 1960s, comic book fandom and underground comix represented the first rumblings of rebellion in the comic book field. Both movements challenged the rules of art in this field where the culture industry simply produced an industrial product with no other value than quick consumption and equally quick disposal. Comic book fandom developed an appreciation beyond the mere consumption of comic books. These fans were not simply readers of comic books, but avid collectors as well. Their deep affection for comic books led fans to develop an expert knowledge and also to elevate comic book artists as celebrated creators of this art form. Underground comix artists, on the other hand, initiated a new movement in comic books that rejected commercial success as the only measurement of achievement. They also rejected the idea of comic books as merely purveyors of popular entertainment. They created comics expressing their own personal visions for a sophisticated young and adult audience. Fandom and comix, however, were initially separate movements in comic books—each approaching the modern American comic book in radically new ways. And similar to the bohemian revolt in French literature, these early movements were not part of a coherent subfield of comic book production. In the 1980s, however, these new approaches to the comic book merged into a more coherent comic book subculture similar to the restricted subfield in the Heroic Age of French literature.

This new comic book subculture marked the beginning of the Heroic Age of comic books. In this subculture, artists, fans, critics, and publishers developed their own set of criteria to judge and appreciate comic books and comic book artists. Also, like nineteenth-century French literature, principles of autonomy emerged in the world of comic books. Against the rules of art in comic books before this age, these new principles rejected the subordinate position of artists in the comic book field. These principles asserted that artists' talents and unique visions were central to the world of comic books. While these principles of autonomy were articulated in a number of different ways during the Heroic Age, depending on the artist, publisher, or fan, in general they transformed the comic book field as a whole. This broad transformation in the rules of art in comic books was made possible in part because, unlike the restricted subfield of French literature, the new restricted subfield of comic books in the 1980s was the dominant market for all comic books: there was no larger commercial mass market for comic books. This new comic book subculture, therefore, significantly determined the economic and symbolic value of comic books and their artists during this new Heroic Age.

The period before the Heroic Age is what I call the "Industrial Age" of comic books. It coincides with what comic book fandom calls the Golden, Silver, and Bronze Ages of the American comic book. Comic books from the mid-1930s through the 1970s were created under a different context than the Heroic Age. It was a period of ingenuity, creativity, and risk-taking. And the period produced a cultural legacy that we continue to enjoy today. But the rules of art were driven by one simple overriding rule: if it sells, keep selling it, and find as many ways to sell it in slightly different packaging. Such a rule has been applied during the Heroic Age, but in the Industrial Age this was the golden rule with no equally compelling ones. It was an age of a mass market where readers, for a period, seemed to have an insatiable demand for comic books. An assembly-line process was essential to produce product for an ever-expanding market and to generate greater and greater profits. There were no principles of autonomy among artists during this age, nor was there an interpretive community to apply independent criteria of judgment to comic books as an art form beyond simply commercial success. Certainly artists during this age had criteria to judge their craft of writing and illustrating, but with no principles of autonomy in the field of comic books they remained mostly craftsmen producing a mass product judged by a very different set of criteria than during the Heroic Age.

The field of comic books from the 1980s to the present has been heroic for another important reason. French writers and critics in the nineteenth century felt that the best and most authentic literature was besieged by market and other external forces. Individuals in the comic book subculture, however, felt the art form itself was under siege and wholly unappreciated. The 1980s to the present has been a heroic age in comic books because artists, publishers, and fans have fought heroically against the possible disappearance of the comic book. And they also have fought heroically for recognition, respect, and appreciation for an art form they believe is as imaginative and entertaining as any of the more popular arts or as serious and sophisticated as any of the more respectable arts. This makes the Heroic Age of comic books strikingly different than the Heroic Age of French literature as described by Bourdieu. Comic book heroes were not seeking to reject market forces or institutional consecration like their heroic literary brethren in nineteenth-century France. The comic book was so marginal and given such low regard that comic book heroes worked hard to regain a mass market for comic books as well as institutional recognition of the comic book as a legitimate art.

Bourdieu also argued that heroic ages in art are chaotic because the rules of art are undergoing radical transformation. The "social space" of an art form, like literature in nineteenth-century France, is no longer occupied with "ready-made" positions for authors to create their work, publishers to promote their books, critics to judge a work of art, or audiences to apply their likes and dislikes. Even the ready-made positions before a heroic age are subject to the chaos that prevails in this new social space. Positions are extremely "elastic" with futures "uncertain" and "dispersed."[6] Such chaotic fields of art invite individuals of different social backgrounds and dispositions to join in what Bourdieu described as "a sort of well-regulated ballet in which individuals and groups dance their own steps, always contrasting themselves with each other, sometimes clashing, sometimes dancing the same tune, then turning their backs on each other in often explosive separations, and so on."[7]

The Heroic Age of comic books was certainly chaotic in exactly this way. The end of the Industrial Age in some ways opened up the social space of the comic book field, since major commercial success in a mass market was no longer very viable. Only three old publishing houses, Marvel, DC, and Archie survived beyond the Industrial Age and they relied mostly on characters created during this earlier age. The field of industrial ready-made positions also was incredibly limited in terms of genres and artistic styles. Positions in this new social space, therefore, were to "be made" as artists and publishers attempted a diverse array of comic books in terms of graphic style, content, and genre. Artists even rebelled in "remaking" the industrial ready-made positions of the old publishing houses. Small independent publishers as well as a self-publishing movement appeared that allowed artists to create comics based on old genres, new genres, combinations of genres, or supposedly genre-free "literary" comics with styles ranging from the traditional mainstream American style to the avant-garde. The chaos of this new social space also provided openings for artists from social groups previously marginal to the field. Women, gays, and minorities joined the dance to make new positions or remake old positions in the field. And debates ensued as artists, publishers, editors, critics, and fans danced about the constantly changing positions in the chaotic field of comic books.

Out of this chaos, however, something miraculous happened. Comic books did become more serious, more complex, and more respected. And this was true from the most pulp to the most literary of comic books. To borrow a phrase commonly used in the general press coverage of comic books: comic books actually "grew up." While comic books originally were based on short stories in serial format, now comic books present long-arced narratives with complex story lines. Now the fastest growing market for comic books, graphic novels, presents this art in book-length format, again allowing for complex and compelling storytelling. Graphic novels also range from pulp fiction, literary fiction, autobiography, and history to even journalism. Graphic novels are reviewed regularly by *The New York Times* and *Entertainment Weekly*. More importantly, they are reviewed regularly by the *Library Journal* and *School Library Journal* as libraries have become one of the more important new markets for comic books. Comic book artists receive prestigious awards from the MacArthur Fellowship to the Pulitzer Prize. They even have their work displayed in art museums like the Whitney Museum of American Art in New York City. And, of course, there does not seem to be a moment when a comic book character is not gracing multiplex screens across the country. The future of the comic book as a respected art form has never seemed brighter, but as this book will show, it was a long, difficult road to respectability.

The Production of Culture

Of course the Industrial and Heroic Ages occurred in the "real" world of actual production, distribution, and consumption. The social history of the

American comic book is also about the way market forces, organizational structure, technology, laws, and government or industry regulation shape the aesthetics and content of an art form. It is also about the logics of cultural production and consumption: how artists and others approach the production of an art form and how audiences and others approach its appreciation and consumption.[8] From the culture of production perspective in sociology, the state of an art form—whether the popular art most commonly produced by mass media industries or the fine art most commonly produced in institutional and commercial art worlds—is less about any intrinsic qualities it may have, the breadth of talent available to realize its full potential as art, or the full range of audience tastes ready to enjoy it. The production of culture perspective is more about how other factors constrain or aid the development of the art form from the creative output of its artists to the access available for those who might want to consume it.[9] And the history of American comic books certainly bears this truth out as anyone in comic book culture would readily attest.

For both the Industrial and Heroic Ages of the American comic book, for example, the dominant logic of production has been the same logic found in most popular culture industries. Todd Gitlin best summarizes this logic as "recombinant culture"—innovation stems from copying or recombining whatever is successful at the moment.[10] In the culture industry, imitation is the sincerest form of flattery. The comic book industry's main concern in both ages has been to publish guaranteed product, and whenever possible, to exploit its properties in other media and consumer products. At the same time, however, the industry had to adapt this fundamental industrial logic to specific circumstances, whether a boom market, a threat of government regulation, a rapidly declining market, or a new comic book subculture. The basic question is how the adaptation of this logic by the industry affected the evolution of the comic book over its long history. So mainstream comic books did evolve more complex story lines and mature content. A star system of artists also emerged as comic book fandom's purchasing power supported the talents and visions of individual comic book artists. And mainstream publishers responded to the interests of comic book consumers as not only readers, but also collectors. But the basic industrial logic never changed as the dominant publishers during the Heroic Age depended on a few tried-and-true properties and genres, repurposed successful product from other media, and relied heavily on the licensing of their properties.

One of the more unique aspects of the social history of comic books was the transition in the 1980s from a mass market to what is referred to as a "direct" market. The old system of distributing comic books via magazine distributors to newsstands and other retailers was collapsing by the early

1980s. In order to survive, commercial publishers shifted to a new direct market based on special comic book distributors and comic book shops. Publishers relied on a new dedicated comic book subculture. Specialty retailers preordered nonreturnable comic books for their local comic book shops. So publishers were able to avoid the problems of overproduction, poor sales, and corruption in the old system. It is a commonly held belief in the comic book field that the direct market saved the American comic book. Unfortunately, this market also became a structural roadblock to ever regaining the mass audience comic books once enjoyed. And by the end of the twentieth century, with six years of declining sales, the direct market seemed more like an obstacle to the survival of comic books than an aid.

This transition to a direct market in many ways set the stage for the Heroic Age in comic books. It was mainstream publishers' dependence on this direct market that forced them to adjust their industrial logic to a new comic book subculture's criteria of judgment and forms of consumption during the Heroic Age. The new power of this subculture also empowered artists to challenge the rules of art in the comic book field as their individual economic and symbolic value increased within comic book fandom. These artists also were empowered by the entrance of independent publishers made possible by a niche, direct market where small publishers could more easily enter the field. Independent publishers and rebel artists, in other words, were able to challenge the old rules of art from the Industrial Age in ways that were not feasible in the declining mass market. The Heroic Age in comic books, therefore, was made possible because this fundamental reshaping of the comic book market allowed new forms of appreciation and new principles of autonomy to enter the field.

Again, what the production of culture perspective highlights is the way factors external to communities of artists, and their potential audiences, significantly shape art forms. Richard A. Peterson, for example, argues that the Rock 'n' Roll revolution in the 1950s was more about mundane changes in industry structure, technology, and regulation than either the creativity of a new generation of musicians or the power of a new generation of listeners.[11] And Herman Gray argues that the rise of black television shows in the 1990s was more about the competition of cable television and new broadcast networks, that is, a fundamental change in the structure of the industry, than a sudden desire in the television industry for a multicultural universe of prime-time programming.[12] So the question is how such factors as market forces, industry structure, technology, laws, or regulations affected the evolution of the comic book as an art form. More importantly, we will see how the opportunity space created by such factors in the comic book field in the 1980s both aided and constrained comic book rebels' attempts during the Heroic Age to transform the field's rules of art and to make the comic book a legitimate and respected form of art.

Demanding Respect: The Status of Comic Books, Artists, and Fans

When I started my research project in 2001, it was not unusual to find a perplexed look on the face of individuals when I told them I was doing an academic study on comic books—or at least a curious look from those unfamiliar with the world of actual comic books. In some ways, this very marginality or invisibility of comic books and comic book culture at the time was what attracted me to this study. As a sociologist I was interested in art forms during moments of radical transformation in their meaning and practice. I was particularly attracted to radical transformations in popular art where those involved believe they faced an uphill battle against a reigning orthodoxy that viewed this art form as less than respectable—or certainly not to be taken seriously. Of course in the case of comic books, it might not be disrespect for this art form that was the sole problem, but also a matter of its invisibility to most Americans. This was particularly the case for new types of comic books created during the Heroic Age of comic books—most peoples' memories of comic books remained locked in the Industrial Age.

In choosing comic books as my object of study I quickly found that "lack of respect" was the common lament of virtually all who have participated in the field of comic books. This lament was not simply about comic books' low regard, but the low regard toward artists and fans as well. Official culture until recently remained convinced that the comic book is an art form best for either childish humor or adolescent fantasy. Comic book artists also struggled in both the Industrial and Heroic Ages with the low status of their chosen field of art. Comic book fans, on the other hand, faced the stigma of collecting, cherishing, and taking seriously an art most considered childish. For most of comic book fandom, official culture looked with scorn or incomprehension at such cult-like devotion. Given the low status of the art form, its artists, and its fans, demanding respect in the field of comic books has had a wide-reaching significance.

Comic book fandom has not been alone in feeling a lack of respect for devoting so much time and energy into a popular art. Fandom of popular culture in general has received little respect from official culture. Joli Jensen, Henry Jenkins, and Matt Hills point to how fans of popular art have faced an official culture that views their fan activities as not only silly and inane, but views the fans themselves as somehow suspect, suffering from some form of arrested development or psychological pathology.[13] Other scholars have discovered similar views about popular art fandom.[14] And Matthew Pustz has dealt directly with the stigma associated with comic book fans.[15] More recent scholarship also has looked at how lack of respect exists *within* popular art fandoms as conflicts and distinctions emerge between competing subgroups and their activities.[16] Once again, Matthew Pustz discovered such distinctions between competing interpretive communities were quite apparent in comic book fandom.[17]

Of course, lack of respect toward popular culture in general was a common attitude of official culture for most of American history. Neal Gabler points to elite distaste in the nineteenth century for popular culture like pulp fiction.[18] Lawrence Levine and Paul DiMaggio also show how elites in the late nineteenth century created high art institutions to separate themselves from this popular art, its artists, and its audiences.[19] Bart Beaty and James Gilbert look at the continued elite disdain in the mid-twentieth century toward what critics at the time called "mass culture"—popular culture created by large mass media industries. Elites not only despised the lowbrow nature of mass culture, but viewed it as a potential threat to American culture and society. Beaty and Gilbert also show how comic books were framed by this mass culture debate.[20] In fact, comic books became the scapegoat of these fears over the power of mass culture in the 1940s and 1950s. This panic over comic books forced a radical shift in the evolution of this popular art form.

Historian Michael Kammen, however, argues that since the mid-twentieth century such cultural authority over popular culture has lost its power. And the distinctions between high, popular, and mass culture have lost some of their purchase—at least in terms of elite and middle-class views toward popular culture.[21] Sociologists have reached a similar conclusion about the "democratization" of American culture in the last half of the twentieth century.[22] In the 1990s, some sociologists even began to refer to the elite and middle class in the United States as cultural "omnivores." Elite and middle-class consumers not only enjoyed both high art and popular culture, but found unique social advantages in such omnivorous tastes. American omnivores' tastes, however, still distinguished them from the working-class American "univore's" taste for only the popular.[23] Therefore, the tastes of the elite and middle class still act as class markers against the tastes of the working class. And Bethany Bryson also found that certain low-status popular art was still less likely to be part of such omnivorous tastes.[24] This was usually the case for popular art associated with specific low-status consumers like country music or rap music.

The low status and stigma associated with comic books for a long time prevented the same reevaluation in official culture enjoyed by other forms and artists in popular entertainment. It also meant that comic books were certainly not enjoyed by most omnivorous consumers. This was due in part to the marginal nature of the comic book market. But it was also due to the stigma of comic books as subliterate art more appropriate for children and adolescents than adults. And again, this is about the entire art form. Scholars have shown how popular art genres like soap operas and talk shows continue to elicit the old disdain toward popular culture.[25] But until only recently, comic books have been as a whole mostly suspect in the eyes of official culture.

In the Heroic Age, individuals began demanding respect toward comic books, their artists, and their fans. But the comic book subculture remained marginal to official culture. When I started my research in 2001, many believed the comic book field was in a deep, life-threatening crisis. As if by some miracle, however, over the last seven years this art form and its subculture have caught the serious attention of official culture and have recaptured the popular imagination. The long struggle to gain respect for comic books seems to have actually made some progress. We will see that a number of changes over the last seven years have opened up a new social space outside of the comic book subculture. And this new social space has the potential to make the comic book a legitimate art form serving a new mass market of diverse readers.

Cultural Politics and Popular Culture

Another theme in this book is how the cultural politics of the American comic book also involved broader social and political currents. For scholars in cultural studies, mass media and popular art are crucial terrains for the articulation of larger social and political struggles.[26] Works in cultural studies have emphasized how economic, political, and social currents translate into the cultural terrain such as the conservative politics in Britain and the United States in the 1980s or the identity politics in the United States in the 1990s.[27] Cultural studies scholars argue that cultural politics is an ongoing part of mass media and popular culture as discourses and representations constantly articulate the social, economic, and political landscape. My social history emphasizes moments when specific social and political currents were articulated in the field of comic books from the Industrial Age through the Heroic Age. The question is how such broader currents intervened in the comic book field to significantly shape its evolution as an art form.

During the Industrial Age, for example, Cold War hysteria in the 1940s and 1950s reinvigorated a social movement bent on the political and moral policing of American culture. This broader social and political movement inspired a more specific anti–comic book crusade. This crusade vehemently attacked comic books as socially dangerous and succeeded in significantly hindering the development of the comic book. On the other hand, the counterculture movement of the 1960s also was articulated in the comic book field as underground artists found a perfect medium to express their rejection of mainstream culture and promote their mission for free and authentic expression. This intervention in the comic book field also significantly affected the development of the American comic book. And during the Heroic Age, the new social space of rebellion in comic books articulated broader social and political currents of gender, race, and sexual identity politics in the United States. A comic book subculture dominated by white heterosexual males and their fantasy world was challenged by artists seeking a greater presence of females, minorities, and gays in the comic book field as wells as their broader representation in comic books.

Certain scholars in cultural studies, however, also emphasize how the mundane factors stressed in the production of culture perspective affect in part how such political movements are articulated in a cultural field.[28] In this sense, as Herman Gray argues, understanding cultural politics involves an analysis of the interaction between broader social, economic, and political currents and the specific structures and logics in a commercial popular art field.[29] The social history of comic books, for example, shows how structural change in the comic book field in the 1980s opened up the field to a broader array of social and political representations—a more open social space for the articulation of a more diverse cultural politics. But this history also shows how these structural changes, as well as the commercial logic of the field, ultimately limited the impact of this new cultural politics in comic books. The social history of the American comic book, however, also shows how broader social and political currents can generate a cultural politics that significantly transforms the structure and logics of a popular art field as the anti–comic book crusade fundamentally reshaped the comic book field in the 1950s. This history in general reveals the complex ways social, economic, and political currents can affect both the development and the ideological content of a popular art form.

Comic Book Culture

My book joins recent academic scholarship that addresses comic books and comic book culture as serious and legitimate objects of study. M. Thomas Inge and William W. Savage produced the first serious academic works on comic books in the United States.[30] These works addressed comic books as ideological texts from a critical perspective. British art historian Roger Sabin has written two histories on British and American comic books.[31] More recently Amy Kiste Nyberg and Bart Beaty have written on the anti–comic book crusade.[32] Bradford W. Wright has written a social history of mainstream comic books focusing on the relationship between their changing content and American culture.[33] Recent works by Matthew Pustz and Jeffrey A. Brown have looked at contemporary comic book culture.[34] And with the introduction in 1999 of the *International Journal of Comic Art*, a number of scholars have approached comic books from across the disciplines.

Academic scholars, of course, are not the only individuals writing about comic books. A number of authors have written general trade books on the history of comic books, for example, Gerald Jones's *Men of Tomorrow: Geeks, Gangsters, and the Birth of the Comic Book*.[35] More importantly, however, individuals in the field of comic books and comic book fandom have created a large collection of writings on comic books and comic book culture. This work is obviously both primary and secondary material in my study. Published work in the comic book field is an important part of the alternative discourse in the subculture of comic books that challenges the low status of the field. This literature also provides a rich source on the history and aesthetics of comic books in America. A glance at the most recent academic scholarship also will show that without the long and hard work of writing about the world of comic books by fans, artists, publishers, and others in the comic book field, none of this academic scholarship would be possible. The low regard held toward comic books meant that it was up to those committed to this art form to write the history of the American comic book. It has been their heroic efforts that made this book possible.

The Boundaries of the Comic Book Field and Fandom

One very important note in the present social history of the American comic book is the international dimensions of the comic book field and comic book fandom. I have so far used "American" in designating the modern English-language comic book. This is because the field of comic books I address began and remained centered in the United States. But in reality, the development of the modern English-language comic book in the United States paralleled its development in other English-speaking nations. The Canadian market for most of the modern comic book's history was dominated by the commercial interests and comic books located in the United States.[36] And while a Canadian subfield of comic books appeared in the Heroic Age, it was interconnected with the same developments in the United States through a shared direct market and comic book culture. Given this strong connection between Canada and the United States during both the Industrial and Heroic Ages, I will refer to the comic book field as "North American" and its market as "North American" to acknowledge what was really the core geographic boundaries of the field.

Britain experienced a more independent development of the modern English-language comic book and established its own field of comic books beginning in the 1930s. But the British comic book market in the 1960s suffered an even greater decline than the North American comic book market. Britain eventually shifted to a direct market of comic books serviced by specialty comic book shops and North American comic books dominated this market and British comic book fandom.[37] The most important effect of this greater interconnection between Britain and the United States was the "British Invasion" of comic book artists in the United States beginning in the late 1970s and 1980s. So English-language comic book culture during the Heroic Age had become international in scope and rebel artists whether American, Canadian, or British shared the ideological discourse of rebellion found in the North American comic book field.

Demanding Respect

In choosing to do a major research project on American comic books, I also rediscovered my love for the art form. I never became a comic book fan, but as a young boy I was part of the Marvel Zombies who devoured Spider-Man, Fantastic Four, X-Men, Doctor Strange, and even Howard the Duck. I was a devout *MAD* magazine reader as well. I left comic books behind in the mid-1980s. My last major comic book purchase at the time was the groundbreaking *Batman: The Dark Knight Returns* series written by Frank Miller. I did purchase Art Spiegelman's Pulitzer prize–winning *Maus* when it was published as a graphic novel. But like many early readers of comic books, I moved on to other art forms. Of course, now I regret having left behind this wonderful art form. In reading the writings of fans, artists, and others in the comic book field, and returning to reading comic books, I was easily convinced of the incredibly creative, inventive, serious, and not so serious potential of a great art form called the comic book. I have become a staunch defender and avid enthusiast of contemporary comic books and the artists who dedicate themselves to creating them. It is unfortunate that I cannot include the great array of comic art created by comic book artists in this book. But I hope the following social history of the American comic book will not only enlighten you to the themes I have outlined here about artistic rebellion, the political economy of art, cultural status, and cultural politics, but also inspire you to pick up a graphic novel or comic book and discover how comic books have truly grown up.

1

The Early Industrial Age I

Pulp Logic and the Rise of the
American Comic Book

The Industrial Age of the American comic book began with the popular success of this new art form in the late 1930s. The comic book, of course, did not appear *sui generis*. The new comic book field in the Industrial Age replicated the structures and logics found in the popular culture industries of its time. During this age, the comic book field had a singular *industrial* logic that determined its structure and the practices that governed it. For those involved in producing this art form, it was simply a commercial entertainment product produced in an assembly-line fashion for a mass market. And for millions of readers, the comic book was simply regular, pleasurable entertainment. Without a doubt artists during this industrial age enthusiastically embraced this new medium of expression and developed a true craft and tradition of comic art. And this industrial age produced popular art that truly captured the imagination of millions of readers. But this singular logic in production and reception significantly determined the evolution of this new art form during the Industrial Age.

Not surprisingly, the Industrial Age and its industrial logic of production and reception covered the rise and fall of comic books as a commercial *mass* market. What comic book fandom calls the Golden, Silver, and Bronze Ages of the American comic book marked the beginning and end of the Industrial Age. The first modern American comic book appeared for sale on newsstands in 1934. But it was the phenomenal success of Superman's

1938 debut in *Action Comics #1* that sparked a boom in publishing that established a mass market for comic books. This mass market continued to grow over the next fifteen years until the boom peaked in terms of circulation numbers and readership in the mid-1950s. This can be considered the Early Industrial Age of the American Comic book. The late 1950s saw a stark decline in the comic book industry and marks the transition to the Late Industrial Age of the American comic book. The Late Industrial Age lasted three decades where the overall trend for the mass market of comic books was slowly declining numbers in terms of publishers, titles, circulation, and readership.

The Early Industrial Age, of course, generated the basic logic of production in comic books that formed what Pierre Bourdieu called the "rules of art" in an art field: the dominant practices in producing and consuming an art form.[1] The Early Industrial Age's assembly-line production of comic books meant that quantity and speed were the primary goals of publishers *and* artists. Publishers' main interest during the boom was exploiting the market to the greatest extent possible by flooding it with as much product as possible. And the new field was mostly filled with very young, working-class artists willing to work under less than ideal conditions, intent on producing as much as was humanly possible to generate a living. During the boom, young artists reveled in the excitement of a new industry and finding a livelihood at a time when few options were available to them. They never questioned, however, the working conditions of the field where publishers paid simple page rates and retained all ownership of an artist's work. And questions about the potential of this art form in terms of narrative and visual breadth, or as a vehicle for the personal expression of artists, were more or less nonexistent. This basic logic of production would remain virtually unquestioned until some rumblings, beginning in the 1960s, and the eventual rebellion in the field during the Heroic Age.

Pulp Logic and the Early Industrial Age

The modern American comic book was the progeny of three popular art forms in the early twentieth century: comic strips, film animation, and pulp magazines. One could trace the genealogy of *comic art* in the United States to the illustrated dime novels of the nineteenth century as well as eighteenth-century political cartoons, illustrated broadsheets, and chapbooks. But the immediate parentage of modern comic books was unquestionably the popular comic strips, film animation, and pulp magazines of the 1930s. And their influence was not merely formal in terms of content and craft, but also in terms of the industry, the market, and the individuals who first made the modern American comic book a great success.

Newspaper comic strips would seem the most obvious influence on the comic book: the comic strip craft of combining paneled illustration with text is the fundamental craft of comic books. The comic strip had entertained newspaper readers since the 1890s.[2] It continued to grow in popularity into the twentieth century. Comic strips witnessed a boom of new strips and genres in the 1920s and 1930s. The first comic books in the 1930s actually were reprints of popular comic strips found in newspapers across the country. Early comic book artists' original work was unquestionably influenced by comic strips and their popular artists. And a number of artists who began in comic books eventually would produce newspaper comic strips.

The 1920s and 1930s also was an important period for American animation. The two powerhouses of Hollywood film animation were established during this time. The 1920s witnessed the formation of the Disney studio, while the animation studio of Warner Brothers made its mark in the mid-1930s.[3] Film animation characters soon found themselves sporting regular comic strips. And the Hollywood tradition of representation in animation certainly had a strong influence on comic books. Film animation not only contributed characters and the unique styles of their artists to very successful comic books, but it also established one of the most enduring and successful genres in comic books—funny animals. One of the most successful comic books in overall circulation in the history of comic books was the funny animal comic book *Walt Disney's Comics and Stories*.[4]

The field of pulp magazines, however, had the greatest direct influence on the structure and rules of art in the new field of comic books. Pulp magazines were the popular fiction of their time and reached their peak of popularity in the 1930s with genres ranging from adventure to romance to science fiction.[5] Most of the publishers that established the comic book as a mass medium were, or had been, involved in the highly profitable pulp industry. The four most successful publishers of comic books in the United States, for example, were from the pulp industry: DC, Marvel, Dell, and Archie. Pulp publisher Harry Donenfeld created National Periodical Publications in 1938, which was the forerunner of DC Comics. Marvel Comics started out as Timely Publications in 1939 under the stewardship of pulp publisher Martin Goodman. Goodman's former associates in pulp publishing, Morris Coyne and Louis Silberkleit, joined John Goldwater to create MLJ Magazines in 1939. MLJ became Archie Comics in 1946 after the phenomenal success of their teen creation. Dell Publishing, under the leadership of George T. Delacorte, was a successful pulp magazine publisher beginning in the 1920s. Dell discovered gold in 1940 with its funny animal comic books featuring characters from popular film animation.

Other comic book publishers who helped establish the comic book market in the late thirties and early forties also came from the pulp industry. These publishers included Aaron A. Wyn, Ned Pines, Wheeler-Nicholson, Billy and Roscoe Fawcett, Lev Gleason, and T. T. Scott. Even the old nineteenth-century pulp publishing house Street and Smith entered the comic book market in 1940 with their pulp characters The Shadow and Doc Savage.[6] In general, most comic book publishers, even with no previous background in pulps, quickly adopted the industrial logic that these pulp publishers brought to the comic book industry. As comic book historian Mike Benton points out, the early comic book field was fundamentally shaped by the formulas, genres, and commercial practices of the pulp field.[7]

The influence of pulp magazines also came from their overflowing presence in newsstands at the time. So it is not surprising that comic book producers borrowed from pulp narrative and illustration as well as the more popular pulp genres. Most comic book genres during the Industrial Age were straight from pulp literature: adventure, romance, western, crime, science fiction, horror, jungle, detective, teen, and war. Even the most successful genre in comic books, the superhero genre, was a hybrid of adventure, hero, and science fiction. Comic book writers and illustrators were heavily influenced by pulp fiction. The dominant tradition of "realism" in comic book illustration came from illustration found in pulp magazines or pulp comic strips. These artists also eventually incorporated elements of the sexuality, violence, and gore found in the more lurid pulp magazines. The "good girl" art of scantily clad and well-proportioned females found in comic book art during its Industrial Age came from the pulp tradition of illustration. Comic book producers also borrowed the common pulp-strategy of publishing anthologies and creating character-based series. Comic book producers, of course, also borrowed the lucrative practice from pulps of licensing characters for use in other media or commercial merchandise.

Interestingly, another pulp fiction influence on comic books was through actual comic art. The comic strip began a transformation in the late 1920s. In its first few decades as an art form it was dominated by humor strips. This early dominance of humor strips explains the terms "comics" and "funnies" that came to refer to this form of panels of illustrations with text.[8] But in the late 1920s and the 1930s popular pulp magazine genres like adventure, detective, science fiction, fantasy, and romance began to appear in newspaper comic strips across the country.[9] So the transference of pulp fiction narrative, illustration, and genres into comic art was already underway before comic books. Comic book artists from the early years of the Industrial Age would refer to the great illustrators of pulp comic strip art like Milton Caniff, Alex Raymond, and Harold Foster as their role models. They also would consistently "swipe" from these famous pulp comic art illustrators in creating comic books.[10] The sexuality, violence, and gore of pulps, however, never made it into the more respectable comic strip; that translation of the pulp tradition into comic art was left to the comic book.

Pulp fiction in the 1930s was part of a long tradition of popular fiction in America including the dime novels and weekly story papers first popularized in the nineteenth century. The birth of pulp magazines in the United States is usually dated in the 1890s with Frank Andrew Munsey's *Munsey's Magazine* and *The Argosy*.[11] Pulp magazines slowly replaced dime novels and story papers as the main source for popular fiction leading to the Golden Age of pulp magazines in the 1920s and 1930s when more than a hundred titles could be found on newsstands.[12] The standard pulp magazine during this golden age was 128 rough-pulp pages with a slick-paper cover, containing about six short stories and up to two longer stories.[13] The tradition of popular fiction found in these magazines influenced not only comic books, but all forms of popular story narrative from popular theatre, to film, to comic strips, to radio, to finally television. One could easily argue that popular fiction was the parent of all subsequent forms of popular narrative. Most of the popular genres first created in pulp fiction would appear in film, comic strips, radio, comic books, and television. But comic books for a variety of reasons would be the true child of this tradition as the new field of comic books fully embraced the basic industrial logic of pulps.

To say the comic book industry was the child of pulp fiction is not meant to be derogatory of the comic book as an art form. Today "pulp fiction" in the popular imagination refers to the more sensational and seedy paperbacks of the mid-twentieth century. Collectors prize the often lurid covers of these pulp paperbacks. But the tradition of pulp literature is far older and broader than our contemporary memory of this medium. Edgar Allan Poe, Nathaniel Hawthorne, James Fenimore Cooper, Horatio Alger, Theodore Dreiser, Jack London, Upton Sinclair, O. Henry, Edgar Rice Burroughs, Dashiell Hammett, Raymond Chandler, and Zane Grey wrote pulp literature. Many popular icons—Buffalo Bill, The Hardy Boys, The Shadow, Tarzan, Buck Rogers, Zorro, and Sam Spade—appeared in dime novels or pulp magazines.[14] The defining feature of pulp literature was that it was *cheap*—a truly mass medium. In truth, pulp literature was *popular* literature.[15] Pulp literature was a creative and inventive art form geared to a mass audience. It happened to include material that more respectable book publishers and "slick" middlebrow magazines would never imagine publishing. These publishers published "literature" for a select readership of upper- and middle-class readers. Pulps published "entertainment" for the popular classes.

Another defining characteristic of pulp magazines as popular art was the field's logic of selling whatever the buyer desired. This logic of selling meant that conventional science fiction and mystery stories were accompanied by sordid crime magazines and risqué magazines of all varieties on newsstands across America. As for the more lurid magazines, pulp publisher Harold B. Hersey admitted in 1937 that "pulpwood paper is comparatively inexpensive; as long as there are people with publishing ambitions and the means to satisfy them, and certain strata among the public, we will find these sheets on the newsstands."[16] The logic of selling also included attracting the attention of as many potential readers as possible. This is what drove some pulp cover illustration toward alluring and sensational imagery whether a western, adventure, aviator, crime, detective, jungle, science fiction, or romance magazine. There were, of course, the more lurid fiction magazines as well, such as the pulp magazine *Spicy Detective*.

The pulp fiction field in general followed common practices found in most commercial popular culture. Ken Gelder points to a number of aspects of the logic in the field of pulp fiction commonly found in other forms of popular art. The use of thematic genres, for example, is a common logic structuring fields of popular art. Another logic is the reliance on serials based on popular characters. A company's brand name or a character's popularity also can be more important in defining a popular work than its creator. Success, of course, is measured in numbers more than critical acclaim. And finally, creators of popular art view themselves more as hardworking craftsmen than artists trying to create a unique, transcendental work of art.[17] In terms of popular audiences, their expectations of pleasure are also shaped by these same logics.[18] Pulp magazines, and their comic book progeny, closely adhered to these basic logics of popular art; other narrative popular arts, such as comic strips, radio, and film, followed similar aspects of these logics as well.[19]

The pulp field also shared one of the most important logics of the popular culture industry; what Todd Gitlin calls "recombinant" culture. In examining network prime-time television, Gitlin discovered that prime-time programming was mostly a recombinant culture based on the theory of "nothing succeeds like success." The dominant rules of art in television were to replicate previous successes with copies, spin-offs, or combining elements from the formulas of several successful shows to create a new one.[20] Such logic, however, had been part of commercial popular culture long before the advent of television. Pulp fiction might even be considered the first industrial level of recombinant culture in American popular art.

According to pulp publisher Hersey, it was "a common practice, neverthe-less, in the pulpwoods, to eye a successful magazine venture, then bring out one almost exactly like it in title and make-up. The ones who complained about this most vociferously are the worst offenders. Contents are likewise imitated . . . It is part of the game . . . Again, I might repeat that imita-tion is still the sincerest form of flattery among publishers, especially those engaged in the pulpwood business."[21]

But recombinant logic works not only within a single medium such as pulp magazines, it acts across media as well. The common practice of "repurposing"—translating a success from one medium to another—is also an example of recombinant culture. The repurposing of pulp characters and series, for example, was common in comic strips, film, radio, and of course, comic books. And pulps also repurposed. The highly popular pulp maga-zines *The Shadow* and *The Lone Ranger* were repurposed from successful radio programs. And both characters would find themselves in film serials, comic strips, and comic books. Eventually *The Lone Ranger* became a highly successful television program as well. One might argue that the 1930s to the 1950s was a "golden age" of recombinant culture with pulp fiction, comic strips, radio, film, and comic books repurposing at a pace even an evil mad scientist would envy.

Like other popular art forms, pulp fiction's success also was based on pro-viding a regular diet of "new" product to a large mass market. And the pulp market was far less constrained in terms of production, distribution, and sales than competing media such as comic strips, radio, and film. This meant that for pulps quality definitely played second fiddle to quantity in terms of the pulp stories created by freelance writers or the assistants in the "fiction factories" of top-producing writers. And writers were paid by the word! In the 1930s, most earned one or two cents a word. Rates could be as low as half a cent, while a few top writers commanded five to ten cents.[22] In a letter to *The New York Times* in 1935, pulp publisher A. A. Wyn estimated the market for monthly pulp magazines at approximately 125 titles, demanding one hundred million words a year (at a cost of $1,500,000), and attracting ten million Americans who put "down their hard-earned cash each month for their favorite magazine."[23] In his reminiscences of the pulp trade, writer Frank Gruber calculated the num-ber of words in weeklies, monthlies, and semimonthlies needed in the 1930s "to fill the hungry maws of the pulps" at 195 million.[24]

Pulp writers like Frank Gruber admired, and envied, the most prolific of their profession. The successful pulp writer Arthur J. Burks—named "King of the Pulps" in *The New Yorker* in 1934—was known to produce 250,000 words a month, three million a year.[25] Publisher Hersey in 1937 was clear about what made a professional pulp writer. "The professional disciplines himself to long, tedious hours at the 'mill,' the amateur has yet to go through the heart-breaking process of inuring himself to the grind. The professional can turn out a yarn on any subject of any length and at any given time . . . whereas the amateur is incapable of adapting his talents to a practical purpose. The professional has attained an objective state of mind about his work, the amateur still talks about inspiration and individuality in self-expression which are so precious to the serious artist and so utterly useless to the quantity writer."[26] The New York Times in 1933 also noted the practical, professional, craftsman-like approach of pulp writers in its description of a successful pulp writer. "Henry Bedford-Jones, one of the best known of the pulp-paper writers, starts work each morning in his home in Hollywood with a repeating phonograph blaring the same record over and over and five stacks of manuscripts on his worktable. He starts on one story, keeps at it until he hits an impasse, then shifts to the second."[27]

The pulp logic of production did see value in the reputation of certain popular authors. Such feature authors were well known to avid pulp readers. But authorship was a negotiable item in the pulp trade. Many writers, including the top of the trade, would use a number of pen names during their careers. One of the most prolific and successful writers, Frederick Faust, wrote under twenty-three pen names—he was notoriously known in the trade as actually hating pulp literature, preferring poetry, although he did pump out ten thousand words, around twenty pages, of pulp a day.[28] But given the nature of producing hundreds of stories in a variety of genres, sometimes in the same magazine, many successful writers used pen names. On the other hand, some publishing houses, particularly with bull pens of writers, had a policy of writers being anonymous and using names other than their own. As publisher Hersey demonstrated in his 1937 book on the pulp industry, editors and publishers were not looking for literary writers expressing their authentic selves in some muse-inspired moment, just craftsmen who could produce good product on a regular basis, under any name—unless the name had market value![29]

Those involved in pulps also were distinctly aware of their low status in the hierarchy of the literary field. Writers for middlebrow magazines like The Saturday Evening Post or Harper's Magazine were certainly hired pens, but they wrote for middlebrow magazines set between pulp magazines and more highbrow journals.[30] Hersey certainly complained about the elitism of middlebrow writers in the slick magazine market. "Too many writers who have been promoted to the smooth-papers are apt to look with scorn upon the pulpwoods where they got their start and earned handsome incomes as they gradually worked into more spectacular and even more lucrative markets . . . The men and women engaged in the profession of contributing to popular fiction magazines do not brag about the literary values involved in their stories; the smooth-paper gentry seem to forget that just as much hack writing goes into shiny-paper sheets as it does into any other branch of the publishing business."[31] Or as an irate pulp writer wrote to *The New York Times* in 1933, "The craftsman who fabricates wood-pulp stories differs from the occasional 'smooth paper' writer, who laboriously constructs one story a year and calls in his friends to rejoice ginfully at his breaking into print, as a deft and capable bricklayer differs from his unprofessional brethren who slowly achieve a result by trial and error. One is an artisan, the other an amateur."[32]

All these elements of pulp logic were to translate easily into the new field of comic books during the Early Industrial Age. Like pulp publishers, comic book publishers were simply businessmen who focused on profits, not art, and certainly not artists. In the collective memory of comic book fandom, many early comic book publishers were not a particularly generous or honest lot of businessmen. Comic book fan and science fiction writer Ted White thirty years later in 1970 minced no words when he claimed "comic book publishers were, all in all, a thieving, grasping lot. Not to dwell too long upon the point, they were crooks . . . The first rule was, do it cheap. Find cheap labor, pay cheap prices. Low overhead. Tie up as little money as possible."[33] Gerald Jones, while less fanatic, certainly confirms that publishers were mostly hard-driven businessmen oriented to the less than aboveboard practices inherited from the tough industry of pulps.[34] Comic book historian Mike Benton also notes the sleight-of-hand tactics publishers employed, including publishing under a variety of names and imprints for financial and legal reasons.[35]

During the early years of comic books, publishers were mostly centered in New York City. And they certainly would come and go. Benton points to the volatile nature of the field as dozens of small publishers in the 1940s and 1950s disappeared as quickly as they appeared. More than half of the forty-five publishers who entered the field by 1943 were gone only ten years later, although over twenty new publishers entered over that same ten-year period.[36] Comic book artist Gil Kane remembers that "most of the publishers were impulse publishers—guys who worked as distributors and decided to go into comics. Some publishers were already established who didn't have a comics department but overnight wanted a comics department."[37] Comic book artist Joe Simon remembers the many fly-by-night publishers during the first years of the comic book field, "It was not unusual for a publisher unfamiliar with the comic book business to take a fling at the field, fail, and come out with a profit . . . the new entrepreneurs: the cloak-and-suiters, investors from the garment industry, taking a fling at the media; the undercapitalized promoter and hustlers with desk space and an answering service. As a rule, though, these publishers were without talent, without savvy, and without a chance."[38]

And comic book artist Joe Kubert jokes about the first decade of the industry, "as a matter of fact, anyone who owned a closet could open a publishing office and was called a publisher."[39]

It was not necessarily by chance that the most successful publishers in the comic book field were those most connected to the pulp industry. The key to success was the national newsstand and rack distribution network of newsprint media that was also key to the pulp industry. National, for example, thrived in part based on owner Donenfeld's access to distribution with his own Independent News Company, formed when he was publishing pulps.[40] Other publishers had independent distribution like Fawcett. Independent distribution was particularly important since the American News Company dominated newsstand and rack distribution at the time.[41] In the late 1940s and early 1950s other comic book publishers would strike out on their own as booming sales allowed them to invest in independent distribution.[42] In the early 1950s, thirteen national distributors were involved in comic books, but American News Company still accounted for over a third of the titles distributed.[43]

The ease with which new publishers entered the market was possible in large part due to a system heavily based on independent comic book shops and freelancing artists and writers. Many publishing ventures were one-room affairs with simply an owner, editor, and possibly a secretary. While major publishers also had in-house art departments that used regular staff, high demand during the boom led even these publishers to outsource to shops and freelancers. The publishers paid a set price for a comic book created by a comic book shop, then packaged and published it for distribution and sale. Remember, the key was distribution. While some small shops serviced only one or two publishers, the more successful shops contracted simultaneously and over time with a number of different publishers. Comic shops ranged in size from large successful shops with over fifty associated artists and writers to smaller shops with only one, two, or three artists/writers. Comic book shops also used both regular, paid staff and freelancers. The shop system and freelancing provided two basic advantages: it allowed new publishers to enter at low cost and allowed established publishers and comic shops to quickly respond to higher demand for their products. An incredible number of comic books during the boom period of the late thirties, forties, and early fifties were created by these independent shops and freelance artists.[44]

The standard comic book during the boom was seven and a quarter inches by ten and a quarter inches. The regular length was sixty-four pages, although in the postwar period the length dropped to forty-eight, then to thirty-two pages.[45] They sported four-colored glossy covers and pulp paper pages. The average length of a comic book story was ten pages, but this varied considerably. The comic book had usually one text-based story, included along with other "fillers" like promotions for superhero clubs or advertisements for such things as muscle building and superhero merchandise. Cartoonist Jules Feiffer fondly remembers the early comic books "as glisteningly processed in four colors on the cover and flatly and indifferently colored on the inside . . . They didn't have the class of the daily strips, but to me, this enhanced their value. The daily strips, by their sleek professionalism, held an aloof quality which comic books, being not quite professional, easily avoided. They were closer to home, more comfortable to live with, less like grown-ups."[46]

Whether working freelance, in-house, or at a comic shop, creating comics was a collective effort involving the roles of editor, writer, penciler, letterer, and inker. Depending on the shop, department, or artist, artists could combine a number of these roles in creating a comic book or occupy a single specialized role like fine-tuning main characters or inking backgrounds. The standard production process for a comic book involved editors approving story outlines, writers writing approved scripts, pencilers creating rough drafts of comic pages and panels, letterers fine-tuning text, pencilers fine-tuning characters and background, inkers with black ink completing the copy, and editors reviewing the final copy. Special artists did the covers for comic books and writers provided the short text-based stories. The shop's or publisher's editor would review the final comic book and package it for printing. The coloring of comic book pages was done separately at the printers. The final step was the printers, through arrangements with distributors, sending the comic book to local wholesalers for distribution to retailers.[47]

It was this production system of publishers, comic shops, and artists that fed the great boom in the Early Industrial Age. The first newsstand comic book *Famous Funnies* appeared in 1934, but the boom really started in 1939 with the national sensation of Superman. According to Benton, twelve publishers had gambled on comic books from 1934 to 1938 with only eight active publishers by the end of 1938. But from 1939 to 1941, twenty-five new publishers entered the field.[48] And the national media by 1941 and early 1942 was noticing that something new was happening in American popular culture. In April 1942, both *Publishers Weekly* and *BusinessWeek* noted the new booming market of comic books with fifteen million sold monthly.[49] M. C. Gaines, one of the originators of the modern comic book and a successful publisher during the boom, reported in *Publishers Weekly* that 120 comic book titles were on sale, including monthlies, bimonthlies, and one-shots with an estimated sixty million readers. Gaines claimed that comic books had "tripled the output of some paper mills, of 6 newsprint rotary color printing plants and other printing and binding establishments," and supported "over 500 script writers and artists." He also boasted that five thousand comic book titles had been attempted since 1936.[50] *Spot* magazine in 1942 reported 140 comic book titles "crowding the newsstands," and noted that in "the course of a year their readers plank out for them a solid $18,000,000."[51]

While the long-term trend after 1942 was a general rise in titles, circulation, and sales, there were momentary bumps along the road with wartime shortages, postwar exuberant overproduction of magazines, scrambling when certain genres lost their appeal, or worse, dealing with vociferous critics, boycotts, and government actions.[52] By 1944 the top publisher National was publishing nineteen comic book titles with monthly sales of 8,500,000 copies. Its closest competitor Fawcett had eight titles with monthly sales of nearly 4,500,000 copies.[53] It's clear the war years did not stop the general boom from continuing. While titles slightly declined, circulation and sales continued to climb.[54] Immediately following the war in 1946 comic production picked up, Fawcett's executive Will Lieberson reported 150 titles on newsstands every month in *Writer's Digest,* and *Publishers Weekly* reported 45,000,000 in monthly circulation for the year.[55] The press in 1949 was reporting industry figures of sixty million in monthly circulation.[56] The boom would eventually reach its peak in 1954 with over eighty million in monthly circulation and boasting 650 titles with estimates of annual profits ranging from 100 to 150 million dollars.[57]

The boom period created a hectic pace of production to maintain the high number of comic titles. The assembly-line production meant a myriad of artists would work on a single comic book series, whether to keep pace with general demand or as artists moved between shops, publishers, and freelancing. Comic book publisher Fawcett actually celebrated its industrial logic of production in the general press. In the early 1940s its Captain Marvel had become the highest circulating comic book character: supporting four separate comic book titles totaling ninety issues annually. In 1942 Fawcett boasted in *Spot* magazine that "the World's Mightiest Mortal has brought mass-production assembly-line methods into the production of comic magazines. Though some leading comics are still written by one man and drawn by another, and there are even cases in which one man does both the story and the art work, no one writer and one artist can possibly put Captain Marvel through his paces 90 times in twelve short months. It takes a group of from six to ten writers—known as 'squinky writers' to the trade—to pen his adventures, and a team of a dozen artists to translate them into pictures."[58]

The frenetic assembly-line nature of the boom period is also celebrated in comic fandom and in the fond, or not so fond, memories of writers and artists from those hectic days. The term "sweatshop" is constantly used in interviews of early comic artists to describe the conditions of production during this time. Will Eisner remembers overseeing the Eisner and Iger comic book shop. "The shop was set up pretty much like an ancient Egyptian slave galley [laughs], and I'd be sitting at the end of the isle, beating the big drum [laughs]."[59] Comic book artist, and eventually publisher of DC, Carmine Infantino recalls his first time visiting the Chesler Studio:

> It was an old factory building, and there was this broken elevator, and it rattled its way up to about the fourth floor—it was a five-story building. And as you got off the elevator, you faced a brick wall. In front of the brick wall was Harry Chesler sitting with his cigar in front of an old, broken-down desk, puffing away . . . to your right there was a larger room where about five or six artists and letterers sat, and did their art work. That was it. But they worked most of the day, they didn't talk much. They rarely kidded around, not that much, because Harry would be sitting out there watching everybody, and puffing his nickel cigars.[60]

The Jack Binder Shop was notorious for its sweatshop conditions as well as its rather poor-quality product. Boards had check-off boxes on their backs so artists could check them when their task was done and hand it off to the next artist.[61] Infantino also remembers the Binder Shop in New York City. "They were big factory rooms, huge rooms, with guys at desks lined up, one in back of the others, just rows of them drawing away."[62] Gil Kane remembers the Binder Shop on Fifth Avenue "just looked like an internment camp. There must have been 50 or 60 guys up there, all at drawing tables . . . It was exactly like an assembly line. You could look into infinity down these rows of drawing tables."[63]

The "art" of comic book making during the Industrial Age like in pulps was speed of craft and quantity of work. Early comic book artists reveled in the hard work, long hours, and craziness in the early years of comic books. A common story was how a new comic book, sporting brand-new superheroes and other characters, was invented over a single weekend with a clear deadline from the publisher to have a packaged comic book by Monday. Jules Feiffer evokes the crazy pace and excitement of the early days:

> The work was relentless. Some men worked in bull pens during the day; free-lanced at night—a hard job to quit work at five-thirty, go home and free-lance till four in the morning, get up at eight and go to a job. And the weekends were the worst. A friend would call for help: He had contracted to put together a sixty-four-page package over the weekend—a new book with new titles, new heroes—to be conceived, written, drawn, and delivered to the engraver between six

o'clock Friday night and eight-thirty Monday morning. The presses were reserved for nine. Business was booming. New titles coming out by the day, too many of them drawn over the two-day weekend.[64]

While a few writers and artists in the early years had spent time in the pulp industry, most writers and artists during the boom started off very young. They were predominantly white, male, and from working-class families. Many artists were still in high school or dropouts when they started their first job in comics. And many artists, and publishers, were from lower status ethnic immigrant communities at the time, especially the Jewish community.[65] The first years of the comic book field were during the Great Depression, so artists, young and not so young, were willing to be exploited and poorly paid.[66] Will Eisner remembers how hard times led artists to accept their fate as comic artists. "We had just emerged from the Depression. Comic book artists were grateful for what they could get . . . The comic book artists grew up in a field which regarded them as unnecessary. We were always told we are replaceable. Everybody knew and understood that if you didn't like the rates, the payment, you would go and they would replace you."[67] Golden Age Fawcett editor Rod Reed remembered how "guys who were trying to make a living writing comics really had to bat out a lot of pages to make a decent income . . . Artist's rates were low, too. They had to turn out a lot of work and stay up late nights and give up many dates to meet deadlines . . . If you were hungry or thirsty, you signed."[68] Infantino comments that the Binder Shop artists "weren't making good money. But that was the way of the world in those days, and everybody just accepted it."[69]

Women artists were few in number in the early years before the war, but there were a few women artists working in comic shops. World War II would lead to a large number of young male artists running off to war, so the number of female artists increased significantly. In Trina Robbins and Catherine Yronwode's history of women in comics, they note that it was unlikely that before World War II more than a dozen women on average worked each year in the comic book field, but during the war and immediately after this number tripled regardless of a high turnover rate. But by 1950, women comic book artists had again dropped back down to their prewar numbers.[70] And while a few women artists worked on action heroes, particularly women action heroines in scanty clothing, most were consigned to work on teen, career, and romance comic books.[71] The comic field was unquestionably a male-dominated field.

With all this frenzied work, artists would earn on average five dollars a page, from a low of two dollars to a high of ten dollars, either based on a page-rate system or on a weekly salary. The average artist earned ten to twenty dollars a week. A very few top artists, however, like Joe Simon and Jack Kirby, were bringing in five hundred dollars a week by the early forties.[72] The war years saw average salaries increase slightly, up to fifteen dollars a page.[73] But low pay was virtually all the credit writers and artists received for their hard work. Most artists remained anonymous. As C. C. Beck, who drew the first Captain Marvel comics, later complained, "We had to wait forty years for recognition. Many of the artists and writers and editors died unknown and unhonored."[74] Benton points out that writers and artists for specific comic titles constantly changed over time, so crediting artists made no sense.[75] This constant change of artists was a result of not only an assembly-line production where artists were easily interchangeable, but also because writers and artists constantly moved between projects and changed jobs hustling for better money.[76]

For comic book fandom, the greatest sin of this era was artists signing away the rights to their original work. Reed remembers the anonymity and lack of rights for writers and artists at Fawcett. "No, they didn't permit an artist to sign his strip and they didn't give writers bylines. A printed statement on the back of your check said you waived all rights to anything you did."[77] Only the very top artists could squeeze high salaries or some royalties out of their creations. And here we run across the infamous case in comic book history of the creators of Superman, Jerry Siegel and Joe Shuster. Their loss of "creator's rights" and battles with National over royalties are legend in comic fandom. They agreed in 1938 to sell the rights of Superman to National for a ten-year contract with a weekly salary of 130 dollars to produce the comic book. When Superman began generating a million and a half dollars in profits in only a few short years, the artists were able only to negotiate profits of seventy-five thousand dollars annually from National, which they used to support their art studio in Cleveland. The artists remained bitter and eventually sued National in 1947 for their rights to Superman. They lost in court, settled all rights with National for ninety-four thousand dollars, and lost their jobs. But the battle for their creator rights continued, and even continues today after their deaths.[78]

Low wages, long hours, anonymity, and lack of creator's rights were not the only ways artists suffered under the industrial pulp logic of the comic book field. To say they got "no respect" would be an understatement. Comic book artists were certainly on the bottom of the graphic-art hierarchy and suffered from the stigma attached to comic books as subliterate fare for children, that is, for "moppets." Again Eisner remembers that "[c]omic book artists then were regarded both socially and in the profession as what the Germans called an *Untermensch*, a subhuman. It was not uncommon for those of us who were doing comic books not to say we were doing comic books; when we were at a cocktail party, we'd say we did illustrations. Cartoons. If you said comic books, some nice lady would stand there and say, 'Oh, really?' This is in very small letters in a large balloon. And then she'd say, 'How nice.' Second pause. And go somewhere else."[79]

Most young comic book artists had art training in high school and post-secondary art schools. Many artists came out of the Pratt Institute in New York City.[80] Their dreams were not to become comic book artists. Joe Kubert remembers that "[m]ost of the people who got into the comic book years ago really didn't have any intention of being comic book artists or cartoonists."[81] Will Eisner recalls the artists working for his shop. "All of them there, by the way, were there as a kind of stepping place, that was a first stop to either, hopefully, dreaming of becoming a syndicated cartoonist for the newspapers, or going into book illustration."[82] Comic book artist Marc Swayze tells the common tale of artists first trying, and then failing, to sell their original ideas for comic strips—a more respected and lucrative graphic art—with his attempt to sell "Judi the Jungle Girl." "And so I went, syndicate after syndicate . . . United Features, the New York News, McNaught, McClure's . . . my list was long . . . Judi and I didn't get our contract." He ended up as an apprentice with comic strip artist Russell Keaton before landing a job at Fawcett making comic books.[83]

While being a comic book artist was not the most respected job, many writers and artists approached their craft seriously, even if others were just putting in time. Comic book artist C. C. Beck always viewed his Fawcett crew as the best in the trade and professionals committed to their craft. "My theory is that at Fawcett we had professional, experienced editors, writers and illustrators, while at other places they had a bunch of illiterate, untalented klutzes. We all used the principles we had learned in other work when producing Captain Marvel stories and art, which we regarded as simply another form of popular literature."[84] Marc Swayze also praises Fawcett artists. "I discovered it to be an unsung, specialized field of commercial art that included people trained and experienced in other artistic endeavors. Those at Fawcett were talented and competent . . . and they were smart."[85] While most comic artists applied a craftsmanlike pride to their work, they were quite aware it was not "Art." Joe Kubert points to the basic view of early comic book artists, "I think the majority of the guys who did comic books years ago approached it as a job."[86] Jack Kirby agrees with Kubert, "I felt at the time that I really didn't want to be a Leonardo da Vinci. I didn't want to be a great artist, but I loved comics and I wanted to be better than ten other guys . . . It was a skill, and it was my way of earning a living . . . We were factories, and we were turning out products thick and fast because they wanted books rapidly and steadily."[87]

The field of comic books during the boom period certainly followed an industrial pulp logic of production. Publishers, editors, writers, and artists were working hard to satisfy the seemingly unquenchable demand of comic book readers. It was assembly-line production where the product or brand, whether Superman or Captain Marvel, Dell or Fawcett, meant more than the names of writers or artists. Only Superman's Siegel and Shuster received any major attention as artists during the boom. It was simply popular entertainment. It was not important if comic book artists enjoyed the stories they wrote or penciled or inked as long as they got the job done.[88] The focus was assuring the flow of comic titles and stories week in and week out.

Without doubt the field of comic books during the Industrial Age, like the field of pulp magazines, showed an amazing dedication to recombinant culture. The very growth of the comic book market was based on recombinant logic. The history of this market was a series of genre bursts—a successful formula replicated quickly across the industry—repeated again and again as publishers continually looked for ways to expand what seemed until the mid-1950s an unlimited market for comic books. The first major comic book genre of superheroes came about from a recombinant logic that replicated Superman in virtually every imaginable way in an incredibly brief period. Comic book publishers and artists also were adept at the art of recombining successful formulas to create yet another successful comic book title or character like the romance and western genres giving birth to romance westerns or Superman and Mickey Mouse bringing forth Mighty Mouse. And comic book publishers would replicate whatever they could from other media like the popular *Green Hornet* radio program or the popular radio and film comedians Abbott and Costello. And comic book publishers were certainly happy to have their own original *licensed* creations appearing in pulp fiction, comic strips, radio, and film, or even on a plastic ray-gun. We will now see this recombinant culture at work in the next section on the evolution of the comic book as an art form.

Up, Up and Awa-ay! Comic Book Art

The birth of the modern American comic book in 1933 was not the result of a highly radical innovation. The first comic book simply repurposed comic strips in a pulp magazine format. Harry I. Wildenberg and M. C. Gaines, employees at the Eastern Color Printing Company in Waterbury, Connecticut, are credited with creating the modern American comic book. This company printed the colored newspaper comic strips for several major northeastern newspapers and also did color printing for pulp magazines.[89] In 1933,

Wildenberg came up with the idea that a standard tabloid-sized sheet printed from several seven by nine inch plates could be folded into a seven and a quarter by ten and a quarter inch stapled book of reprinted comics. The salesman M. C. Gaines sold the idea of this new book of reprinted comic strips as a promotional giveaway to Proctor and Gamble. They published ten thousand copies of *Funnies on Parade* for Proctor and Gamble in 1933.[90] The modern American comic book was born.[91]

The first few comic books were produced by Eastern Color Printing as premium giveaways for companies like Proctor and Gamble, Kinney Shoes, and Wheatena. Like *Funnies on Parade* these giveaways featured reprints of comic strips. Eastern and the pulp magazine publisher Dell Publishing quickly entered into a joint effort in 1934 to sell a comic book at retail. Dell ordered thirty-five thousand copies of *Famous Funnies* and distributed them in department stores where they quickly sold out at ten cents a book. But Dell was not convinced that this small success warranted continuing with this venture, so Eastern convinced the distributor American News Company to distribute this comic book in newsstands. American News ordered 250,000 copies. This new joint venture then released a new version of *Famous Funnies* (*Famous Funnies #1*) as an ongoing series in May 1934: it was the first ten-cent regularly published comic book title. While operating in the red for the first issues, *Famous Funnies* began generating profits by the following year. This first successful serial comic book remained in publication until July 1955.

Most of the first wave of comic books from 1934 to 1938 used reprinted comic strips. The aim in these first comic books was simply to repurpose comic strips to a new medium to squeeze additional profit from proven properties: the least creative logic of recombinant culture. These reprint comic books were anthologies populated with various characters and stories. They simply copied the diversity of comic strip genres found in the popular Sunday funnies, including humor, adventure, romance, detective, science fiction, and the western.[92] M. C. Gaines packaged three reprint comic books for Dell Publishing after it decided to test the potential of this new market once again. Newspaper syndicates also saw the potential of this new market. Both the King Features Syndicate and the United Features Syndicate published their comic strips in new reprint comic book titles. The success of these reprint books once again was demonstrated by *Famous Funnies* in the first half of 1938. The Audit Bureau of Circulation had *Famous Funnies* with an average monthly circulation of around four hundred thousand.[93]

The first wave of comic books did involve a few publishers who experimented with anthologies of original material. This approach, however, remained minor in comparison to the use of reprinted comic strips. But pulp writer Major Malcolm Wheeler-Nicholson's comic books *New Fun* (1935),

More Fun Comics (1936), and *New Comics* (1936) were good examples of how early comic book publishers borrowed from the pulp tradition in creating original material. These comic books featured original adventure, western, detective, jungle, teen, and science fiction. Wheeler-Nicholson also introduced the classics genre in these anthologies with stories like "Ivanhoe" and "Treasure Island." There were also pages of only text that were dedicated to covering popular topics found in pulp magazines such as sports, movies, hobbies, books, and popular science. There was even a letters section in *New Comics*. Wheeler-Nicholson also borrowed advertising genres from the pulps such as muscle-building ads like Charles Atlas. These titles, like most of the early comic books, had something for everyone in the variety of their material.[94]

A single-genre strategy, however, emerged as the dominant approach in the second wave of comic books that began around 1939. A few single-genre comic books appeared during the first wave. Wheeler-Nicholson's single-genre comic book first published in 1937, *Detective Comics*, actually remains the longest continuously running comic book in the United States. The second wave also was driven by original material as more and more publishers entered the field, helped along by new comic book shops. Oriented toward creating original material, publishers and shops relied heavily on recombinant culture in creating new single-genre titles. Publishers introduced a number of pulp genres during the second wave of comic books such as adventure-aviator, mystery-detective, crime, western, war, fight, science fiction, jungle, and teen. The other main strategy was directly repurposing successful popular art from animation, pulp magazines, radio, and movies into comic books. Most western comic books in the second wave, for example, were repurposed from comic strips, radio, and film.[95] The most creative strategy, however, was not replication or repurposing, but creating a hybrid of previously successful genres or formulas. The new hybrid superhero genre in this sense was the high moment of creative innovation in the field of comic books during the Industrial Age. This second wave of comic books and publishers generated a booming market in only a few years.

National became the undisputed leader in the second wave of new comic books that generated the boom market in the early 1940s. The pulp publisher Harry Donenfeld was one of the creditors for Wheeler-Nicholson's publishing venture. Faced with financial difficulties, Wheeler-Nicholson sold his interests in 1938 to Donenfeld who created National Periodical Publications. National published the most important comic book in the history of American comics. *Action Comics #1* came out in June 1938 and featured a new comic book character called Superman. The success of *Action Comics* and its new action hero was swift with monthly sales after the first few issues reaching five hundred thousand.[96] Within a year Superman had his own comic book. In 1941, National boasted a monthly circulation of nine hundred thousand for *Action Comics*, which still featured Superman, and a monthly circulation of 1,300,000 for *Superman* with annual sales of this series at 950,000 dollars. [97]

Superman was certainly a product of recombinant culture: a new hybrid born from pulp fiction and comic art. The creators of Superman, Jerry Siegel and Joe Shuster, were young science fiction fans and aspiring comic artists. Pulp fiction had already introduced costumed heroes in science fiction and detective comic strips and magazines like *Buck Rogers*, *Flash Gordon*, *The Shadow*, and the *Green Hornet*. Before the success of Superman, Siegel and Shuster were creating comic book characters for Wheeler-Nicholson. Their talent at recombinant culture was evident in their Dr. Occult series that deftly combined the comic strip characters the Phantom and Mandrake the Magician. Whatever other influences went into the creation of Superman, it was clear that Siegel and Shuster were perfecting the art of recombinant culture, dreaming of the glory of pulp success, and found their mark with Superman.

With the phenomenal success of Superman, National would follow the dictum that "nothing succeeds like success" by following a strategy of superhero comics in capturing the new market in comic books. Its two divisions, *Detective Comics* and *All-American Comics*, introduced superheroes in old titles and published a number of new superhero titles. Batman appeared in *Detective Comics* in 1939 and in his own comic book in 1940, joined by Robin, The Boy Wonder. *Batman* reached circulation figures of eight hundred thousand by 1941. [98] Of all the new superhero titles *Sensation Comics #1* in 1942 stands out in featuring another icon of American popular culture, Wonder Woman, who would have her own comic book later that year. By 1942 all National titles except for *Detective Comics* were all-superhero comic books.

Other publishers quickly recognized the success of Superman and the superhero strategy at National. This strategy unquestionably dominated the new field of comic books. When Martin Goodman formed Timely Publications (Marvel) in 1939, he immediately tried to cash in on what seemed to be a potential fad for superheroes. His first comic book *Marvel Comics* (1939) introduced the superheroes Human Torch and Sub-Mariner. Many of the more than ten comic book titles Timely published from 1939 to 1943 featured superheroes or costumed crime-fighters. [99] The most popular superhero in the 1940s, Captain Marvel, was created by the pulp magazine company Fawcett in their first comic book, *Whiz Comics*, in 1940. By 1942, he was joined by the other members of the Marvel Family: the Lieutenant Marvels, Uncle Marvel, Captain Marvel, Jr., Mary Marvel, and Hoppy the Marvel Bunny. With other new publishers joining National, Marvel, and Fawcett, literally hundreds of superheroes appeared, trying to capture the attention of young readers. According to comic book historian Mike Benton, by 1943 thirty-six publishers had published superhero titles.[100]

Replication, however, was not the only aspect of recombinant culture evident in the superhero genre burst in the early 1940s. Superheroes were repurposed too. National was quick in seeing the repurposing potential of its new Superman property. Superman quickly had his own syndicated comic strip in 1939 and his own radio program by 1940. Paramount Pictures was producing animated Superman cartoons in 1941, while Superman was licensed to over thirty consumer products of one sort or the other. There was even a Superman Club of America with certificates, code cards, and buttons. National claimed overall profits from Superman at 1,500,000 dollars for 1940 to 1941.[101] "Three times a week, millions of young spines tingle as Superman thunders hollowly over the air waves, 'Up, up and awa-a-y!'" noted *The Saturday Evening Post*. "His noble profile confronts them in two magazines and 230 newspapers with a combined circulation of nearly 25,000,000. That boy is growing rare who has no Superman dungarees in his wardrobe or no Superman Krypto-Raygun in his play chest."[102]

Other superheroes were repurposed in the 1940s. Spy Smasher, Batman, and Captain America appeared in Saturday matinee film serials, while Blue Beetle and Batman had their own comic strips. Blue Beetle even had a short-lived radio program. Unlike National, Fawcett was not as successful repurposing its widely popular Captain Marvel. Fawcett, however, did launch a successful Captain Marvel Club that claimed 573,119 members in 1944.[103] Fawcett publisher Roscoe Fawcett remembered what a huge endeavor it was to maintain the club. "Oh yes! We had to go out and rent an entire building just for the Captain Marvel Club . . . overnight! I couldn't believe the response we got; we were flooded with mail . . . all those dimes, quarters and dollars that came in! We had to hire six women who did nothing but open envelopes and empty out money. We must have had between 30 to 35 employees hired solely for the handling of the Captain Marvel Club."[104]

The only other genre strategy that created a burst of imitations during the second wave was a matter of repurposing too, but in the other direction. Funny animals were anthropomorphic animals popular in early comic strips like George Harriman's Krazy Kat, and they became a mainstay of film animation from Walt Disney's Mickey Mouse to Warner Brothers' Bugs Bunny.[105] Funny animal comic books began by repurposing successful animated film series or comic strips.[106] Dell Publishing obtained rights to Walt Disney Studio's animated characters in 1940. That year it published the first all funny animal comic book *Walt Disney's Comics and Stories*, which went on to be one of the most successful titles in overall circulation in the history of comic books.[107] It began as a reprint comic book, but within two years was presenting original material. Dell followed up in 1941 with Warner Brothers cartoon characters in *Looney Tunes and Merrie Melodies.*[108] Other publishers quickly caught on to the funny animal strategy repurposing film animation or creating original material. The success of funny animal comic books also led publishers to try funny people with a number of humor comic books such as *Comedy Comics* (1942).

The bursts of superhero and humor genre titles in the second wave of comic books revealed the future pattern of development for the market of comic books: a series of "genre bursts" expanding the market until its peak in the mid-1950s. So while various pulp genre titles appeared at the beginning of this market, such as adventure, teen, war, jungle, crime, and science fiction, the uncertainty of the new market led publishers in the second wave of comic books to rely heavily on the proven product of superheroes. Just like National Periodical Publications, which transformed itself into a virtual superhero brand, other publishers dropped potential genres to join the superhero bandwagon. So except for the funny animal and humor comic books, few genres created a slew of imitators in the early 1940s.

By 1944, the second wave of comic books established the comic book as a major form of popular entertainment. But who was reading comic books? Comic books were quickly associated with young preadolescent children. But in reality, while young children were the main market, comic books were being enjoyed by almost everybody. The Market Research Company of America in 1944 reported that 95 percent of boys and 91 percent of girls between the ages of six and eleven read comic books, while 87 percent of male and 81 percent of female adolescents aged twelve to seventeen read them. But 41 percent of male and 28 percent of female adults aged eighteen to thirty read comic books as well, with 16 percent of men and 12 percent of women thirty-one and older reading this new medium. The company claimed more than seventy million comic book readers with boys and girls reading twelve to thirteen comic books a month, young men and women seven to eight, and older adults six per month. These statistics were presented by Dr. Harvey Zorbaugh in 1944 in a special issue on comic books in the *Journal of Educational Sociology.* A defender of comic books, Zorbaugh exclaimed that comic books, "like comic strips, are read by all sorts of people who make up America—young and old, poor and rich, those who never got beyond the sixth grade and Ph.D.'s, soldiers and civilians . . . True, education and economic and occupational status somewhat influence the reading of comic books. But their influence is less than one might suppose."[109] While adults from all walks of life over eighteen read comic books, in the next wave of comic books publishers definitely aimed to beef up this market demographic.

The postwar period from 1945 to 1954 represents the third and final wave of the comic book boom. It was first marked by the fall of the superhero genre. By 1947, circulation numbers were declining for virtually all superhero titles. 1949 put the nail in the coffin with superhero titles disappearing from newsstands and superheroes like the Green Lantern, Sub-Mariner, and the Human Torch disappearing from the comic book universe.[110] Publishers initiated a variety of genre strategies to build successful titles and reach new audiences. The fall of the superhero led to genre bursts for previously tried genres like teen and war, as well as brand-new genres like romance and horror. Two major marketing strategies clearly defined the third wave. The first strategy was to retain the large base of young audiences. The second strategy was to tap into audience segments with further potential; whether adolescent female and male readers, as well as young, and not so young, female and male adult readers. These two strategies were an unquestionable success as the annual number of comic titles went from a low of 130 in 1944 to a high of 650 in 1954.[111]

Publishers in the third wave certainly did not abandon their most avid readers, children between the ages of six and eleven. New funny animal titles like *Funny Frolics* (1945) and *Animal Antics* (1946) continued to appear on newsstands in the postwar period and the genre remained strong throughout the boom period. Funny animal comic books were certainly bringing in the very youngest readers, but publishers also went for kids comic books in the third wave.[112] These comic books featured the funny adventures of little kids. The first star of third wave kid comic books was the character Little Lulu who appeared with her own title in 1945. Two of the most successful kid comic books appeared during this period: *Casper, the Friendly Ghost* (1949) and *Dennis the Menace* (1953).

Following the war, publishers also seemed intent on growing the audience of female readers of all ages for comic books. The biggest audience for teen comic books was young girls, so it was not surprising that a burst of teen comic books occurred in the postwar period.[113] Teen comic books were basically humor comic books featuring teen characters. Timely pursued the teen genre with a vengeance, beginning with career-teen comic books like *Tessie the Typist* (1944) and *Millie the Model* (1945).[114] It released over ten teen titles by 1947. Other publishers also joined the teen genre burst with titles like *Candy* (1947), *Dotty* (1948), and *Archie's Girls, Betty and Veronica* (1950).[115] According to comic book historian Trina Robbins, this genre burst led teen comic books to outnumber the more male-oriented genres of crime, horror, and superhero.[116]

The teen burst was quickly eclipsed by the new romance genre replicated from popular romance magazines. Romance comic books became the fastest genre burst in the history of comic books.[117] The first successful romance comic book was *Young Romance* (1947). The industry responded to its success with a storm of romance titles in 1949. One hundred titles appeared in 1949 with the words *love* or *romance* in their titles.[118] Over twenty publishers were pushing romances that year.[119] *Young Romance* was selling two million copies an issue by 1949.[120] *Time* magazine noticed the sudden barrage of romance comic books in August 1949. "Love is sweeping the country. On newsstands all over the U.S. last week, new-style comic books with such come-on titles as *Sweethearts, Romantic Secrets, Teen-Age Romances* and *Young Love* were out-selling all others, even the blood & thunder variety. The sexy, slick-covered romance-mongers—souped-up soap operas in new wrapping—were rolling off the presses as fast as publishers could think up names . . . America's girls & boys, aged 8 to 80, would soon have their pick of 100 love & romance books, published by two dozen different concerns, with an average press run of 500,000."[121] Timely became the king of romance, publishing over thirty titles between 1948 and 1954.[122] In 1950 over fifty new titles were added to newsstands with another sixty or more new titles appearing until the end of the boom in 1954.[123]

As Trina Robbins points out, romances covered a variety of themes to capture the female audience's imagination.[124] Given the over two hundred titles introduced during the boom it was somewhat unavoidable as the recombinant genius of publishers, writers, and artists went about creating the right replicated mix of style, story, and genre. Different publishers adopted certain house styles. Timely, for example, combined romance with drama and adventure, while other publishers went for a more sordid approach to romance comics.[125] But publishers were adept at trying any approach to generating a new title from *Hi-School Romances* (1949) and *Campus Love* (1949) to *Love Adventures* (1949) and *Love Mystery* (1950). They even tried linking romance to genres geared more for male readers like the western genre. Thirteen western-romances appeared in 1949 alone with such titles as *Frontier Romance* and *Cowboy Love*.

While publishers were successful in capturing the attention of millions of female readers, they were equally interested in male readers. Two genre bursts in the late 1940s were clearly geared toward male readers. The first of these genre bursts was the crime comic book. The crime genre quickly gained a reputation for its violence and gore, even if not all crime comic books emphasized this aspect of the genre. And this genre presented "true-life" crime stories and fictional crime stories. A veritable crime wave hit newsstands in 1948. Mike Benton notes that with only three crime titles in 1947, suddenly thirty-eight appeared in 1948 covering 15 percent of comic book titles for that year.[126] Another twenty-two new titles sporting the word *crime* on their covers appeared in 1949 and 1950.[127] This genre burst included titles like *Gangbusters* (1947), *All True Crime* (1949), and *Crime Can't Win* (1950). The second male-oriented genre was the western. This burst occurred in 1948 and 1949 with over fifty new titles.[128] This genre was built on both original material and repurposing successful characters and stars. Repurposed comic books of popular characters and stars included Red Ryder, Tom Mix, Gene Autry, Roy Rogers, and the Lone Ranger. But major publishers would produce a slew of new historical and fictional characters to shoot up the newsstands with titles like *Blazing West* (1948), *Kid Colt Outlaw* (1948), and *Wild West* (1948).

Between 1950 and 1953 three other genre bursts appeared in the comic book market. Entertaining Comics, best known as EC, launched the next genre burst with *Vault of Horror* (1950), *Crypt of Terror* (1950), and *Haunt of Fear* (1950). In the following two years a horror genre burst hit the market. EC also was involved in the final two genre bursts of the boom period: science fiction and war comic books. EC published *Weird Science* and *Weird Fantasy* in 1950 joining *Flying Saucers*, *Strange Adventures*, *Strange Worlds*, and *Captain Science*. Space became the major theme in 1951 and 1952 with eleven new titles about space, such as *Mystery in Space* (1951) and *Space Squadron* (1951). In 1950, EC also published the war comic book *Two-Fisted Tales*, which joined two other new war titles *War Comics* and *G.I. Joe*. But in 1952, the war genre burst with over thirty new titles with the words *war* or *battle* or *combat* on the cover.[129]

More evidence of the recombinant culture generating the development of comic books was the mixed-genre comic book, which was an important strategy of publishers in the third wave. As already shown with western-romances this strategy was most dominant in exploiting the booming female readership in comic books by linking other genres to the romance. But publishers also tried western-crime, science fiction–western, crime-horror, and even funny animal–science fiction. While genre bursts and their mixed genres dominated the third wave of comic books, there were other genres of comic books. For example, publishers repurposed media stars and stories from Hollywood film and radio in such titles as *Movie Comics* (1949), *Ozzie and Harriet* (1949), and *Dean Martin and Jerry Lewis* (1952).

During the boom a few attempts were made to publish comic books outside the pulp fiction tradition. Gilbert Publications published *Classic Comics* in 1941, later changed to *Classics Illustrated* in 1947. This comic book featured stories from the great classics of literature. *Classic Comics* had sold one million copies of its twenty-eight titles by 1946.[130] Yet, the pulp logic of the field saw no future in replicating classic literature. *Parents Magazine* also launched a campaign to make clean, wholesome comic books. This publisher released three wholesome comic books in 1941: *True Comics*, *Real Heroes*, and *Calling*

All Girls. The publisher boasted a combined circulation of 750,000 copies in 1942.[131] *Parents* published seventeen other wholesome titles between 1941 and 1950. But *Parents* stopped publishing comic books with the last June 1950 issue of *True Comics*. Religious comic books also were published. The most successful was the Catechetical Guild with *Topix Comics* (1942), which remained in publication until 1972.[132]

Alternative strategies like literary, nonfiction, and religious comic books, however, had little impact on the pulp logic defining the field of comic books during the Early Industrial Age. This section has shown how a series of genre bursts, based on an industrial recombinant logic of production directly borrowed from pulp fiction, defined comic books as an art form and as an entertainment. The development of the comic book occurred both in the breadth of genres that appeared and in the expansion to a broader readership. While comic books were enjoyed by readers from every age, gender, and walk of life, the third wave was important in creating a large female and adult readership for comics.

Conclusion

In the Early Industrial Age, the comic book field energetically embraced the logic of the pulp fiction tradition. As the field of pulp magazines faded into history in the mid-twentieth century comic books easily replaced them as readers' favorite popular magazine. By 1954, the 650 comic book titles found on newsstands dominated the magazine industry. And they provided avid readers with a menagerie of funny animal, kid, teen, romance, crime, western, war, horror, and science fiction comic books. The Early Industrial Age shows how the recombinant culture of the popular culture industries was the foundation of the pulp logic that fed this booming market of comic books. Whether the replication or remixing of old pulp genres in the series of comic book genre bursts, the successful repurposing of Hollywood animation, or the anonymity of the artists toiling in the assembly lines of comic shops, the comic book field fully embraced the industrial logic dominating the culture industries of the period.

The comic book also epitomized what new media scholars call "remediation."[133] A new medium usually begins by incorporating elements of previous media. It then articulates them with new elements particular to its own qualities of communication. In this sense, comic books were good old pulp fiction in a new comic art package. But remediation is not simply about the experimentation of formal elements of old and new media. As Raymond Williams argues, remediation occurs within a social and institutional context.[134] So the process of remediation of pulp magazines, comic strips, and film animation was not simply an aesthetic process of transferring elements of old media into a new medium. It was fundamentally shaped by the industrial logics of production, and the organizational structures, of previous industries, particularly the pulp magazine industry. To put it in another way, the commercial interests and commercial assumptions guiding the old industry of pulp magazines were "remediated" as well as the stories and illustrations found in pulp magazines. And this remediation of the pulp logic was to have considerable consequences for the comic book field.

The success of comic book publishers and their pulp logic unfortunately generated a barrage of criticism on the perils this form of popular entertainment held for American children of all ages. An interim report in 1955 to a congressional subcommittee made this point clear:

> It has been pointed out that the so-called crime and horror comic books of concern to the subcommittee offer short courses in murder, mayhem, robbery, rape, cannibalism, carnage, necrophilia, sex, sadism, masochism, and virtually every other form of crime, degeneracy, bestiality, and horror. These depraved acts are presented and explained in illustrated detail in an array of comic books being bought and read daily by thousands of children. These books evidence a common penchant for violent death in every form imaginable. Many of the books dwell in detail on various forms of insanity and stress sadistic degeneracy. Others are devoted to cannibalism with monsters in human form feasting on human bodies, usually the bodies of scantily clad women.[135]

Parents, teachers, librarians, ministers, academics, and politicians would make up a growing anti–comic book crusade dedicated to stopping this new deviant form of popular entertainment. And their ire would have severe consequences for the future of the modern American comic book.

2

The Early Industrial Age II

The Crusade Against Comic Books and the
End of the Comic Book Boom

*C*riticisms and fears about comic books appeared immediately following the popularity of this new medium. The rising voices against
comic books came from parents, librarians, teachers, and others worried about the avid comic book reading of young children and adolescents.
The rapid success of the superhero genre and the impressive rise in young
readers quickly placed in the popular imagination an association of comic
books with children. As Lovell Thompson wrote in the *Atlantic Monthly* in
1941, "That's what gets Kid-brother America to put up twelve million a year:
twelve million in greasy small coins, warmed by dirty small palms; twelve
million chivvied or cheated for, earned by sweat or by swindle."[1] Children
were the largest and most dedicated readership of comic books, but a large
number of adults read comic books as well. However, whenever surveys of
readership appeared in the press, the existence of adult readers was usually
treated as an unexpected surprise. This association with children made comic
books vulnerable to anxieties over their effect on the developing minds and
values of American youth.

The postwar genre burst of crime comic books only made matters worse.
The early criticisms and fears morphed into a nationwide crusade against
comic books. And western, romance, horror, and war comic books stoked the
fires even more. From the very beginning of the boom, comic book publishers
tried to assuage fears about their comic magazines. And they certainly took

notice of this postwar crusade. They even made some early efforts to thwart this rising tide of anger and the demand for censoring comic books. But they mostly counted the rising numbers in circulation and sales and continued to publish what readers seemed all too willing to buy. Eventually, however, the attacks of the crusade and government action became too much to bear and publishers finally acted collectively to self-regulate their industry.

Scholars Amy Kiste Nyberg, Bart Beaty, and James Gilbert provide the social context for understanding this anti–comic book crusade. Nyberg focuses on the defense of children's culture in America against the supposed ill effects of popular entertainment. Crusades over children's culture hark back to Anthony Comstock's campaign against dime novels following the Civil War. And in the first three decades of the twentieth century film found itself the object of fears about its effect on children.[2] Beaty views the crusade in light of the "mass culture" critique dominant in the first half of the twentieth century that held all popular art as suspect. It viewed mass culture as not simply lowbrow, but also dangerous. Mass culture was framed as a narcotic, a stimulant to violence, or a promoter of a totalitarian mind-set.[3] Gilbert takes a somewhat different approach than Beaty in viewing this crusade as more the unfortunate timing of postwar comic books with the periodic fears about mass culture during times of major social change in America. In this case, the postwar hysteria over juvenile delinquency found an easy scapegoat in comic books and the supposed anomic effects of mass culture.[4]

While Nyberg, Beaty, and Gilbert provide crucial insights on the anti–comic book crusade, they never place it in the context of what was clearly a broader movement of censorship in the postwar period. By ignoring this broader movement one fails to fully understand how the anti–comic book crusade became such a huge nationwide movement that successfully transformed the American comic book. From both a sociological perspective and a historical perspective the broader movement of censorship was crucial. Social movement theory in sociology provides us with an understanding of how a movement is able to mobilize so quickly and effectively at a national level. Resource mobilization theory emphasizes how social movements are possible, and successful, based on the organization and resources available for mobilization and action.[5] The anti–comic book crusade's success was based on religious and civic associations already in place, mobilized in a general movement of censorship around obscenity and anti-Americanism. Such broad censorship forms the historical context of the anti–comic book crusade. In other words, the comic book unfortunately found itself in the confluence of several social factors in the postwar period: the defense of children's culture, elitist views of mass culture, an obsession with juvenile delinquency, and a general Cold War movement of censorship. But it is the last factor that ultimately made the anti–comic book crusade one of the most successful movements of censorship in the history of the United States. This general censorship movement provided the organization, resources, and general dispositions to successfully attack comic books.

The crusade's success finally forced the comic book industry into self-censorship, radically changing the direction of the comic book field. The Comics Code of 1955 marked the end of the Early Industrial Age of the American comic book. Immediately following the implementation of the code publishers, artists, titles, and profits began to disappear. There were other reasons, of course, for the bad fortunes in the comic book field, such as the popularity of television. But the important point is that after 1955 the overall trend in the field was a declining market for comic books. And in response to the poor state of the field, the dominant publishers in the field would gradually commit themselves to a limited set of genres that helped further limit the diversity of comic book readers. The national prominence and success of the anti–comic book crusade, and the implementation of the Comics Code, also solidified the perception of the comic book as a subliterate, children's medium. And this stigma associated with comic books would continue to resonate with many Americans up to the end of the twentieth century.

Can Archie and Veronica Read?
The Early Debates about Comic Books

The early debates about the ill effects of comic books involved a more or less equal amount of detractors as well as defenders of this popular art. Detractors at times portrayed comic books as the greatest evil yet mounted against American children, possibly even turning them into little Nietzsches or Hitlers. As Margaret Frakes argued in the *Christian Century*, "superheroes are supposed to be dedicated to the service of freedom and democracy, their virtues and methods are purely fascist in nature."[6] Defenders of comic books, on the other hand, at times portrayed the fear of comic books as so much nonsense. Catherine Mackenzie, in the *New York Times* column "Parent and Child," remarked in 1941 that the "harmful influence of 'comic' books has been so vigorously protested by educators and by parent-and-teacher groups that some fathers and mothers begin to think that only a special providence saved their own nervous system from blood and thunder in childhood."[7] The core of the early debate was on the general effect of comic books on young children's physical, mental, and moral well-being.

In the early 1940s, comic books attracted the attention of the guardians of children's culture. And the main moral entrepreneur of this criticism was

Sterling North, literary critic at the *Chicago Daily News*. He wrote the first major attack in the press against comic books. His "A National Disgrace: And a Challenge to American Parents" appeared as an editorial in the *Chicago Daily News* on May 8, 1940. He did not mince words in his critique of comic books. "Ten million copies of these sex-horror serials are sold every month. One million dollars are taken from the pockets of America's children in exchange for graphic insanity. . . . we found that the bulk of these lurid publications depend for their appeal upon mayhem, murder, torture and abduction—often with a child as the victim. Superman heroics, voluptuous females in scanty attire, blazing machine guns, hooded 'justice' and cheap political propaganda were to be found on almost every page." But the stories and images were not the only problem. "Badly drawn, badly written and badly printed—a strain on young eyes and young nervous systems—the effect of these pulp-paper nightmares is that of a violent stimulant . . . Unless we want a coming generation even more ferocious than the present one, parents and teachers throughout America must band together to break the 'comic' magazine."[8] The following year North claimed in *National Parent Teacher* that forty newspapers and magazines republished his editorial, and requests for reprints averaged one thousand a day.[9]

Early critics presented a number of critiques of comic books. Some focused on the violent, sexual, racist, and graphic nature of the content. Thomas Doyle claimed in *Catholic World* that "gaudy" comic books introduced children "to an unreal world peopled by scheming sirens and cold-blooded murderers and are the worst possible education for children whose minds are too impressionable not to retain some residue of the dangerous non-sense poured into them."[10] Critics also viewed comic books as nihilistic or promoting a totalitarian mind-set. In *American Mercury* James Frank Vlamos was dismayed by superhero adventure comic books. "One epic of violence will perhaps be studied in future times in the adventure 'comics' which now load the newsstands . . . They live and struggle on a nihilistic level of colossal crimes, supreme scoundrels and supernatural avengers . . . the 'funnies' demonstrate all the arguments a child ever needs for an omnipotent and infallible 'strong man' beyond all law, the nihilistic man of the totalitarian ideology."[11]

Critics also condemned the unrealistic fantasy in comic books that seemed to mesmerize young readers, but little prepared them for the real world. Frakes claimed in the *Christian Century*, "Educators point out that the 'superman' element encourages daydreaming, convinces children that ordinary procedures are unworthy of consideration as ways of meeting problems, leads them to expect miracles instead of everyday means of solving difficulties."[12] The poor quality of comic books also was viewed as potentially harming children's eyesight. And the seeming addiction of children to comic books inspired fears they would never put them down and move on to dealing with reading good books and developing a high quality of mind. In 1941, *Time* concluded, "Young America now gobbles up about 10,000,000 comic books a month—an overseasoned, indigestible, nerve-shattering, eye-ruining diet of non-comic murder, torture, kidnappings, sex-baiting. Traceable to these hyperthyroid thrillers are many a midnight scream in the nursery, many a juvenile nervous tantrum."[13]

What was to be done? North suggested that the best antidote to comic books was good books. "Through the substitution of good literature for the trash which the children have been reading, we can stir the deepest feelings and emotions, contribute positively to active human experience, and help children identify themselves with fictional characters worthy of their name."[14] Others had more inventive solutions to wean kids off comic books. Nyberg and Beaty point to how this early criticism was hotly debated among teachers and librarians in their professional journals.[15] Teachers and librarians were concerned about subliterate comic books and their effects on the reading habits of children. Countermeasures against the ill effects included making lists of quality reading material with a similar appeal as comic books or focusing on children at their own literary and aesthetic level to guide them to better material.[16] One librarian labeled a few shelves "Heroes and Supermen" to suggest comic book material, but placed better children's books on them. She claimed it was a success![17]

Parents Magazine editor Clara Savage Littledale announced that the magazine's publisher had a different plan to attack the comic book menace:

> [T]o launch a new and different comic magazine . . . It is of the same size, the same general appearance as the other comic magazines. There are the same 64 pages of bright-colored pictures, the same patches of text. The difference is in the subject matter, which deals with current and past history . . . Every page in this new comic magazine is filled with action and excitement. But the heroes are not impossible characters . . . They are the men whom children should know and admire, with whose achievements they should be familiar . . . Instead of helplessly bemoaning the fact that children are devouring time-wasting comic magazines—the publishers of *Parents Magazine* have accepted the challenge inherent in the situation, and are seeing what they can do about it.[18]

Littledale was referring to *True Comics*, the first of the wholesome comics that appeared in the early 1940s to counteract what many felt was the pernicious influence of comic books. But Nyberg notes that educators and librarians had mixed views on whether this strategy was appropriate.[19] The article "Librarians, to Arms!" in the *Wilson Library Bulletin* voiced doubts about this strategy for already damaged comic book readers and argued that children's reaction to *True Comics* was "a pale imitation of the 'real thing.'"[20]

Academics quickly entered the fray of the comic book debate. Many of these academics were associated with the comic book industry. The industry brought them in as advisors and sought their help in studying the reading habits of children and the effects of comic books. Both Fawcett and National made use of advisory boards of academics.[21] And in 1941 National published a brochure, *Comics and Comic Magazines,* highlighting these findings. Overall, academics studying comic books found the fears of parents, educators, librarians, and others mostly unfounded. They found the fantasy element a positive aspect of comic books similar to old folktales or ancient myths; both traditions, they pointed out, also had violence and gore. They found comic books improved children's vocabulary and aided in the development of literacy. They also suggested that the use of comic books by parents and teachers could aid in the general intellectual growth of their children. While these academics published their findings in academic journals between 1941 and 1945, their findings and views appeared in professional journals as well as the general press.[22]

Catherine Mackenzie, in her regular "Parent and Child" column, picked up on the early research of academics. In March 1941, she discussed the work of Dr. Loretta Bender and Dr. Reginald S. Lourie, who "made a thorough study of children's reactions to contemporary folklore as represented in the comics . . . By and large they have come to the conclusion—from evidence too long to give here—that the comic book 'presents very little in concept and fantasy that is not present in the fairy tales the child encounters and must early learn to differentiate from reality . . . ' Maybe the authors have something there: the exploits of Perseus in decapitating Medusa gave some of us a turn in our time."[23] Their findings also were published in *Science News Letter*: "Let the children read the 'funnies.' Comics provide folklore of this modern age. Science finds that children need the lurid, blood-and-thunder adventures of Superman, Buck Rogers, the Bat Man, Flash Gordon, Popeye or the Red Comet, and their magic triumphs over space, time and gravity . . . Even the obviously emotionally unstable child should not be deprived of the possible benefits he will gain from reading the comics, these psychiatrists advised."[24]

Child psychologist William Moulton Marston defended comic books and his own creation Wonder Woman in the *American Scholar* in 1944. "This phenomenal development of a national comics addiction puzzles professional educators and leaves the literary critics gasping. Comics, they say, are not literature—adventure strips lack artistic form, mental substance, and emotional appeal to any but the most moronic of minds . . . But by these very tokens the picture-story fantasy cuts loose the hampering debris of art and artifice and touches the tender spots of universal human desires and aspirations . . . Comics speak, without qualm or sophistication, to the innermost ears of the wishful self." Marston compared comic books to old mythic traditions. He then mentioned how he entered the comics field in "the role of reformer. I was retained as consulting psychologist by comics publishers to analyze the present shortcomings of monthly picture magazines and recommend improvements." He goes on to list the "outstanding" authorities on National's advisory board and lets readers know that "the active efforts of these and others and the cooperation of the publishers, headed by M. C. Gaines, and his associates, have raised considerably the standards of English, legibility, art work, and story content in some twenty comics magazines totaling a monthly circulation of more than 6,000,000."[25]

Marston also mentioned the efforts of National in educational comic books and promoting literacy, another strategy used by publishers in defense of the business. National was at the forefront of this effort by comic book publishers. A 1942 editorial in *The Elementary School Journal* noted National's participation in these positive efforts, especially since the:

[R]apid increase in the popularity of comic magazines during the past five years has stimulated a great deal of thought and discussion among parents, teachers, and others concerned with child development . . . Several attempts are now being made to utilize children's interest in comics as a means to securing desirable educational goals. One such attempt is that of the Superman D.C. Publications, which are prepared with the assistance of an editorial advisory board including educators, child psychiatrists, and child-study authorities. The materials published include the Superman comic magazine and workbook and the Superman Good Reading Project. The workbook contains vocabulary exercises of various kinds in addition to the picture stories. The Superman Good Reading Project attempts to stimulate interest in reading library books through the use of posters and book lists.[26]

Academics and publishers were not the only ones defending comic books. Others found the fears surrounding comic books unwarranted, even if some comic books were as bad as critics believed. In a 1941 "Contributors Club" section of *The Atlantic Monthly,* Lovell Thompson, publisher at Houghton

Mifflin, agreed that in comics "there is some sadism, and a great deal of brutality. The themes and plots of the picture stories are completely formless . . . The kid brothers revel in it, just as their grandfathers reveled in the gruesome details of Grimm—and just as their grandfather's grandfathers reveled in the Old Testament . . . Let's not be too eager to take them from our children, brutal and supernatural as they may be."[27] Thompson would again defend comic book reading in a later article in the *Atlantic* titled "How Serious are the Comics?" Here he would add "that a few of the thoughtful people interested in child education have begun to point out that the children who read comics are also the children who read books. They are, in fact, simply children who read."[28]

The detractors of comic books were not very impressed by academic studies, public relations ploys, or the arguments of others. Margaret Frakes, in the *Christian Century*, expressed the general view of critics about these efforts to defend comic books. She found scholar Josette Frank's argument about comic books as modern day folktales ridiculous. "No better answer to Miss Frank's contention could be found than a reading of the gory pages of some of the magazines in this series." As for the educational efforts of comic book publishers, she also was adamant. "One has more respect, somehow, for publishers who frankly stress the 'thrill' of their offerings and leave all mention of education out of it."[29] Comic book publishers eliciting the aid of professionals to clean up their comic books did not impress Harold C. Field from the Parents Institute, which published *True Comics*. "Mr. Marston has tried to 'sell' worried parents on the harmlessness of the 'Superman' type of comics by hinting that there are 'don'ts' set up for writers and artists contributing to the comic books. The publicizing of these 'don'ts' serves as pretty window dressing, but it is a fact that the 'don'ts' are not lived up to by even the leading magazines in the field. The struggling magazines pay absolutely no attention to them."[30]

The early debates about comic books covered in the media were mostly before the start of World War II. Nyberg presents a number of convincing reasons why this debate never caught the momentum that the next phase of anti-comic book furor would. First, cultural critics and scholars were more focused on the new electronic media of film and radio. Second, right when comic books were becoming a national sensation and attracting negative attention a major war broke out, so more serious matters occupied everyone's attention. And her final reason is that in the postwar period comic books were linked to something more fearful than lurid content and poor quality: now comic books promoted juvenile delinquency.[31] The comic book also would become enmeshed in a postwar period of increasing censorship as an anti-comic book crusade resonated with the Cold War hysteria of the time.

The Postwar Movement for Censorship

It is important to set the postwar anti–comic book crusade in the context of a general movement of censorship in America during this period. Following World War II, censorship became a major public issue as various forms of print, ranging from serious fiction to textbooks to comic books, confronted growing attempts at censorship. The specific crusade against comic books, therefore, is linked to a Cold War hysteria that generated fears of a morally, socially, and politically vulnerable America threatened by oppositional voices and deviant culture. While the crusade against comic books had its own specific critiques of this popular medium, the resonance of this crusade with the American public, clergy, politicians, educators, and public officials was strengthened by the general Cold War hysteria at the time.

Paul S. Boyer argues in his book *Purity in Print* that the first half of the twentieth century was actually most remarkable for a gradual shift against censorship among cultural elite and professionals such as librarians, academics, lawyers, and judges. At first, this shift against censorship revolved around the question of obscenity, but just before World War II debate began to shift to include defense of political expression in fiction and nonfiction as claims of "anti-Americanism" were targeting books and magazines. This shift, however, in "liberal" elite sectors of the American public, and their success in circumscribing government intervention, generated a backlash in civil society that once intertwined with Cold War hysteria led to a moral crusade to rid America of seditious, obscene, and violent writing.[32]

Two crucial events related to censorship occurred before the war. The first was the establishment of the National Organization of Decent Literature in 1937 under the auspices of the Catholic Church. This organization was established after the success of the earlier Catholic National Legion of Decency's campaign against motion pictures. This new organization on "decent literature" would be one of the most important organizations during the censorship movement of the postwar period. The other crucial event before the war was the publication of *The Grapes of Wrath* by John Steinbeck in 1939. This classic work of fiction sparked avid attempts at censorship nationwide based on questions of obscenity and leftist politics. The level of attacks against this book led the Council of the American Library Association to approve the first "Library's Bill of Rights" in 1939. The association believed this declaration was necessary because of "indications today that point to growing intolerance, suppression of free speech and censorship affecting the rights of minorities and individuals."[33] This marked an important turning point in the library profession, a profession that previously had viewed its role as a gatekeeper of "good" literature.[34]

There were also attempts at this time to ban books considered "anti-American" in libraries and colleges. With the war, however, people's attention was redirected to other concerns. This was reflected in press coverage shifting to government censorship of news related to the war. The next major national debate on book censorship was reignited in 1944 when officials in Boston began concertedly to ban obscene material. It hit national attention with attempts to ban a book on interracial love titled *Strange Fruit*. Library journals, literary magazines, and opinion magazines almost unanimously condemned these efforts. *The Saturday Review of Literature* expressed the general view of critics of this censorship in its featured article "Boston is Afraid of Books" in 1944.[35] Attacks against *Strange Fruit* and other books rose over the next few years as publishers, booksellers, and librarians confronted a growing movement to ban serious literature with supposedly obscene content. The question of political censorship also arose at this time with the censoring of textbooks and the banning of the "left" periodical *The Nation* across the country beginning in the summer of 1948. Ironically this move was triggered by a *Nation* exposé in 1948 on the influence of the Catholic Church in the United States, including the "The Catholic Church as Censor" by Paul Blanshard.[36]

That same summer, *The New Republic* in the article "Burnings Next?" warned readers of the rising tide of censorship:

> Thus far, there have been no book bonfires in the U.S. Yet there are many developments throughout the country which look ominously in that direction . . . In California, the State Board of Education, under pressure from professional patriots, has been making changes in a series of books called *Building America*, published by the National Education Association . . . Philadelphia police, acting without warrants, raided 50 books shops and seized 2,000 books on charges of obscenity . . . The *Nation*, following a series of articles on political and social activities of the Catholic Church, has been banned from the public school libraries of New York and other cities, and from some colleges.[37]

The American Library Association, fearing the rising tide in censorship, reaffirmed a "Library Bill of Rights" at its national convention in 1948. It also formed seventeen state committees on intellectual freedom with hopes of forming similar committees in other states. *The New York Times* reported that the "question of censorship over-shadowed all others at the conference, which was attended by 6,000 librarians, educators and authors. Many of the spokesmen of the association were plainly worried by the trend toward censorship . . . Particular notice was taken of religious, political and govern-mental attempts at censorship. The librarians cited instances of interference by various individuals or groups, who, for various reasons, insisted that a certain book or magazine be withdrawn from circulation."[38]

Despite efforts to combat censorship, including court rulings against cer-tain attempts at banning books, the movement grew in momentum in the early 1950s. Matthew Josephson warned readers of the political ramifica-tions of the movement in 1952 in *The Nation*. "Sober reports of the Ameri-can Library Association *Bulletin* indicate that there have been "hundreds" of incidents throughout the United States in which self-constituted guardians of the public safety have taken action to remove, censor, suppress, or destroy teaching material or books deemed by them 'subversive' or 'un-American'."[39] The growing movement to ban books and magazines relied mostly on citizens and religious groups.[40] In 1952, *The New York Times* did a special series on attempts across the country to ban books. It noted how "self appointed com-mittees are being organized in many areas to 'screen' the books used by col-leges or by the general population . . . Voluntary groups are being formed in nearly every state to screen books for 'subversive' or un-American statements. These organizations, not accountable to any legal body, are sometimes doing great harm in their communities."[41]

Leading the political crusade were civic organizations like the American Legion. In her 1951 article, "Why You Buy Books that Sell Communism," Irene Kuhn made clear the secretive threat interwoven through American life for *American Legion Magazine* readers. "Each phase of American life and activity could be explored almost endlessly for proof of the success of this sin-ister foreign propaganda that has but one aim: the destruction of free, capi-talist society and the conversion of thinking, independent men and women into plodding mindless slaves . . . Books have become transmission belts for insidious propaganda for treason."[42] Religious organizations also were lead-ing the moral crusade in the early 1950s, including the National Organization for Decent Literature (NODL).[43] While officially NODL claimed their lists were only meant to aid Catholics in choosing appropriate reading materials, these lists were used by Catholic organizations and others in pressuring the removal of books from libraries, booksellers, and newsstands.[44] John Fischer criticized the efforts of NODL in 1956 in *Harper's*: "Its chief method is to put pressure on news dealers, drug stores, and booksellers, to force them to remove from their stocks every item on the NODL blacklist."[45]

That censorship rose as a major public issue and debate in the late for-ties and fifties was evidence of both a major crusade against literature and a major shift among many in the United States against censorship. I believe this reconfiguration of the debate around censorship in the thirties, forties, and fifties set the social context for the comic book to be the most vulnerable to censorship. This debate was reshaped along the old standing differentiation of the highbrow and lowbrow found in the mass culture ideology of the period. There was a cultural hierarchy in which arguments against censorship defended serious hardbound literature over paperback books over picture magazines over comic books.[46] And there was a cultural hierarchy between print and image where arguments against censorship defended literature over magazines with provocative images. And finally, there was the reconfiguration in censorship that defended the right of adults to virtually any content and focusing censorship in defense of vulnerable children and adolescents. All these reconfigurations would make the comic book the least defendable against censorship in America in the mid-twentieth century.

In 1955, former associate editor of *Harper's Magazine* Eric Larrabee noted the gradual shift in censorship to less legitimate forms of literature like pulp paperbacks. "The older or more established the medium, generally speaking, the greater the freedom from attack. When it is new, or exploiting a new audience, it must expect to be regarded as a potential outlet for the obscene . . . The common element in each instance is the status rivalry between the lower-middle-class censor, who feels responsible for the morals of the class immediately below him, and the aristocrat, to whom the threat to literature is as nothing compared to the threat of censorship."[47] Such an approach was confirmed by book distributor Samuel Black in an address to the Atlantic Coast Independent Distributors Association Annual Convention in 1952. "It is imperative that we free ourselves, without delay, from the constant fear that haunts us every time we put out a pocket-sized book which causes one to wonder what manner of diseased mind can contrive such tripe."[48] Or as Edward A. Weeks, editor of *The Atlantic Monthly*, informed his audience at a booksellers meeting in Chicago in 1953, "we can ask that our publishers raise their sights and respect our standards instead of pandering to the pulp market. We can show our disgust with the bosomy, blowsy novel whose heroine—to judge from the jacket—is always undressing or being undressed."[49]

By the early 1950s, the NODL also began emphasizing the policing of newsstands and bookshops for obscene paperbacks, magazines, and comic books. Reverend Thomas J. Fitzgerald of the National Council of Catholic Men pointed in 1952 to the NODL's "guide to individuals and groups who desire to take steps to minimize or eliminate the damage caused by objectionable literature, a list of objectionable magazines, pocket-size books and comics."[50] The prejudice toward censoring obscenity in more image-based magazines was evident too among Catholic groups' attacks against newsstands. A 1952 article in the *Christian Herald* lamented to its Christian readers that "all in all, filth adds up to a profitable business . . . Twilight publishers issue about one third of the 1,200 magazine titles that may be found on news-stands, and are powerful, even cocky . . . Your town can do a housecleaning job on its magazine stands—with or without police backing . . . It requires no great amount of literary acumen or Puritanism to label each and every one of these magazines as obscene."[51]

By the mid-1950s a number of books appeared defending intellectual free-dom and attacking the rising tide of censorship as undemocratic, irrational, and foolhardy. In 1955 several books were published critical of the censorship movement: *The Censorship of Books, The Right to Read,* and *Banned Books.* As the study "The Freedom to Read," commissioned by the National Book Committee, a committee organized by the American Library Association and the American Book Publishers Council, noted in 1956. "[T]here is now, much public agitation over the problem: various kinds of censorship were being proposed, and practiced, on various kinds of communications. Public officials and private groups sought to limit the freedom to read on various grounds, primarily political and moral. Battle-lines were formed between those who feared the effect, especially upon the young, of what they deemed to be subversive or immoral books, and those whose fear was rather of the damage to society itself resulting from the limitation of freedom inherent in such restrictions."[52]

So this was the general climate in which the more specific crusade against comic books grew in the late forties and early fifties. While so far we have seen censorship based on political viewpoint and obscenity, violence was to be the death knell for an uncensored comic book medium, although issues of sexuality would appear in condemning comic books too. Since comic books were viewed as children's literature, moral entrepreneurs were able to posi-tion them in the general hysteria of censorship as a morally corrupting influ-ence on children through violence, sexuality, and other supposedly antisocial behavior. With the Cold War hysteria in the late forties and early fifties giv-ing rise to a general fear of an exploding juvenile delinquency problem in America, moral entrepreneurs were able to position comic books as a major social problem demanding drastic action.

The Anti–Comic Book Crusade and Juvenile Delinquency

The postwar period witnessed a shift in emphasis and momentum in attacks against comic books. A nationwide movement emerged that truly could be called an anti–comic book crusade. John E. Twomey reflected on the rise of this movement in *Law and Contemporary Problems* in 1955. "No other medium of American popular culture has been subjected to such wide-spread, vehement and continuing attack as the so-called comic-books . . . the public outcry against crime and horror comic-books has persisted and now seems to have assumed the character of a permanent, grass roots, citizen's crusade . . . their elimination has become the cause célèbre of women's clubs, church groups, and community action organizations."[53] The level of attacks against comic books was truly remarkable. Even more remarkable was how the comic book industry weathered this storm for so long before events finally convinced enough publishers to enact a permanent code of self-regulation necessary to survive.

While the old criticisms of comic books persisted, they were quickly overwhelmed by a new framing of comic books as a social problem related to children's *identification* with the violent, criminal, and sexual behaviors and images found in the new, postwar comic book genres. Comic books now became active agents for deviant behavior. The greatest fear was that the epidemic of juvenile delinquency, which authorities assured the public was threatening the very foundation of American life, was a symptom of the wide popularity of these new comic books. Comic books now would be constantly linked to juvenile delinquency in announcements from various organizations and experts that would elicit a slow trail of news articles in the press. In 1947, for example, the Fraternal Order of Police, at its twenty-eighth annual national convention, passed a resolution that described comic books as "one of the contributing factors to the cause of juvenile delinquency" and as "unrestrained, bold, vicious, salacious and immoral."[54] Reports of copycat crimes inspired by comic books also would appear in the press.

The main clinical studies on juvenile delinquency and comic books were presented by the moral entrepreneur and psychologist Fredric Wertham. He launched a one-man crusade against comic books in the late forties and early fifties. His work with juvenile offenders eventually led to his total commitment to the role comic books had in juvenile delinquency. He always defended his work as not a simple deterministic argument that disregarded other social factors behind juvenile crime, but he clearly viewed comic books as a menace. His various writings, talks, symposiums, radio appearances, and interviews across the country made him the public figure of the crusade and its strongest advocate. The general reading public would be introduced to Wertham in two articles in 1948. The first was in *Collier's* in the article "Horror in the Nursery" written by Judith Crist.[55] And the second was his own article "The Comics . . . Very Funny!" in the *Saturday Review of Literature*. This latter article would be reprinted three months later in the *Reader's Digest*.[56] Both Nyberg and Beaty point to these two articles as the spark that quickly ignited the crusade.[57]

In "The Comics . . . Very Funny" Wertham begins with a number of stories of violent or criminal behavior of young adults, all who read comic books. He then presents a litany of more violent and criminal acts of young adults across America. "All these manifestations of brutality, cruelty, and violence and the manner in which they are committed—that is the folklore of the comic books."[58] He goes on to ridicule seventeen points in defense of comic books. And to bolster his argument he then attacks the defenders of comic books:

> The apologists of comic books, who function under the auspices of the comic-book business (although the public is not let in on that secret), are sociologists, educators, psychiatrists, lawyers, and psychologists. They all agree that this enormous over-stimulation of fantasy with scenes of sex and violence is completely harmless. They all rely on arguments derived from misunderstood Freud and bandy around such words as "aggression," "release," "vicarious," "fantasy world." They use free association to bolster up free enterprise. The worst sector of comic books is increasing and the best, if there is a best, is getting smaller. The comic-book publishers seduce the children and mislead parents.[59]

Wertham was not alone in discussing the new threat of comic books. The debate would reemerge in professional journals for librarians and educators as well as parents and religious magazines. In 1948 Ruth Emily Smith sounded the alarm in the *Library Journal*, stating that comic books "sold in greater numbers annually than books" and presented statistics showing comic book publishers in the ranks of the top magazine publishers in the country.[60] The link to violent and criminal behavior appeared in an editorial in the *National Education Association Journal* that same year.[61] By the end of the year, Jean Gray Harker, in the *Library Journal*, was calling for teachers and parents to act against the comic book menace. "So these are the comics, a misnomer if there ever was one. What are we going to do about them? Are we going to give up and let children read them! I will buy all the good books I can afford. I will encourage my children to go to the library, and I will discuss their reading with them. I'm going to talk to groups of parents in our local P.T.A.s. I shall ask conscientious parents and other citizens to urge swift passage of a state crime comic censorship law."[62] An article in the *Christian Century* in late 1949 alerted readers to local efforts to curb objectionable comic books.[63] And in 1950, Jesse L. Murrell warned readers of *Parents Magazine* that while many "parents, teachers, communities are upset about the comic books and the influence they are having on children today . . . they have taken no steps to evaluate the comics now on the market." His organization, Cincinnati Committee on Evaluation of Comic Books, stepped into the fray by developing their own list of rated comic books.[64]

The movement against comic books quickly accelerated across the country. *Newsweek*, in July 1948, reported on this sudden surge of hostility toward comic books. "Comic book publishers were feeling the pinch of two forces as midyear arrived. Educators, clergyman, and spokesmen for parents' organizations had made sweeping criticisms of comics which overplayed sex or glorified crime and criminals. Detroit police had stopped newsstand sales of some comic books. And in recent months a flood of new productions had increased the number of comic book titles to more than 450."[65] This movement would include law enforcement, city and county government, national civic organizations, local civic organizations, and local self-appointed committees. It would include both official and civic action against comic books. By 1949 state legislatures entered the fray and by 1951 comic books were being discussed in congressional hearings in Washington DC.

Law enforcement and local government either took legal action or threatened action if newsdealers and publishers did nothing to eliminate "objectionable" comic books. Thomas W. Ryan, director of the New York State Division of Safety, asked the New York State Sheriffs Association to "take action against comic books because of the relationship that 'clinical studies have shown between crime and comic books.'"[66] The National Association of Prosecutors joined other organizations and agencies in passing a resolution that strongly suggested "that legislation be adopted designed to prohibit the sale of objectionable crime, sex, and horror comics to juveniles."[67] The Los Angeles County Board of Supervisors passed an ordinance in 1948 with a fine or jail term for selling crime comic books to children under eighteen. *Time* reported, "Outraged by comics that piously headline their pages 'Obey the Law' while dripping with murder by meat cleavers, quicklime, axes and buzz saws, the Los Angeles County Board of Supervisors took action."[68] *The New York Times* reported in November 1948 that the "lurid type of comic books have become such 'a headache for city governments' that about fifty cities have taken steps toward regulation of sales, the United States Conference of Mayors reported today. These steps range from laws banning objectionable comic books to cooperative efforts among sellers . . . Emphasis on murder, mayhem, sex and glorification of crime constitute the 'new look' in comics for a large segment of this particular publishing industry."[69]

Civic and trade organizations also quickly moved to clean up comic books. *The New York Times* reported in September 1948 that the "National Council of Parents and Teachers today demanded that state laws be passed prohibiting objectionable comic books and urged the formation of local committees to evaluate comics, radio programs and motion pictures."[70] In November the same organization formed a national committee to "help wipe out" comic books.[71] Mrs. George C. Porter, Historian of the New York State Federation of Women's Clubs, declared at this organization's annual meeting "that if publishers would not improve their comic book material, 'it must be done by legislation.' She recommended censorship boards in each state to pass on comic-strip material similar to boards for motion pictures."[72] In 1949 delegates of the Council of the National Federation of Catholic College Students voted "to expand the fight against magazines featuring sex and glorifying crime. . . . the plan called for students armed with lists of what they consider offending publications."[73] The New York State Pharmaceutical Association in 1948 called "on its 6,900 member drug stores to ban the sale of comic books until the publishers guarantee that they comply with the standards of the National Organization for Decent Literature."[74]

Church and civic leaders and groups across the country urged government officials to take action and lobbied local newsdealers to take down "objectionable" comic books.[75] Many of these groups threatened to boycott retailers; and for those who complied, some groups even provided a monthly certificate of compliance.[76] Two major organizations provided lists of objectionable comic books used by individuals and groups fighting comic books. The first was the Cincinnati Committee on Evaluation of Comic Books formed in 1948. The Cincinnati Committee's list appeared in *Parents Magazine* beginning in 1950.[77] The second organization was the Catholic NODL; it joined the fight against comic books in 1947.[78] Besides distributing regular lists, however, NODL also distributed instruction manuals for local action in its general campaign against indecent literature of all varieties. These guidelines were intended to help local committees to organize Parish Decency Crusades and encourage other groups to participate in these efforts to promote decent literature. The template developed for local action that NODL put in place in its general campaign of censorship was clearly replicated for the anti–comic book crusade by Catholic and non-Catholic civic groups—policing of retailers, suggesting removal of books, threatening boycotts, and offering certificates of compliance.[79]

In late 1948 and early 1949 the press reported a few actual burnings of comic books. In Binghamton, New York, in December 1948 a "mound of 2,000 comic books and picture magazines" were burned "as students at St. Patrick's Parochial School sought to dramatize their movement to boycott publications which they say stress crime and sex."[80] In Albany, New York, that same month children of "S. S. Peter and Paul Parochial School made a bonfire of comic books that dealt with crime and sex."[81] In Rumson, New Jersey, Cub Scouts planned to burn comic books in January 1949, but local opposition to this book burning convinced them to donate them to the Salvation Army.[82] The burning of comic books, however, did not move beyond these isolated incidents.

In the late forties, it was clear this movement was growing and succeeding in censoring comic books either through official sanction or voluntary policing. At the end of 1948 *Publishers Weekly* noticed that the "public opposition to comic books—especially those which run to themes of crime and violence—has increasing repercussions. Local committees are formed . . . local ordinances are scanned or new ones proposed, and newsstands visited. These efforts are headed toward a general censorship which is as mistaken a plan for improving comics as it is in the case of newspapers, books, movies or radio."[83] Henry E. Schultz, Executive Director of the newly formed Association of Comic Magazine Publishers (ACMP), noted the hysteria of the moral crusade against comic books:

> Women's clubs, churches and civic organizations took up the cry and finally the great National Congress of Parents and Teachers with a membership of six million made the drive against comics a cornerstone of its national program . . . In towns, villages and municipalities throughout the country sheriffs, prosecutors, mayors, councilman and the law-makers were goaded and prodded into action and many did their best to please and appease the angry torrent which has been loosed . . . finally to cap the climax mass burnings of comic books were publicly held in several communities. . . . In almost one hundred communities some form of organized suppression of comic books appeared. . . . communities where legislation was not attempted, committees representing organizations and church groups threatened news dealers with boycott, and with the support of public officials embarked on programs to rid their states of "undesirable literature."[84]

The formation of the ACMP in July 1948 was a direct result of the growing crusade as publishers attempted to defend the industry. The ACMP was quick to get its efforts to self-regulate out to the general public. A *New York Times* headline announced "Clean-Up Started by Comic Books as Editors Adopt Self-Policing Plan: Publishers with Circulation of 15,000,000 a Month Approve Moral Standards to Overcome Objections of Critics."[85] *Newsweek* and *Time* also announced the new efforts of the industry. *Time*, noting recent attacks on comic books, claimed that the comic book industry "bending before this blast . . . agreed to a cleanup campaign of their own."[86] Readers of the *Library Journal* were also introduced to the efforts of publishers to clean up comic books and the new code.[87]

Unfortunately, the publishers who joined the ACMP represented less than a third of comic book publishers and the fourteen to fifteen million circulation of association members' comics fell far below the fifty to sixty million overall circulation reported at the time. A report from the United States Conference of Mayors in November 1948 made light of such an attempt by so few in the comics field and the nation's mayors remained unimpressed.[88] By early 1949 *Publishers Weekly* reported that major publishers National, Dell, Fawcett, Marvel, Harvey, and others left the association and rejected the code. National and Dell made clear they were not the publishers that needed to be policed. As Henry E. Schultz later testified before a U.S. Senate subcommittee, this effort at self-regulation eventually collapsed and the industry returned to its old ways, good and bad.[89] The year of the mass defections from ACMP brought more bad news to comic publishers as the Canadian Parliament passed a law to bar all crime comic books with up to two years imprisonment for violation of the statute.[90]

While comic book publishers felt the ire of Canadian legislators, they had at least one thing in their favor: the U.S. courts. Both Steve Mitchell and Edward L. Feder point to the importance of the March 1948 Supreme Court decision on the appeal of bookseller Murray Winters's conviction in New York City.[91] Winters was arrested for selling a crime pulp magazine. He violated the penal code against books and magazines devoted to crime and featuring violence and sexuality. The Supreme Court struck down the conviction based on the vagueness of a law no retailer could possibly be sure they were violating. Immediately following the decision eighteen state statutes similar to the New York State law were no longer constitutional. And while the decision left room for carefully and narrowly defined statutes, it would quickly discourage such efforts at both the local and state levels.[92] The 1948 Los Angeles County ordinance also was struck down a year later by the California Supreme Court.[93] So while state legislators and local councils continued debating and investigating comic books, attempts at actual ordinances or legislation were few and virtually unsuccessful.[94]

Local police still had ways of forcing distributors and retailers to eliminate certain publications from distribution and sale. Authorities in Detroit were particularly adept at such "unofficial" censorship; so successful that the term "the Detroit Plan" was attached to this approach in censoring books and magazines. Law and political science professor Walter Gellhorn spelled out the Detroit approach to censorship in 1956:

> In few cities are they distributed by more than two wholesalers, whose trucks also deliver magazines and comic books to newsdealers and other retailers. The police need not attack upon a broad front, but can

entirely control the situation by squeezing this narrow bottleneck. Truck operators are usually heavily dependent on police tolerance of brief violations of parking regulations, during unloading operations; wholesaler's warehouses are subject to being especially closely examined by building, fire, and health inspectors. Moreover, the retailers may be municipal licensees. Both wholesalers and retailers . . . are therefore readily influenced by police "suggestions" that particular books be suppressed. In mid-1955 the Detroit police department, upon request, was proudly distributing its list of banned books to at least a hundred other cities.

Gellhorn also pointed to how local authorities helped religious and civic groups police retailers.[95]

Now certainly there were those defending comic books besides comic book publishers. Defenders of comic books usually admitted that many were horrid and objectionable, but that was no reason to mount such virulent criticisms and robust actions. Katherine Clifford, in *Parents Magazine* in 1948, defended children's desire for comic books:

The furor over comics waxes, but never wanes. Parents worry; psychologists predict dire consequences; and my children and yours go right on reading comics, with or without our parental sanction . . . Of course some comics are trash. So are some of the day's best sellers. But we don't advocate censoring books, or abolishing them, just because some aren't worth the paper on which they're printed . . . I hold no brief for lurid sex and crime-ridden comics, but I heartily approve of those which treat of historical events, past and present, which poke fun at human foibles, which offer good adventure and entertainment, or which subtly infuse an exciting story with arguments for racial tolerance and other worthy aims.[96]

Dorothy Barclay, in the *New York Times* in 1950, stated frankly, "After more than ten years of claims and counter-claims, book-burnings and bannings, rulings and reversals, the comics are still with us." She suggested that regulating the comic book diet of children—"democratically decided"—was the best approach.[97] In general, however, Clifford and Barclay's assurances were rare voices simply defending comic book reading. In part this was because the debate had shifted to the question of juvenile delinquency, self-regulation, and censorship.

The content of new comic book genres and the success of the crusade meant that most defenders felt compelled to admit the problems with content, but warn against creeping censorship. *The New York Times* editorialized against state laws to regulate comic books in February 1949:

> [M]any people are deeply concerned over the moral and social effect of this flood of pulp paper that has been loosed on the newsstands in the last decade or so. Its publishers are reaping the whirlwind of indignation that is the result of their own failure of self-restraint. That official censorship should be proposed or effectuated, at it has in many cities, was inevitable. No doubt there have been and are offensive abuses by some comic book publishers. But it is a dangerous invasion of freedom of the press, with which all freedoms are joined, to set aside for governmental pre-censorship one form of publication.[98]

An editorial in *Harper's* in 1951 expressed a similar qualified defense while criticizing the link between comic books and juvenile delinquency. "This is not to say that we should encourage or support those who ignore the code and publish the 'vile and immoral' comic books which still in fact exist. What it does suggest is that it would be dangerous oversimplification to blame the current wave of juvenile delinquency and crime upon comic books or any other reading matter which is available to youth."[99]

Academics associated with the industry continued to publish academic articles. They repeated the old defense of comic books, attacked the link between juvenile delinquency and comics, and warned against censorship. The *Journal of Educational Sociology* featured a symposium of these academics in 1949. Josette Frank addressed the old fears of comic books with the assurances that there was nothing to fear. She also assured readers there was no link with juvenile delinquency.[100] Harvey Zorbaugh surveyed adult attitudes and actually discovered that a majority found comic books unfavorable or expressed serious reservations about them. He ended, however, on a high note. "There is a considerable and healthy ferment of criticism . . . but it is unlikely to cause any great devaluation of the first amendment."[101] Henry E. Schultz felt differently and alerted readers to the rising tide of censorship, but felt comfort that "[o]ther sane forces began to make themselves heard. The Civil Liberties Union, The Author's League, The National Cartoonists Society, The National Association of Magazine Publishers, and many other groups traditionally interested in the fight against censorship urged caution and expressed deep concern over the trend towards political and legislative censorship."[102] Frederic M. Thrasher mounted an attack of Wertham's work and warned that scapegoating comic books was a failure to face responsibility for "providing our children with more healthful family life and community living."[103]

Other academics' voices occasionally appeared in the press easing the fears of parents about the link between juvenile delinquency and comic books, but just as many voices claimed the opposite. In 1948, Edwin J. Lukas, executive director of the Society for the Prevention of Crime, claimed at a meeting of Christ Church in New York City, "Parents who blame comic books for juvenile delinquency are using them as 'twentieth century scapegoats' to which to shift their own responsibilities."[104] Sociologist Paul W. Tappan spoke at a meeting of the Institute of Probation in New York City where "comic books, recently much assailed by sociologists as contributory to juvenile delinquency, were absolved from much of the blame."[105] The New York Times also reported Lawrence A. Averill's talk in front of the American Association for the Advancement of Science. "The main danger probably comes from comic books dealing with crime, horror, hate, fear and lust, Dr. Averill added. Some of these, he said, assume their readers to be little monsters with 'the brain of a child, the sexual drive of a satyr, and the spiritual delicacy of a gorilla. . . . but in many cases they are no worse than the movies, radio or the more sensational and erotic literature of the day.'"[106] Averill was not giving a ringing endorsement for comics!

Several organizations fighting the general movement of censorship in the United States did feel compelled to fight efforts to censor comic books. But such efforts never openly defended crime or other comic books. The American Civil Liberties Union (ACLU) and the American Book Publishers Council attacked efforts of the New York State Legislature to enact censorship laws against crime comic books. Morris Ernst, counsel for the ACLU, believed these efforts on comic book censorship were something "Stalin or a Hitler might have invoked . . . In the opinion of the American Civil Liberties Union the passage of this bill by the Senate is a direct threat to the freedom of the press and by the press we mean daily press. If this bill were constitutional— which it is not—every daily newspaper could be brought under it."[107] Curtis W. McGraw, president of the American Book Publishers Council, sent a telegram to state legislators with a prepared statement by the chairman of the Council's Anti-Censorship Committee. "Although books in general do not appear to be directly affected by the proposed New York State comic books censorship bill . . . we as book publishers respectfully but in the strongest terms protest such a bill as an unnecessary, illegal and subversive invasion of the constitutional guarantees of freedom of the press and as a dangerous repressive precedent . . . such administrative procedure or delegation of power will inevitably invite unjustifiable attacks on all kinds of publications by pressure groups and other special interests and will undermine and harass genuine freedom to publish."[108]

The late 1940s certainly showed a rash of heated debate, concerted civic action, and official efforts of censorship in relation to postwar comic books. But as Beaty points out, by 1951 there was a brief lull in the storm of anti–comic book attacks.[109] Local and state efforts in the crusade certainly continued.[110] But the flurry of official announcements, association proclamations, and debates about juvenile delinquency in comic books lost its strength by 1951. In 1950, the Senate Crime Investigating Committee, headed by Senator Estes Kefauver, investigated comic books because, in the words of the senator, "juvenile delinquency has increased considerably during the past five years and that this increase has been stimulated by the so-called crime comic books." Unfortunately, the report of the views of sixty-five officials and eight child guidance experts before the committee showed the majority to see "no direct connection between the comic books dealing with crime and juvenile delinquency."[111]

Two events in 1954 would reinvigorate the crusade. The first was the U.S. Senate Subcommittee to Investigate Juvenile Delinquency's meeting in New York City. Its objective was to investigate the relationship between comic books and juvenile crime. The hearing was nationally televised and attracted wide press attention. David Park's analysis of these hearings argues that they were meant as a "show trial" designed to balance the pressures of the crusade with the need to protect the commercial interests of the comic book industry. In other words, the hearings were designed to pressure the industry into self-regulation that would eliminate the most offensive comic books. Park makes a further argument that it was not the link to juvenile delinquency that made these show trials powerful, but the framing of crime and horror comic books as simply vulgar, tasteless, and unworthy of support.[112] The agenda of the committee was clear from the outset. Richard Clendenen, executive director of the committee, admitted that there was no consensus on the link to juvenile crime in all the studies and other material reviewed for the committee.[113] But between his opening and closing remarks he presented examples of crime and horror comic books that easily confirmed all the worst claims on the vulgar, violent nature of the two genres.[114]

The opposing views of "experts" on the link to juvenile delinquency were certainly presented, including the testimony of Fredric Wertham. But the most damning part of the hearings was virtually all the representatives of the comic book industry agreed that certain comic books were detestable and worthy of no defense. Only publisher William Gaines attempted to defend crime and horror comic books and failed miserably even in his own eyes.[115] Henry E. Schultz of the ACMP admitted that efforts at self-regulation had failed. But he asked the committee not to confuse the broader problem of juvenile delinquency with "the bad taste and the vulgarity sometimes bordering on obscenity that occurs in these publications. I think many of the comic-book publishers have failed in their duty to mothers to take this great medium which was 7 years ago a wonderful vital thing and they have debased it in many ways."[116] Helen Meyer, vice president of Dell Publications, noting that this publisher produced wholesome comic books that represented 15 percent of all titles, went on to state, "Dr. Wertham, for some strange reason, is intent on condemning the entire industry. He refuses to acknowledge that other types of comics are not only published, but are better supported by children than crime and horror comics." When asked by Senator Robert C. Hendrickson if she supported eliminating horror comics, she replied, "We certainly are. And we would love to help you do it."[117]

The second major event of 1954 was the publication of *Seduction of the Innocent* by Fredric Wertham. Wertham not only argued for the link between juvenile delinquency and comic books, but in his chapter "I Want to Be a Sex Maniac!" he also argued that comic books threatened the psychosexual development of children. Comic books stimulated children sexually, led to early masturbation, promoted sadomasochistic fantasies that mixed sexuality with cruelty, and sparked confusion around homosexual impulses with homoerotic images and story lines. He argued that Batman and Robin, and Wonder Woman, were homoerotic characters. He repeated the claims of comic book reading's effect on literacy; claiming that comic books led to "reading retardation," "reading disability," and actual damage to the eye movements necessary for reading regular texts rather than paneled comic art.[118] He lambasted the manipulation of readers in advertisements. He criticized the scholarship defending comic books. He even ridiculed the courts for hindering the censorship of comic books. It was a universal damning indictment of the entire comic book field and those who produced, published, and defended comic books.

Wertham's book was widely reviewed. As Beaty argues, almost all the reviews in journals, magazines, and newspapers were in agreement that comic books were a threat to America's children, even if some admitted that Wertham's arguments and prose was at times over the top or unconvincing.[119] Wolcott Gibbs argued in *The New Yorker* that at "the moment, the comics are under attack again, and 'Seduction of the Innocent' has provided their enemies with some of their most potent ammunition. In many ways, it is an absurd and alarmful book . . . but the concrete evidence it offers is a real crime against the children seems to be practically unanswerable. I like to think that Superman and his pals are up against the battle of their perverse, fantastic and foolish lives."[120] In the *Library Journal*, Louis Barron, while admitting Wertham at times overstated his case, agreed that "the shocking facts are there and cannot be laughed away by comic book publishers and their hired psychological experts. This important book is certain to attract a great deal of attention, and will help make many parents and educators more aware of the very real dangers of comic books on our children and society."[121]

The U.S. Senate hearings and Wertham's tirade against comic books certainly reignited the crusade against comics. Most debates and demands, however, followed the lead of the senate hearings by focusing on the threat or depravity of crime and horror comic books. An editorial in the Catholic publication *America* in September 1954 celebrated how "the ground swell of public opinion against the crime-horror comics is mounting to a tidal wave. From dozens of places over the country . . . there is mounting evidence of more vocal public protest and more vigorous police action against this type of comic book, which is more and more being indicted as an incentive to juvenile crime."[122] In *National Parent-Teacher* in December 1954 Myrtle Gourley urged "every parent who cares about his child, every adult who cares about his community, to leaf through the crime and horror comics and see for himself the realm through which a child can wonder for a dime . . . my personal opinions should be perfectly clear by now. Crime and horror comic books must be wiped out, removed forever from the reach of children."[123]

The rising tide against crime and horror comic books is evident in Edward L. Feder's report, *Comic Book Regulation*, for the California legislature in 1955. Feder noted that the National Institute of Municipal Law Officers issued a model ordinance in 1954 to help local officials draft anti–comic book ordinances that could survive constitutional review. He reviewed thirteen cities and counties in California that considered ordinances in 1954. He included another twenty cities outside of California that also considered ordinances against comic books in 1954. He also reviewed a rise in legislative deliberation and action across the country that same year.[124] Feder also noted that the National Council of Juvenile Court Judges, at their 1954 annual convention, demanded the "outlawing of 'comic books and horror magazines depicting crime, sadism, vulgar, sex, and horror scenes' . . . The resolution called for action at all levels of government to 'outlaw, curtail, and prohibit the publication, dissemination and distribution of so-called comic books, picture magazines and horror magazines depicting objectionable features.'"[125] Meanwhile, local and state associations also were acting or demanding action, and the General Federation of Women's Clubs urged its members "to continue efforts to abolish crime comic books . . . we must not relax our efforts to abolish crime comic books." The clubs were asked to appoint volunteers to visit newsstands regularly and to write letters to publishers and retailers protesting the magazines.[126]

While pressures and actions to ban the distribution and sales of crime and horror comic books increased significantly in 1954, many commentators or associations were against any form of censorship. This was particularly the case for those involved in the general press. Ward Moore, reviewing *Seduction of the Innocent* for *The Nation*, expressed this general view: "No matter how menacing comic books are, censorship—even disguised as regulation—is more menacing still."[127] Even organizations calling for government action and the banning of comic books suggested self-regulation on the part of the industry. The American Legion, for example, which had previously supported government action against comic books, committed itself in 1954 to supporting industry self-regulation, admitting that most comic books were harmless.[128] And when the comic book industry began to respond to criticism by moving toward a self-regulatory code in late 1954, the General Federation of Women's Clubs commented that this "is an effort to regulate the comic book business within itself and, if it is carried forth vigorously, a most commendable one."[129]

The reinvigoration of the crusade against comic books, particularly the resurgence of government action, finally woke up comic book publishers to the need to respond in a concerted and collective manner. In September 1954 a new Comics Czar was announced by the newly formed Comics Magazine Association of America (CMAA). New York City Magistrate Charles F. Murphy, "a vigorous campaigner against juvenile delinquency," was the new czar. He promised "'the new program of self-regulation will be based on a strong and effective code of ethics and a competent staff of reviewers' . . . He promised the 'strongest code of ethics ever adopted by a mass media industry.'"[130] In October the CMAA approved a Comics Code and by the end of December Murphy announced the initiation of the code for the first week of January 1955 with twenty-eight of the thirty-one major publishers on board, representing 75 percent of the sixty million comic titles published each month.[131] The new CMAA also mounted a major public relations campaign to convince critics that the industry was finally taking self-regulation seriously.[132]

The new code was quickly covered by the press. *Time* reported that "publishers of 'good' comics are as much opposed to horror books as anyone . . . the Comics Magazine Association of America, a newly formed group representing 90% of the comic-book industry, moved against 'the aggressive minority trying to make a fast buck with horror comics' . . . Thus the comic-book publishers hope to police themselves and avoid being put out of business."[133] The biggest public relations coup, however, was DC editor Mort Weisinger's article in *Better Homes and Gardens*, "How They're Cleaning Up the Comic Books," in March 1955:

During the course of this month, some 50 million moppets and teen-agers will plunk down one or more dimes of their pin money for brightly colored comic books . . . Some anxious parents concerned with the reading habits of their children will note something new has been added to the familiar gaudy product . . . This seal is another and the latest answer to the comic-book industry's bitterest critics. During the next 30 days, as millions of comic books introducing this seal flood the magazine racks of candy stores, supermarkets, and pharmacies throughout the country, the public will be informed that the seal is the symbol of the industry's new policy of stern self-censorship . . . Comic-book houses are on the hot seat today as a result of conscienceless editing by a minority of unethical publishers within their ranks . . . it is because of the past activities of the lunatic fringe that the entire industry has been smeared . . . Released to civic groups, law-enforcement agencies, and church groups, the code drew unprecedented acclaim.[134]

While at first crusaders and government officials were not impressed by the new Comics Code,[135] within a year, as industry self-regulation took greater effect, this policy worked to ease their minds. In February 1956, T. E. Murphy argued in *Reader's Digest* that "[t]wo years ago newsstands in this country were piled high with comic books that dripped depravity, obscenity and violence. Today there is a new look. . . . In a spontaneous grass-roots movement groups of citizens across the nation rose up and, with nothing but the spirit of their decency to guide them, drove the dirty books off the stands and their peddlers to cover, and forced the adoption of a new code by comic-book publishers."[136] And that summer the director of the Cincinnati Committee, Charles F. Wheeler exclaimed, "The comics are really getting better! Not so many of them are being published. . . . It looks as though the recent efforts of parents and legislatures and the comics publishers themselves to clean up the comics and prevent the most objectionable ones from getting onto the newsstands are beginning to have effect."[137]

Mrs. Guy Percy Trulock became the new code administrator for the Comics Authority in October of 1956. She was former president of the New York City Federation of Women's Clubs. It seemed that the crusaders had truly won. In January 1957, Margaret Hickey, editor of the Public Affairs Department of *Ladies' Home Journal*, expressed crusaders' satisfaction with the success of their movement since the crusade's resurgence in 1954. "Two and a half years have passed since the crusade began. What have been the actual results? The worst of the crime and horror comics no longer are sold. Though there is no organized system for checking stands now, individual club members are taking the responsibility of constant vigilance. But there are intangible results too . . . they have been able to mold tastes of the youngsters so that many no longer care for comics."[138]

Hickey's satisfaction must have been widely shared. By 1958 press reports of civic action, proclamations, and government action against comic books faded away. Articles on the social dangers of comic books also faded away. Nyberg points to both the NODL and the Cincinnati Committee for the Evaluation of Comics acknowledging the effectiveness of the code.[139] Nyberg also points to the courts once again ruling against ordinances and state laws against comic books, although most ordinances and state laws were never challenged simply because few actually led to police action given the cleanup of the industry.[140] Even the old elite mass culture criticism of the lowbrow, subliterate, poor quality, and fascist nature of comic books disappeared. The comic book industry had dodged a bullet in terms of government censorship and a vibrant movement to police newsstands across America; but at what price?

The End of the Early Industrial Age

The implementation of the Comics Code in 1955 had an almost immediate negative effect on the mass market for comic books. Estimates of circulation suggested that monthly sales of comic book titles by the end of 1955 had dropped from eighty million to forty million. The new crisis in the comic book field certainly was not only the result of the crusade and the Comics Code. Publishers also faced major problems in their distribution system and with competition from children's television.[141] But the immediate loss of such lucrative genres as crime and horror dealt a severe blow to the comics industry. Regardless of how important the various factors undermining the comic book market had in its decline, the last years of the 1950s would be disastrous for the industry.

Mike Benton, in his history of the American comic book, presents the terrible state of the comic book industry in the years following the Comics Code. By the end of 1955, the number of comic book titles fell to around three hundred compared to an estimated high of 650 titles in the early 1950s. The number of publishers in the field collapsed. Small publishers began folding up shop in 1955. Many comic book publishers struggling in the declining market folded up shop in 1956. Successful publishers like Ace Comics, Avon Publications, and Superior Comics left the field that year. And Benton points to 1958 as the nadir in the collapse of publishers as the few remaining small publishers closed shop, setting the stage for a new era in the comic book field.[142]

Twenty-four of the original twenty-nine publishers of the CMAA formed in 1954 were gone by 1958.[143] The comic shops that thrived during the Early Industrial Age also fell under the crisis. They were already fading by the time of the crisis. Most folded up, however, as smaller publishers disappeared from the field, and major publishers cut costs to survive the falling market by relying on their own bull pens and freelancers.[144]

In April 1959 John L. Goldwater, president of the CMAA, tried to inspire his membership at the annual meeting of the association in New York City. He claimed that "circulation had risen to 600,000,000 copies annually, an increase of 150,000,000 over circulation immediately before the code was adopted."[145] Unfortunately, Goldwater's historical memory was a bit off since most press reports before the code had circulation at around eighty million a month, totaling 960,000,000 annually. The report to the 1954 U.S. Senate Subcommittee made what it called a very "conservative" estimate of a 756,000,000 annual circulation, while Edward L. Feder's report to the California legislature in 1955 had annual circulation at one billion in 1953.[146] Goldwater's figures, however, indicated that the industry had recovered from the nadir in sales in 1955, but it certainly had not returned to the sales figures of the boom period. The future of the industry did not look promising.

Artists remembered the tough times and gloomy outlooks in the comic book field in the late 1950s. Carmine Infantino remembers working at DC during the crisis. "We got hurt financially because the people at DC called us all in and told us we were going to have to take a page cut. I believe it was a $2 or $3 page cut. Of course we were horrified by it. But they said it was either that or nothing. The company had to save some money because they were getting beaten up . . . We did it because the sales were not good at all. And the books were just about keeping their heads above water. So that's how we floundered along."[147] Artist Neal Adams remembers his dream of entering comics in 1959. "Everywhere in the field in 1959, people discouraged hopeful kids from going into the comics business—1959 was not a good year for entering the comics business. I went to DC and I got a lecture. They wouldn't let me in the door . . . I learned that no one had gone into the field for five years . . . There were no new guys, new artists, coming into the field." Adams also remembered how seasoned comic artists also were "having a hard time finding work . . . There was a scattering effect. People who pick up work picked up work, and others did commercial work. It was a terrible, terrible time, and it was reflected in the educational field. When I told people that I wanted to get into comics, they said, 'It's dead. There's nobody . . . forget about it.' And I found it to be true."[148]

Conclusion

The American comic book in the postwar period found itself in a maelstrom of Cold War hysteria. Plastered across newsstands and racks, outnumbering all other newsstand publications, even outselling books, the comic book took center stage in the movement to clean up American literature. Labeled a child's medium in the popular imagination, the comic book was especially vulnerable to fears of the power of the word and image. The fatal blow was the link, however dubious, between juvenile delinquency and the comic book. The fatal flaw was an industry clueless to the events that were happening around it. Whether the comic book was destined to suffer such an attack and its consequences is unanswerable. But I believe that the crucial factor in this story was the rise of a general movement toward censorship in the postwar period that provided the organization, resources, and ideological power to mount a major nationwide campaign against the comic book.

The social history of the anti–comic book crusade also demonstrates how broader social, political, and cultural currents can articulate themselves in specific fields of mass media or popular art. The comic book became the ultimate victim of a national social, political, and cultural movement to rid America of supposedly deviant and subversive literature. The story of this crusade shows, following the production of culture perspective, how such external factors can radically reshape the social organization and evolution of a popular art form such as comic books. Leading into the 1950s, the American comic book was replicating the breadth of genres and readers previously enjoyed by the pulp magazine industry. In its own fashion, the comic book was simply reproducing as well the diversity found in other popular mediums like radio and film, only unfortunately far more graphically. But the stigma attached to the comic book during the anti–comic book crusade would have a devastating effect on the evolution of this popular art field. The ultimate cost in the crusade against comic books was the arrested development of the comic book as a form of popular entertainment. The tragedy of the Cold War hysteria and the crusade to censor literature in America is how the comic book as a medium was not allowed to evolve into a diverse market of genres and readers. The American comic book would now take a far different path as an art form.

While the usual "culprits" in this story as told by scholars and fans have appeared in this chapter, I have left one important factor out. The other factor in the rise of an anti–comic book crusade and the implementation of the Comics Code was the unfettered pulp logic of the comic book field. While pulp magazines certainly attracted the wrath of censors, the transference of pulp stories from text to graphic presentation in what was considered a child's medium was the comic book publishers' fatal mistake. The easy entrance into the field meant publishers and artists could stretch the bounds of story and image in their comic books. If one looks at the comic book in relation to other children's literature, film, or programming of the time, it becomes readily apparent how the comic book came to be the focus of all the censorious fervor of the period. The graphic detail of violence and gore in comic books far surpassed any other popular culture geared to children.

The great boom period of the American comic book was clearly dead by the end of the 1950s. The crusade had done its job and the Early Industrial Age was over. The coming years would be more about maintaining stability in the mass market, not dreams of another great boom in comic book production. The comic book field had now entered the Late Industrial Age of the American comic book. The industrial logic of the Early Industrial Age would continue to be the "rules of art" during the Late Industrial Age. But other events would soon set the stage for a radical transformation in the field of comic books by the end of the Industrial Age.

3

The Late Industrial Age

The Return of the Superhero and the
First Comic Book Rebellion

The Late Industrial Age of the American comic book was a period of transformation and uncertainty in the comic book field. In the 1960s, many in the comic book industry would constantly point to television as a major culprit in their inability to return to the good old days of the postwar boom. But other forces in the comic book field were working against a revival of the comic book market. These forces ranged from mounting problems in distribution to new corporate strategies emphasizing licensing of properties over reinvigorating the comic book mass market. The social organization of the comic book field that made the Early Industrial Age such a success was collapsing and the small number of publishers left in the field during the Late Industrial Age struggled to survive. DC, Marvel, and Archie were the only old publishing houses left in the field by the end of this age in the mid-1980s.

Despite the economic woes in the comic book field, this period also witnessed a second renaissance in superheroes. In their desperate attempt to survive the comic book crisis, publishers, editors, and artists "reinvented" the superhero genre. They quickly brought a new graphic freshness to this genre. They also began to work against the perfect universe of superheroes of the Early Industrial Age. At first they simply made superheroes less than perfect individuals with identifiable personalities. Then in the early 1970s editors and artists began making superhero stories socially relevant. And by the early

1980s, the superhero and his or her universe became more dark, violent, and mature. The success of this reinvention also led to this genre dominating the comic book field. It cemented in the popular imagination the superhero genre *as* the American comic book.

While commercial publishers were struggling to maintain a viable mass market for comic books, others began working to more radically transform this field. The underground comix movement, as a counterculture movement of the 1960s, challenged the pulp logic and rules of art of the comic book field. Rejecting the "straight" world of mainstream comic books, these pioneers of comic art in the late 1960s and early 1970s radically disrupted the preconceptions of the potential of comic books as art. They also rebelled against the subordinate role of comic book artists in the field. Underground comix artists were the first comic book artists to claim principles of autonomy from dominant commercial forces. They were the first comic book artists also to approach this art form as a medium of authentic self-expression.

The comix movement returns us to the work of Pierre Bourdieu on heroic ages in art discussed in this book's introduction.[1] The underground comix movement was a *charismatic* movement that contributed to the ideological foundations of the Heroic Age of comic books that followed in the 1980s. The comix movement had striking similarities to the bohemian revolt championed by Charles Baudelaire in the mid-nineteenth century. This revolt also occurred in a restricted subfield of artists, publishers, and readers that Bourdieu argued set the stage for the Heroic Age of French Literature. Both charismatic movements challenged bourgeois and conventional values, morals, and politics. Both also celebrated a Dionysian approach to life, emphasizing sexual pleasure and drug-induced euphoria. Both demanded art be a vehicle for free expression. And both began an artistic rebellion that would eventually radically change the rules of art in their chosen art fields. It's just that underground rebels chose comic books as their medium!

The Late Industrial Age

At the beginning of the 1960s, publishers continued struggling with the crisis in the comic book market that began in 1955. Peter Bart, in *The New York Times* in 1962, was informed of the conditions of the comic book industry by Jacob S. Liebowitz, president of National Periodicals, and Mort Weisinger, the company's managing editor:

> The comic book industry as a whole, it was noted, has narrowed considerably in recent years. Today comic books sell at a rate of about

350,000,000 a year compared with 800,000,000 a year a decade ago. Where once more than 50 comics publishers prospered, today there are less than a dozen publishing houses of any magnitude . . . Moreover, the comics industry once a major advertising medium for reaching the teen-age and younger market, today has lost much of its revenue to rival media. Even National Periodical, Superman's publisher, presently derives only about $176,000 a year from advertising, compared with nearly $1,000,000 a decade or so ago. [2]

But Liebowitz and Weisinger could at least be satisfied that in these terrible times National had survived. It accounted for around 30 percent of total sales in the industry and generated about 21.6 million dollars in annual revenue in 1962.[3] National and Marvel made a successful price hike to twelve cents that same year. The typical comic book now was thirty-two or forty-eight pages. Unlike National, however, the comics giant Dell was faltering by 1962. With its most popular titles' circulations falling, Dell gave most of its lucrative licenses to Western Printing and its new imprint Gold Key. Dell survived the 1960s mostly repurposing television shows and movies. The onetime giant of the comic book field left the industry in 1973.[4] By the end of the 1960s, National's major competitor would be Marvel Comics, which rose to be one of the top two publishers in the industry by copying the strategy that made National the most successful publisher of the 1960s: the superhero strategy.

Comic fandom credits National editor Julius Schwarz with the successful reintroduction of the superhero genre after its fall from grace in the late 1940s. National actually maintained some of its most popular superheroes in the 1950s like Superman, Batman, and Wonder Woman. Schwarz, however, reintroduced retired superheroes Flash and Green Lantern in 1958 and 1959 in *Showcase* with completely revamped story lines and characters. Flash had his own title by 1959. The sales for these comic books indicated that readers were ready once again to thrill to a new updated generation of costumed superheroes. National introduced Justice League of America (JLA) in 1960 featuring Flash, Green Lantern, Superman, Batman, Aquaman, Wonder Woman, and Martian Manhunter. Schwarz then had the old superheroes Hawkman and the Atom revamped in 1961. National also expanded its Superman franchise. Liebowitz told Peter Bart of *The New York Times* that it was this stock of superheroes and related characters that was responsible for National's 30 percent of annual comic book sales in 1962.[5]

Marvel had not fared well in the late 1950s.[6] In 1961, however, it adopted the superhero strategy. Within three years Marvel established itself primarily as a purveyor of superhero comic books. The first of the Marvel superhero lineup was the Fantastic Four who appeared with their own title in 1961. The following year *The Incredible Hulk* was published. The new superheroes Spider-Man, Thor, and the Ant-Man appeared in 1962. In 1963, Marvel introduced its version of the JLA with the Avengers featuring the Hulk, Thor, Ant-Man, and Iron Man. Spider-Man had his own title by 1963 and the new superhero Daredevil was introduced with his own title in 1964. Marvel was finding success with its new strategy but remained hindered by a 1957 distribution arrangement with Independent News that limited it to eight monthly titles.

In comic fandom Marvel's early success is linked first to editor Stan Lee. Lee initiated what is commonly called the "Marvel Method," which, unlike the old style of comic book making, involved a more collaborative effort between writers and artists. Artists developed full paneled storyboards, with suggestions for dialogue, from brief synopses or story ideas from Lee. Lee would then provide the final dialogue. This method gave more creative control to some of the most seasoned and accomplished artists in the field, like Jack Kirby, Steve Ditko, Bill Everett, Joe Orlando, and Wally Wood. But even more important to the success of Marvel was the style of storytelling. Marvel introduced imperfect characters who were vain, malcontent, misunderstood, or confused. Stan Lee told *The New York Times* in 1971 that in those early years he wanted to do something different with the superhero genre. "New ways of talking, hangups, introspection and brooding . . . I talked to Jack Kirby about it. I said, 'Let's let them not always get along well; let's let them have arguments. Let's make them talk like real people and react like real people.'" Lee presented the example of Spider-Man who could "still lose a fight, make dumb mistakes, have acne, have trouble with girls and have not too much money."[7]

Historian Bradford W. Wright argues in *Comic Book Nation* that the new Marvel universe stood in stark contrast to other superhero titles of the past and for most of the 1960s. This was particularly the case with National's line of superheroes. These superhero stories presented ideal narratives of handsome superheroes in perfect suburbs and ultramodern cities all populated by perfect white citizens. These stories also were totally unambiguous. For Wright, the National model was reflective of the conforming years of the Cold War. But Marvel was resonating with the more combative and rebellious time of the 1960s.[8] Artist Frank Miller, part of the young generation of artists who loved Marvel comics as kids before entering the field of comic books in the 1970s and 1980s, expressed the sense of change in the superhero genre. "Stan Lee combined his talents with those of Jack Kirby and Steve Ditko, and added a new chapter to the Mythology of the American Superhero. They created a host of new characters, fresh born to feed a new generation of readers who found in *Spider-man* and *The Fantastic Four* the vitality that had been drained from the DC heroes."[9]

The Marvel formula would start the superhero genre in a new direction not only toward irreverence and more engaging characters, but also away from young readers toward adolescent and college-age readers.[10] Ronin Ro's book on the Marvel Revolution highlights this sudden surge of college readers and fans in the mid-1960s. College students "sent two hundred to five hundred letters a day and told reporters from *Esquire* that Stan was their Homer, and Spider-man and Hulk were more relevant than Sartre, Camus, Dostoevsky, and Marx."[11] Stan Lee was even invited by college groups to give lectures on their campuses.[12] An article in *The New York Times* on the revolt of a new college generation noted in 1967 that students actually still read Marx, but along with New Left politics, long hair, LSD, and producing their own art, they also enjoyed *MAD* magazine and Marvel comic books that gave them "a chance to laugh at what they see as the absurdities of society."[13] The loyalty of teenage and college-age readers also was based on the Marvel persona projected in the comic books. Marvel was hip, irreverent, and spoke to readers as part of the whole enterprise. This not only included revitalizing the letters section of comic books, but also special columns like the "Bullpen Bulletin" and "Stan's Soap Box." Readers were introduced to the real editors, writers, artists, and even secretarial staff at Marvel. As Stan Lee remembers, "I wanted the readers to feel the same way, to feel that we were all part of an 'in' thing that the outside world wasn't even aware of. We were sharing a big joke together and having a lot of fun with this crazy Marvel Universe."[14]

By the mid-1960s indications were that the target audiences for *new* titles were teenagers and college students. Publishers were still publishing comic books for children, but mostly old established titles. Gold Key continued to successfully publish funny animal titles. And Harvey Publications survived the 1960s based on its old kid titles like *Casper the Friendly Ghost*, *Little Lulu*, and *Richie Rich* as well as multiple spin-offs. Other titles geared to children were repurposed animated characters from Hollywood properties like Gold Key's *Beep-Beep the Roadrunner* (1966) or Dells' *Alvin* (1962). Archie Publications also continued to maintain a third position in the market with its teen comics, the most successful new title being *Josie and the Pussycats* in 1969.

In general, however, it seemed that publishers were looking to a slightly older demographics in adopting new titles. This was clear in the other genre burst in the 1960s besides the superhero genre: repurposed television shows and movies. Dell adopted this strategy in the 1960s mostly focusing on television shows including *Ben Casey* (1962), *Get Smart* (1966), and *The Mod Squad* (1969). Gold Key also emphasized the same repurposing strategy in terms of new titles including television shows like *Bonanza* (1962) and *Gunsmoke* (1969), and movies like *Beneath the Planet of the Apes* (1970). Of course another indication of the orientation to new demographics was how the other publishers besides National and Marvel all introduced superhero titles in the 1960s.[15]

The superhero strategy would get a shot in the arm when Hollywood discovered the potential of superheroes on television. The January 1966 debut of the camp comedy *Batman* on ABC was a smashing success. *The New York Times* reported that ninety companies licensed Batman from National looking to generate seventy-five million dollars in merchandise sales.[16] Comic historian Ron Goulart puts the final Batman merchandise sales for 1966 at 150 million.[17] As for the actual comic books, circulation skyrocketed for Batman achieving nearly nine hundred thousand per month, the highest circulation it ever had in its entire history and greater than any superhero comic book since the 1950s. And it was the best-selling comic book for 1966 and 1967.[18] But Batman was not alone. National also anticipated that its Superman franchise would "exceed, by Superman dimensions" the predictions for Batman merchandising.[19]

Suddenly comic books and superheroes were the hip fad of the moment. Articles appeared trying to figure out how such lowbrow fare could resonate so broadly. Earlier articles already were puzzled by college students' identification with comics, but now everyone seemed hooked on comic books. Betty Rollin in *Look* was flabbergasted, and a bit annoyed, by the new hipness of superheroes. "Superman, Batman and Co. are with us now in the most hotsy-totsy of digs; not only on primetime television, at art movie theaters, on the ruins of Broadway stage, but also in pop-art galleries, on cocktail-circuit conversation lists . . . superheroes and comics in general were discovered by an altogether foreign legion: pop painters."[20] *The New York Times*, noting the "subcultural and pseudocultural" fascination with popular culture, pointed to the rise of the comic book. "From billboards to book jackets, from the most prestigious galleries and museums to the most garish souvenir shops, the public is faced with a bewildering variety of comic-strip advertisements, paintings, pinups, posters and all sorts of visual splendors . . . What makes this vogue for comic-strips so phenomenal is that it cuts across widely disparate levels of commercial, intellectual and esthetic activity in one form or another."[21]

Of course, whether this was a natural appreciation by the public for comic art or simply a fad in merchandising, marketing, and art was another question. At least for pop artist Roy Lichtenstein his art was not about his reverence toward comic books. "I was drawn to the bland stupidity of their appearance . . . I deliberately wanted to take something tasteless and lowbrow and organize it into art."[22] Most cognoscenti of high art taste were not embracing the comic book as legitimate art, although Marvel would point to European artists like Alain Resnais and Federico Fellini as big fans of its comics in the 1960s. Marvel also publicized Stan Lee's "reputation with *cognoscenti*" as "very, very high."[23] On the other hand, sales certainly boomed for superhero and other comic books, although publishers did not rush in with new titles to take advantage of the new craze.[24] But comics publishers soon discovered the true faddishness of the comic book craze in only a few years when the short boom in superhero sales collapsed, with Batman's monthly circulation plummeting to around 350,000.[25] The Batman boom ultimately further underscored the troubles facing the industry in revitalizing its mass market for comic books.

At the end of the 1960s the future of the comic book field did not look any brighter than when the decade started; if anything, it looked gloomier. According to comic book historian Mike Benton, 1969 was clearly the most disappointing year for comic books for this decade with sales declining, no new characters or titles, and a general lack of direction in the comic book field.[26] A major change in the industry was the change of ownership of Marvel and National from their original publishers to larger corporate concerns. The merchandising bonanza of the Batman boom made these comics publishers attractive properties and their sale to larger corporations signaled a major trend in the comic book field to view comic books as licensed properties more than stand-alone popular entertainment products. In 1969, Warner Communications bought National and DC Comics was born. Marvel was bought by Cadence Industries in 1968, which allowed Marvel to find alternative distribution in order to break away from the constraints of its old contract. Marvel launched a burst of new superhero titles featuring their most popular characters, but by 1969 Marvel unfortunately could not escape the general slump in the industry and dropped many of these new titles.[27] The industry responded in part by raising the price of a comic book to fifteen cents in 1969 and twenty cents in 1971. And the standard length of a comic book now was thirty-two pages.

By May 1971, *The New York Times* reported, "for an industry that wields considerable influence, comic book publishing has only a small fraternity of workers. There are something like 200 million comic books sold each year, a volume produced by less than 200 people, including writers, artists and letterers . . . most poorly compensated . . . now the industry consists of perhaps half a dozen companies with annual sales of about 200 million."[28] The industry was desperate to find a way out of a slumping market. The success of "hipper" superhero comics suggested that the best strategy was to target a new generation of slightly older readers who were living in a time in which the inhibitions and conservative politics of the 1950s held little, if any, relevance. In fact, immediately following the collapse of the Batman boom, DC and Marvel began bringing in young writers and illustrators to help make comic books resonate more with a new generation of readers.

With the media linking the success of Marvel to a new rebellious generation of college students, both Marvel and DC moved to be even more in sync with this demographic by becoming more, in the terms of the industry at the time, socially relevant. Bradford W. Wright shows that by 1969 the Marvel Universe was not just about superheroes with actual personalities, real personal troubles, and not necessarily perfect decision-making skills. The alien Silver Surfer began to observe the foibles of the human race plagued by racism, war, and pollution. Meanwhile, the young Peter Parker, Spider-Man, confronted the growing upheavals on his college campus. Daredevil confronted an anticommunist, right-wing villain, the Tribune, who pursued antiwar protesters and draft dodgers. Marvel introduced the first black superhero, the Falcon, in *Captain America*, while another black superhero, Black Panther, lectured members of the Black Panther party.[29] DC joined the social revolution in 1970 with Green Lantern and Green Arrow. Editorial Director Carmine Infantino, seeing the success of Marvel, had writer Denny O'Neil and artist Neal Adams revamp this title and for fourteen issues they dealt with slumlords, racism, environmental pollution, sexism, and the legal justice system.[30]

A new "liberalized" Comics Code was introduced in 1971 to supposedly allow for more socially relevant content, although the industry in reality only reedited a few points in the original code. The industry did add an amendment that allowed for stories on the perils of narcotics. The tinkering of the code, however, was intended not to truly open up the content of comic books, but to allow for slightly more freedom in the use of language and in the portrayal of violence, official authority, romance, and female images. The new code, for example, prohibited profanity, obscenity, smut, and vulgarity as "judged and interpreted in terms of contemporary standards" and deleted the old rule that romance "shall emphasize the value of family and the sanctity of marriage." The only significant change was in terms of horror comics where vampires, ghouls, and werewolves were now permitted in the comic book universe. But the moral and censorious bedrock of the old code remained. Crime still did not pay, illicit sex or "sexual abnormalities" were still prohibited; and if now some authorities could be portrayed as corrupt, it had be shown to be "an exceptional case and that the culprit pay the legal price."[31] Amy Kiste Nyberg argues that the revamped Comics Code did not allow for greater development of the comic book as an art form. For Nyberg, publishers were happy with the status quo with no immediate incentives to take economic risks by experimenting with comic books in ways that could possibly challenge the reigning public view of this popular art form.[32]

With the new code, however, the industry immediately launched into a public relations campaign to let college students know that comic books had become socially relevant. As a *New York Times* headline announced, "Shazam! Here Comes Captain Relevant." "Combining 'new journalism' with greater illustrative realism, comics are a reflection of both real society and personal fantasy . . . Captain America openly sympathizes with campus radicals, the Black Widow fights side by side with the Young Lords, Lois Lane apes John Howard Griffin and turns herself black to study racism, and everybody battles to save the environment . . . Today's superhero is about as much like his predecessors as today's child is like his parents."[33] *Time* in late 1971 also reported on the turn to socially relevant material. "Today almost all comic book characters have problems. As in many fields, the word is relevance. The trend may have begun a decade ago, but in the socially aware '70s it has reached full blossom. The comic's caped crusaders have become outraged about racial injustice as the congressional Black Caucus and as worried about pollution as the Sierra Club."[34]

Publishers and editors did bring a little social relevance to comic books in a few of their titles; but the turn to social relevance announced by the public relations arm of the comics industry left as quickly as it came. It was a very short-lived strategy.[35] Over the long term, the new code led less to the increased social relevancy of comic books than to more graphic, dark, and violent superhero comic books. The revamped X-Men in the mid-1970s introduced Wolverine, whose violent temperament was distinctly different than previous superheroes, while the violent vigilante Punisher also appeared at this time. The most influential work was the artist Frank Miller's stewardship of the Daredevil series in 1979. Miller also was responsible for hyping up the already intemperate personality of Wolverine in 1982. Other characters from Marvel and DC that characterized the darker superhero in the early 1980s were Moon Knight, Thor, and the Vigilante.[36] Part of this transformation in mainstream comic books came about when new independent comics publishers entered the field in 1982 without the Comics Code. Without the code, these independents moved even more into mature content, including darker themes, more violence, and more sex.

In the 1970s, Marvel and DC also made halfhearted gestures toward racial equality with a few black, Native American, and Asian characters following the turn to social relevance. Before the Late Industrial Age comic books replicated the same stereotyped images and representations found in comic strips, animation, and Hollywood film. Marvel introduced the black hero Luke Cage in *Hero for Hire* in 1972, and then moved the hero to *Power*

Man in 1974 with this title lasting until 1986. The Black Panther had his own feature comic book in *Jungle Action* in 1973—Marvel seemed clueless on the "signification" of the title and character in terms of racial stereotyping, although the title "emphasized the character's innate dignity" and was drawn by one of the few black artists in the field, Billy Graham.[37] The title changed to *Black Panther* in 1977 and lasted two more years. DC introduced a black hero in 1977 called Black Lightning. Marvel also introduced a Native American hero in *Red Wolf* from 1972 to 1973. The popularity of martial arts movies and television shows led to the Asian hero Shang-Chi in *Master of Kung Fu* in 1974, this title lasted until 1983. These limited attempts at diversity, however, had little effect on transforming the white world of the American superhero.

Publishers also gave an equally halfhearted attempt in the 1970s to rope in feminism. Female superheroines always existed in comic books, so inclusion of superheroines, like Marvel's Invisible Girl, Marvel Girl, and the Wasp, was nothing radically new. DC, however, promoted their popular Wonder Woman as protofeminist when *Ms.* magazine featured an article in 1972 on the feminist power of this superheroine. *The New York Times* announced an effort to summon the heroine for the feminist cause. "Wonder Woman will soon step from the pages of the comic book and appear as the heroine of a text-and-picture book, garnished with feminist essays by Gloria Steinem and Dr. Phyllis Chesler . . . 'If we had all read more about Wonder Woman and less about Dick and Jane, the new wave of the feminist revolution might have happened less painfully and sooner,' Miss Steinem writes in her introductory essay."[38]

In the late 1970s, Marvel and DC had four titles featuring female heroines, and new female heroines appeared in a few other titles. *Newsweek* announced that "Superwomen Fight Back!" in 1978. But nothing had radically changed in the portrayal of female characters except a few references related to women's equality or women's rights. *Newsweek* noted that regardless of the "raised consciousness" in "comic-book land . . . Not all feminists are delighted at the trend, however. Some question whether superheroines are proper symbols of liberation . . . Ms. Marvel and friends still live in a man's world. Virtually all of the 200 titles published each year are written by men, and the 250 million copies sold annually are read predominantly by boys. Moreover, the comics are drawn almost entirely by males."[39]

If the new code allowed for a few attempts at social relevance in comic books, the return of the horror genre in the early 1970s was the new code's most significant accomplishment. This was truly a genre burst with publishers flooding the market with mystery, horror, and monster titles. Certain older horror titles from the 1950s and 1960s remained on the roster of publishers, toned down to pass the 1955 Comics Code.[40] But in 1972 horror comics flooded the market. Marvel was the biggest producer of horror titles with titles like *Werewolf by Night* (1972) and *Vampire Tales* (1973). DC, Charlton, and Harvey also released new titles like *Swamp Thing* (1972), *Ghostly Haunts* (1971), and *Spooky Haunted House* (1972).[41] By 1974 horror, mystery, and monster comic books were second only to superhero comic books in the 250 titles that appeared that year.[42]

During the early 1970s, while the superhero and horror genres dominated the market, other genres still maintained a presence in the market. The sword and sorcery genre became a staple of the market with Marvel's highly successful launch of the old pulp classic *Conan the Barbarian* in 1970. A popular early 1970s Marvel sword and sorcery character was Red Sonja, she received her own title in 1977. DC also launched sword and sorcery titles. Another successful strategy was the repurposing of fantasy and science fiction movies and shows sparked by the incredible success of Marvel's series *Star Wars* (1977) and *Battlestar Galactica* (1978). Archie comics still remained the third largest publisher with its solid teen genre, while Gold Key remained with their funny animal comic books. Harvey had continued success and released a number of spin-offs from Richie Rich in 1974. Charlton's best sellers were repurposed properties like Yogi Bear, Beetle Bailey, and the Flintstones. And these publishers also published a few titles in other genres like war, western, romance, and adventure.

In 1974, Marvel, DC, Archie, Gold Key, Harvey, and Charlton were the only comics publishers left in the field. The last time there were only six publishers in the field was 1936.[43] Comic book circulation grew in the early 1970s and continued to grow for most of the rest of the decade. But this growth was mostly reflected in a saturation strategy mounted by Marvel and DC. They were facing declining circulations for each title, but compensated by publishing more titles.[44] And it certainly worked to the extent that overall sales figures grew. But the industry was not in a healthy state when it came to the bottom line. Publishers desperate for revenue had even reduced stories to seventeen pages of a thirty-two-page comic book. The top publisher in the field, Marvel, was barely surviving.[45] DC was in a similar state. The other publishers watched their sales drop over the whole decade. In 1975, both Marvel and DC boosted their saturation strategy even more, publishing almost one hundred new titles over the next three years.[46] The saturation strategy for both DC and Marvel collapsed by 1978 and led to what comic fandom calls the "DC Implosion."[47] DC canceled a third of its titles,[48] while Marvel dropped down to thirty-two titles. Marvel reported in 1979 an operating income of only 1.5 million dollars and sales at 23.1 million dollars.[49] National reported sales at 21.6 million dollars in 1962, over seventeen years the annual sales for the top publisher in comics increased only 1.5 million dollars, not accounting for inflation!

The industry struggled during the Late Industrial Age with a number of production problems such as the cost and supply of paper and failing to get their products out on time. In the early 1970s, however, the biggest problem was the collapse of their traditional system of distribution and retail. A number of factors were working against this system. The first factor was the low profit margins of relatively cheap comic books for both retailers and wholesalers. The second factor was the suburbanization of America, which was accompanied by the rise of chains serving as retailers in suburban shopping centers. The old urban retail outlets suffered from low sales, and the new suburban chains were not interested in selling comic books. In terms of the old system of distribution, independent distributors also were suffering from a drop in retailers, a decline in the magazine market, and the move of paperback publishers to direct distribution. Where once large numbers of comic book titles rested on newsstands and racks across America, now far fewer titles were appearing at each retail outlet. The comic book had simply lost favor with distributors and retailers all across the country.[50]

The low regard held by retailers and distributors was accompanied by corrupt practices by distributors in the system. By the early 1970s, things were unraveling. In some cases upwards of 50 percent of comic books never left the warehouses of distributors. By this time a new affidavit system was in place where distributors simply reported unsold comics without the traditional practice of returning them to publishers, either whole or just the cover page. As will be discussed in the next chapter, a considerable fandom of comic books had developed by this time. These fans' interest in collecting comic books led to the development of specialized fan dealers. Some distributors would claim unsold copies and then sell them to these new dealers under the table. Publishers were confused as guaranteed popular titles would see their sell-through rates—percentage of distributed copies actually sold—suddenly fall.[51] And sell-through rates in general fell to untenable levels. By the late 1970s, Marvel was looking at a sell-through rate of 35 percent![52] The distribution system had basically broken down. Harvey had cut back to only two lines of titles by 1981 and suspended publication in 1982. Gold Key folded shop in 1984. Charlton hobbled along until 1986. As one of the early specialized retailers for comic fandom, Steve Schanes, remarked on the problems haunting the industry moving into the 1980s, "Comics were on their last breath. They couldn't have lasted another four years."[53] It was up to an emerging subculture of comic fandom to save the American comic book.

The dire problems the comics industry faced by the late 1970s and early 1980s accelerated a process of transformation in readership already begun with the superhero strategy in the 1960s, which relied almost exclusively on genres geared to teenage and young adult males. Teenage and adult female readers were the first to disappear as romance comic books rapidly declined in the 1960s with only a few making it into the 1970s. The last of the Industrial Age romances, *Young Romance*, ceased publication in 1977 after thirty years in circulation.[54] Patrick Parsons, in his analysis of comic book readership, argues that with competition from other media the industry was losing male and female children readers as early as the 1960s. And Marvel and DC dominated the market by the 1970s with only Archie, Harvey, and Gold Key targeting children readers. And with Harvey and Gold Key folding in the early 1980s, this readership was left with only the limited line of comic book titles published by Archie, a minor third player in the industry. By the end of the Late Industrial Age, comic books had become virtually the sole reserve of teen and young adult male readers.[55]

While the corporations that owned Marvel and DC were not particularly pleased by the poor sales of their comic book lines, they were not necessarily losing money on their comic book properties. First, Marvel and DC were bringing in significant foreign revenues from reprints from their large catalog.[56] But more importantly, they were bringing in large revenues from the licensing of superheroes for repurposing on television and in film and for marketing of a large array of consumer products. In 1979, reporting on problems at Marvel, *The New York Times* noted that "licensing monies have ballooned to the extent that they now contribute more revenues than the comics. These revenues stem from some 300 items—such as superhero bath towels, sheets, drinking cups and toys—as well as TV shows and movies. They prompted one Marvel writer to grouse, 'Marvel seems to be becoming a toy company rather than a publisher.'" Marvel editor Jim Shooter disagreed, "The folk wisdom about this industry is that characters are being kept alive only to allow licensing . . . It's totally untrue!"[57] Whether comic books characters were simply on creative life-support to allow licensing, the trend toward greater profits from licensing than publishing would continue up to the present.

The biggest coup for DC was the success of the 1978 and 1980 Warner Brothers movies *Superman: The Movie* and *Superman II*. *The New York Times* reported in 1981 that Warner's Licensing Corporation of America "awarded 200 licenses for more than 1,200 products on the movies, including belt buckles, underwear, watches, pillowcases, soap packaged like a telephone booth and expensive velour sweatshirts at Bloomingdales; Warner Publishing has churned out calendars, pop-up books, novelizations of the movies, the behind-the-scene story and even a Superman dictionary for children."[58] In 1985, Jenette Kahn, president and publisher of DC, was clear that this company was a "creative rights company." She noted that William Sarnoff, president of the publishing division at Warner Communications brought DC into the fold in 1969 with licensing clearly on his mind, particularly for movies. Kahn arrived at DC in 1976 and quickly revamped its superhero line of comic books. But she was equally aware of Warner's main strategy for revenue generation. "Her formula worked. DC now gets about a third of its approximately $70 million in revenues from comics, with the other two-thirds fairly equally divided between licensing and other products. Superman and his heroic colleagues now are commonplace on clothing and toys, and are spreading into food."[59]

While the licensing of comic book properties is as old as Superman himself, comic book sales for most of the Industrial Age were the main source of revenue for comic book publishers. But by the late 1970s, licensing for television and film, and product merchandising, became the main source of revenue for the major publishers Marvel, DC, and Archie. Many artists and fans truly believed that by the mid-1970s the comic book survived mostly based on its licensing power, complaining that the innovative days of the 1960s were truly dead.[60] Whether or not comic books suffered aesthetically in the 1970s and early 1980s, what was clear is that most Americans would consume superheroes via film, television, and all variety of cute toys and kitsch products. This logic of production would remain the overarching logic of mainstream comic books, regardless of the ups and downs of their sales and the moments of wonderful creative work. The age of the comic book as a mass medium was inarguably over. The only question that remained was whether it was on its deathbed.

While the two dominant publishers, Marvel and DC, entered a new phase of corporate control and a dominant strategy to profit on the "synergy" of their properties, their struggle to survive the declining market for comic books ironically moved them to market comic books as more than just clean, wholesome, unchallenging popular entertainment. In trying to be hip and relevant to a new generation of teenagers and young adults, these old publishing houses were opening the doors to perceive the comic book as not simply a children's medium, but a medium equal to popular film, fiction, or television. For these publishers, comic books remained unquestionably mass products to be churned out on a regular basis. But in their commercial drive to attract an audience they perceived as wanting more engaging and relevant comic book material, they unwittingly set the stage for others, both artists and readers, to take comic books even more seriously. By the early 1980s, the industry was witnessing a new generation of artists and fans intent on transforming the meaning and practice of comic book production and consumption.

Underground Comix

In the late 1960s, an underground comix movement emerged from the countercultural movement of the period. Articulating the rebelliousness, politics, and free spirit of the time, underground artists radically reshaped the American comic book. The social relevance and maturing of mainstream comic books paled in comparison to the social, political, and cultural politics of underground comix that were unquestionably for an "adults only" audience. But the radical and in-your-face content of underground comix were the fruits of a far greater contribution of this movement to the future of the American comic book. Underground artists were the first to articulate a complete rejection of the rules of art in the comic book field. They were the first to claim principles of autonomy that rejected the conventions of the field and the pure commercial ethos that remained its raison d'être. They also established the possibility of criteria of judgment that viewed comic books as a serious art form open to expressions comparable to any other art form. And they were the first to suggest that comic books could be the vehicle for an unmediated authentic expression of their artists.

Several underground artists first connected as high school students in the late 1950s in fanzines dedicated to EC comics.[61] But many of the underground artists attended college, so the first major development in this movement was the network of artists who worked on college newspapers and college humor magazines. Across the country these artists published and exchanged artwork for college humor magazines like the University of Texas *Ranger* and the University of Florida *Charlatan*. Jay Lynch remembers the underground artists making connections in these magazines. "Skip, Artie, and I worked for Chicago's *Aardvark* mag, and Gainesville's *Charlatan* mag. In *Charlatan* we were exposed to the work of Joel Beck, Jack Jaxon, Foolbert Sturgeon and Gilbert Shelton. As another genre, the college humor mags of the early '60s, was also an important forum for seminal underground comix innovators."[62] Jack Jackson (Jaxon) also remembers the connection to other young artists. "I exchanged humor magazines with other colleges, and kept touch with a lot of people who later on you met in the scene. Jay Lynch, and various people from around the country who were in the humor scene, were familiar just from correspondence."[63]

During the early 1960s, underground artists also found freelance work in magazines and novelty cards. Some did work for humor magazines. Harvey Kurtzman's *Help!* featured work by Robert Crumb, Skip Williamson, Jay Lynch, and Gilbert Shelton. Jay Lynch also did work for the humor magazines *Crack* and *Sick*. As early as 1959, Bill Griffith did work for the surfer magazine *Surfer* and created the popular cartoon character Murphy. A few other underground artists worked on hot-rod and motorcycle magazines. A number of artists also found work through Woody Gelmen at Topps Chewing Gum creating novelty cards. Jay Lynch later wondered "if there would have been underground comix without Topps and Woody Gelmen."[64] Underground artists in Texas and California also attempted to self-publish a few actual comic books like Jack Jackson's (Jaxon) *God Nose* (1963), a surreal story based on his experiences on peyote, and artist Joel Beck's humor comic book *Lenny of Laredo* (1963).[65]

The most important catalyst for underground comix was the rise of the "underground" press in 1965. With the advent of cheaper offset printing, new radical press periodicals appeared across the country. The earliest undergrounds included New York City's *East Village Other* (*EVO*), Los Angeles' *L.A. Free Press,* and San Francisco's *Oracle.* By 1967 the underground press had its own news syndicates with the Underground Press Syndicate and the Liberation News Service, which provided articles and art to members. The syndicates spurred a boom in the underground press from 1967 to 1969 with hundreds of underground periodicals appearing across the United States and Canada. The largest circulating press, *L.A. Free Press,* reached a peak circulation of ninety-five thousand.[66] In 1969, *Fortune* noted who was reading these undergrounds, "Hippies and doctrinaire Leninists, anarchists and populists, the 'campus cong' and peaceful communards, militant confrontationists and mystics, Bakuninists and humanists, power seekers, ego trippers, revolutionaries, Maoists, rock bands, and cultural guerillas."[67] Underground artists as cultural guerillas quickly found a home in these new periodicals. The *EVO* in particular featured a number of underground artists like Trina Robbins, Nancy Kalish, Bill Beckman, Kim Deitch, Spain Rodriguez, Gilbert Shelton, Robert Crumb, Jay Lynch, and Art Spiegelman. Eventually the *EVO* published a special all-comics magazine, *Gothic Blimp Works,* edited by underground artist Vaughn Bode. Suddenly, underground artists had a national network and readership to collectively identify themselves as a distinct movement in comic art.[68]

The "official" beginning of the underground comix movement is usually associated with the publication of three comic book anthologies in 1968. The first was *Zap* by Robert Crumb released in early 1968. It featured two of his most popular creations, Mr. Natural and the Keep on Truckin' character. Published in San Francisco, the first five-thousand-copy print run sold out after a Haight Street distributor for counterculture merchandise agreed to distribute the comic book. Meanwhile Gilbert Shelton arrived in San Francisco from Austin, Texas, in the summer of 1968. He arrived with a box of his new comic book *Feds 'n' Heads,* which he handed over to the San Francisco Comic Book Company in exchange for a used car. The third comic book associated with the birth of the movement was Jay Lynch and Skip Williamson's *Bijou Funnies*, published in Chicago in 1968. San Francisco would become the center of the underground comix movement with the Chicago Midwest as the second largest producer of comix.

Between 1968 and 1970, a number of underground artists moved to San Francisco from across the country to join those already in the city to create a community of artists who became the vanguard of the movement, including Robert Crumb, S. Clay Wilson, Gilbert Shelton, Kim Deitch, Trina Robbins, Lee Mars, Willy Mendes, Justin Green, Bill Griffith, Victor Moscoso, Spain Rodriguez, Jack Jackson, Fred Todd, Dave Moriarty, Dan O'Neill, and Dave Sheridan. Bill Griffith remembers:

> There was no resisting the pull of San Francisco . . . It was like an art movement. You joined an art movement; that was the feeling. It was a lot of things. First of all, it was a definite part of the hippie movement, the counterculture. We were part of the whole Haight-Ashbury scene . . . There was a kind of party atmosphere to some degree; and then there was the sort of salon atmosphere. We hung around a comic book store—the San Francisco Comic Book Company . . . We would hang out at the comic book store, and we would have regular parties at the publishers' offices, Rip Off Press and Last Gasp.[69]

Artist Ted Richards remembers the spirit of this art movement: "For me, the whole explosion, and the opportunities that this presented, is hard to describe. You could do about anything. It was an incredible, eclectic vision of art, design, storytelling, writing, color."[70]

The next step for artists was to find publishers to print and distribute their comix. A group of underground publishers quickly appeared between 1968 and 1970.[71] In the San Francisco Bay Area the Print Mint became the biggest publisher of comix, relying on its already successful poster printing and distribution business to promote new comix. Other publishers included Apex Novelties, San Francisco Comic Book Company, Rip Off Press, and Last Grasp Eco-Funnies. Publisher Gary Arlington remembers the burst of energy at the time, "In 1968, when Crumb started selling his *Zap #1*, I was working at a record store in the Mission District. About eight weeks later, I opened the San Francisco Comic Book Company, having no idea what was to come. The first year was pure energy. People came from everywhere to form a team . . . I really loved those early days. All that great stuff happened around me!"[72] In Chicago, Jay Lynch and Skip Williamson started Bijou Enterprises, while Denis Kitchen in Milwaukee established the largest underground publisher outside of San Francisco with Krupp Comic Works. As the boom in undergrounds continued, larger publishers helped distribute smaller imprints from around the country as well as self-publishing artists.

Publishers relied on mail-order catalogs and distribution through the counterculture network of head shops, record stores, and other alternative retailers. The extreme sexual, violent, and drug-infused content of comix made it impossible to go through conventional channels of distribution. The distribution system developed by underground publishers was essential for the success of comix. Artist Jack Jackson noted the importance of this alternative means of distribution. "And since none of the mainstream distributors would touch this outrageous material, it was really essential that we had that 'underground' system. If we hadn't had that system of head shops and various alternative outlets like that, the comix movement just wouldn't have gone anywhere. We all would have been sitting around with boxes of unsold comix."[73]

Once the distribution system was in place, underground publishers experienced a booming underground market for comix. Within a few short years there were around three hundred comix titles available and first print runs averaged twenty thousand copies. Publishers couldn't keep up with the demand.[74] Denis Kitchen remembers that the "demand for underground comix was mushrooming. During the period from 1971 to 1972 we literally could not keep up with the demands of distributors."[75] By 1973, Kitchen's Krupp Comic Works was publishing thirty-six titles with total monthly runs for the publisher at ninety to one hundred thousand and an annual production of over one million copies.[76] By 1972, Print Mint's anthology series *Zap Comics*, which now featured not only Crumb, but also Clay, Shelton, Griffith, Moscoso, and Rodriguez, had sold a total of over one million copies.[77] In 1972, *The New York Times* noted the new market for underground comix: "[S]ince the publication of 'Zap' in 1968, a whole underground comics industry has begun to flourish not only in San Francisco, but also in Chicago and Milwaukee. Although it is still a minor phenomenon accounting for only a small percentage of the 200-million-plus comics sold in America today, the market is growing."[78] Art Spiegelman remembered at the time, "any underground could find an audience for 20,000 copies, even if it really sucked."[79] Denis Kitchen was so enthused about the boom in comix that he informed the fanzine *Comixscene* in 1973 that "the only thing the straight comics have on us right now is money and distribution . . . But we have the talent, the ideas, the real future in comix . . . I can foresee the day when the undergrounds will be bigger than the straights. Of course, then we won't be underground anymore."[80]

Underground publishers treated their artists differently than mainstream comics publishers at the time. First, underground artists kept the copyrights to their work. They also received payment not simply on a per-page rate, but based on the sales of the comic book featuring their work, receiving additional payments for reprint runs, which were common in the underground market. The fanzine *Comixscene* praised the new attitude of underground publishers like Denis Kitchen and his Krupp Comic Works. "Krupp, for example, pays artists $30 a page for a 20,000 run of comix. The artist gets another $30 for a second run of 20,000, another $30 for another run, and so on. Some of the more popular artists get up to $150 a page. The straight comix pay artists a flat rate from $35 to $60 a page, and the company keeps the rights to the artwork. Most ug firms take only the first rights (and the right to reprint in the same book), and give all other rights back to the artist."[81] Patrick Rosenkranz, in researching for a book on underground comix, *Artsy, Fartsy, Funnies*, in the same period discovered similar practices among underground publishers. While there were some differences in payment schemes, the standard practice during the boom was considered twenty-five dollars per page for a print run of twenty thousand.[82]

Mark Estren, however, in researching for his history of underground comix in the early 1970s boom, also found a strong tension between "capitalist" publishers and their radical, libertarian artists. Rip Off Press was created by artists unhappy with the Print Mint. Other artists formed short-lived collectives. Underground artists also formed the United Cartoon Workers of America whose imprint appeared on several underground comix.[83] The union was credited with assuring standard payment practices among publishers. Robert Crumb expressed the view of underground artists in an interview for *Cleveland Magazine* in 1972. "Like a lot of the publishers of underground comics tend to be like . . . uh . . . try to rip off a little bit, but they're just real small time so they can't do that much. They're not really good at being crooks, you know, we manage to deal with them . . . publishers and managers always assume that artists and musicians are dum-dums and they can rip you off. . . . But now we have a union going, see, an underground cartoon workers union. Whatever schemes come up, we get together and talk about it and usually we hash it down to the fact that it'd be a bad thing to do, then forget about that."[84] Where such tensions between publishers and artists would have led the underground movement became a moot point when the market went bust in 1973.

What attention the underground comix movement got "above ground" was mostly to do with the success of Robert Crumb. *New York Times Magazine* in "Who is this Crumb?" noted in 1972 the recent success of Crumb outside of the underground market. His Keep on Truckin':

[S]eries of screwball cartoon characters with tiny heads, funky old clothes and huge clodhoppers, strutting down the street . . . can now be found almost everywhere: scrawled on subway walls and on sidewalks; plastered on bumper stickers; and imprinted on posters, buttons, T-shirts, baseball caps and sneakers—even in the remotest corners of the country . . . His work has been scorned as filthy and obscene, and indeed on the surface one finds a Boschian world of raunchy cartoon characters who curse, cavort and fornicate as if they inhabited an X-rated Disneyland. And yet, his work has been praised by others as comparable to the genius of Toulouse-Lautrec or Picasso. Whatever the verdict, Crumb's work has nevertheless established him as the most important underground cartoonist—and, by extension, social satirist—in America today.[85]

In 1968, Viking Press published the book *R. Crumb's Head Comix* as a trade paperback, albeit with a few swipes of a censor's pen. The following year Ballantine published the paperback *R. Crumb's Fritz the Cat* with Warner Brothers picking up the movie rights. Crumb had certainly caught the attention of the press and public, but the X-rated film *Fritz the Cat* in 1972 was not close to entering the mainstream of American media or culture.

So what were counterculture consumers clamoring to read in underground comix? What was the rebellious and taboo-breaking nature of these comix? San Francisco freelance writer, Thomas Maremaa, in his 1972 *New York Times Magazine* piece on Crumb, described to readers the general nature of this new art form:

> Soon Crumb, along with such artists as Gilbert Shelton, S. Clay Wilson, Manuel "Spain" Rodriguez, Rick Griffith and Victor Moscoso, had started a comics renaissance based in San Francisco. These comics, now changed to "comix," deliberately broke the taboos and defied the self imposed censorship of the traditional comic-book industry . . . They satirized fundamental American values by using old lovable cartoon characters in new, and often unspeakable, situations, turning the culture's own ammunition against itself . . . the non-linear art form of "head comics" began to fulfill some of the functions of social commentary once reserved to the novel. Indeed, Crumb brought "trash" art into cultural mainstream and made it respectable: For Adult Intellectuals. His work also connected more directly with the changing social consciousness of the young, both reflecting and defining many of the common attitudes toward sex, drugs and violence shared by a growing counterculture.[86]

In the simplest of terms, comix were humor comic books geared to the counterculture reader, many basing their humor on some form of social satire. While they gained a reputation for their exaggerated portrayal of sex, drugs, and violence—and were criticized for their misogynistic and sadistic content—comix also articulated the antiauthoritarian and radical politics of the counterculture. But for critics the difficulty was in the anarchistic way all these elements of the undergrounds often existed simultaneously in any one anthology or single story. For underground artists, breaking taboos and violating bourgeois tastes was in itself radical for the time, but the white male artists who dominated the underground scene violated these sensitivities from their own perspective. This led a number of these white male artists to portray women and blacks in demeaning ways. And while a number of underground artists expressed a clear radical politics, most had a libertarian attitude toward American politics with equal parts anti-establishment satire and equal parts antiradical satire. Artist Hall Robins remembers, "That is one thing about undergrounds that does definitely click in young people's minds: constant antiauthoritarianism."[87] As one of the most radical of these artists, even Spain Rodriquez remembered becoming "interested in Marxism, but from a libertarian perspective."[88] Regardless of others' perceptions of their work, however, all underground artists viewed themselves as critical artists challenging the mainstream "straight" society of Middle America.[89]

While underground politics was mostly found in general anthologies like *Zap*, a few specifically political comix were published. Paul Buhle, editor of *Radical America*, recognized the political potential of comix. "Like any potentially subversive cultural mechanism, komix serve at best to destroy an old view of the world and replace it with a new one."[90] He financed *Radical America Komix*, edited by Gilbert Shelton and featuring his antiwar character Smilin' Sergeant Death. Last Gasp Eco-Funnies started off looking to promote environmental awareness with its first comix. Founder Ron Turner remembered how he and his friends at a new ecological center in Berkeley "felt that this new art form, underground art, was a clear way to communicate. As propaganda went, it was as pure as anything we had seen."[91] He published *Slow Death Funnies* in time for the first Earth Day in 1970. Other strictly political comix included Skip Williamson's *Conspiracy Capers* (1969) and Frank Stack's *Jesus Meets the Armed Services* (1970), written under the pen name Foolbert Sturgeon. Spain Rodriguez's *Subvert Comics* (1970) also featured the radical superhero Trashman.

Drug culture and violence also were a regular part of underground comix. Reflecting the counterculture of its readers, drug culture permeated underground comix, but certain series and titles specifically emphasized this culture. The most successful drug-culture comix series was "The Fabulous Freak Brothers" created by Gilbert Shelton. It was featured in his 1968 *Feds* 'n' *Heads* and went on to have its own title and books. Ted Richard's "Doping Dan" also was a popular drugged-out character that spoofed army humor strip characters like Sad Sack. A few other drug-culture titles also appeared like *Stoned Picture Parade* (1968), *Tooney Loons and Marijuana Melodies* (1971), and *Dr. Atomic's Marijuana Multiplier* (1974). There were a few titles that actually addressed the downside of drug use including Jay Lynch's *The Great Marijuana Debate* (1972) and Print Mint's *Tuff Shit Comics* (1972).[92] Extreme violence also appeared in underground comix with some artists like S. Clay Wilson, Gilbert Shelton, and Spain Rodriguez gaining reputations for their extreme graphic representation. But following the tradition of EC comics, violence seemed to pop up everywhere from the sometimes absurd renditions of Crumb to the darker representations of Jack Jackson (Jaxon). Even the underground "romance" comic book *Young Lust* would have bullets flying through bodies.

While every imaginable, and unimaginable, sex act and theme appeared in a majority of comix stories, Robert Crumb and other artists brought it to the forefront in comix titles focusing exclusively on pornography. In 1968 and 1969, Apex Novelties came out with pornographic comix including *Snatch Comics* and *Jiz Comics,* while Rip Off Press published the pornographic comix *Big Ass Comics.* But Crumb, Clay, Shelton, Rodriguez, and others would create equally graphic and demeaning images and stories in *Zap Comix, Yellow Dog,* and other comix anthologies. The most controversial character was Crumb's Angelfood McSpade a black female character based on the old racist caricatures found in old comic art. While most sexual content in comix was satirically exaggerated and often considered misogynistic, a few underground comix attempted a tamer approach to sexuality, albeit still satirical, like *Young Lust* featuring the work of Bill Griffith, Jay Kennedy, Justin Green, and other underground artists.

One set of critics of the misogyny in underground comix were the women artists in the movement itself. In 1974, Trina Robbins expressed the outrage of female underground comix artists to underground journalist Mark James Estren as he was interviewing for his history of the underground comix movement. "What *does* concern me is the hostility towards women I see in this work, especially by Crumb. It's hard to relate to him as a person when you see what he does to women in his strips. . . . Crumb's porn upsets me, as does the work of a whole lot of other guys who think underground comix means porn. Rape is NOT FUNNY!!!"[93] The iconoclasm and intellectual depth of the underground comix appealed to underground comix artist Lyn Chevely, "but the men who wrote most of the comix generally represented women as fantasy objects of sex and violence."[94] Underground female comix artists also felt marginalized in the movement, not part of what artist Lee Marrs called the "boy's club" that excluded women from working in comix.[95]

Strongly influenced by the beginnings of the feminist movement at the time, female underground artists fought back at the misogyny in the comix movement. Trina Robbins joined the staff of the feminist underground newspaper *It Ain't Me Babe* and created, with the help of other female underground artists, the comix *It Ain't Me Babe Comix* for Last Gasp in 1970. A few attempts were made of single-issue, female-friendly comix like *All Girl Thrills* (1970) and *Girl Fight* (1972). Upset with the state of the movement, Robbins gathered in 1972 with ten other female artists—Pat Modian, Terre Richards, Sharon Rudahl, Lee Marrs, Michelle Brand, Lora Fountain, Karen Marie Haskell, Janet Wolf Stanley, Shelby Sampson, and Aline Kominsky—and formed the Wimmen's Comix Collective. These artists collectively produced *Wimmen's Comix* (1972) for Last Gasp featuring stories on marriage, work life, and abortion. As Terre Richards remembers, "As a result of the Women's Movement there was a growing awareness of women in all areas of the arts as well as a newly developing market for women's work in publishing, so the time was right for an all-woman's comic."[96] Almost simultaneously, Lyn Chevely, who used the pseudonym Chin Lyvely, and Joyce Farmer created Nanny Goat Productions in Los Angeles. They published *Tits and Clits* in July 1972, featuring the theme of "menstrual periods and how they affect a woman's life."[97] These pioneering female underground artists were the first to open up the comic field to female artists with a feminist perspective on everyday life, sexuality, and the crucial political issues confronting women at the time.

Other comix by underground women artists began appearing following the first two attempts to break the male monopoly over the movement. Lee Marrs began publishing the series *The Further Fattening Adventures of Pudge, Girl Blimp* with three issues between 1974 and 1977. It was a humorous underground comix about life as a hippie. Chevely and Farmer, who worked as counselors at a women's free clinic, published *Abortion Eve* (1973), where the stories of five pregnant women explained the choices, problems, and experiences of women having abortions. The first lesbian (and gay) comix, *Come Out Comix* (1974), was published at the Portland Women's Resource center by Mary Wings. Roberta Gregory followed with a lesbian comix *Dynamite Damsels* in 1976; Mary Wings published *Dyke Shorts* in 1978. Trina Robbins published her own comix *Trina's Women* with Krupp Comic Works in 1976. She introduced a female-oriented, but decidedly underground in style, erotica in Last Gasp's anthology comix *Wet Satin* (1974, 1978).[98]

Women underground artists as self-identified feminists in the seventies, while like all underground comix artists pushing the envelope of acceptable conventional norms, presented a more coherent politics in their intervention in the underground comix movement. They focused on feminist political positions related to sexism, homophobia, physical abuse, and abortion. Like other underground comix artists, their politics were up front and, so to speak, in your face. Fellow comix artist Diane Noomin dubbed their strategy or style as "twisted sisters"—feminists with an underground transgressive attitude—which also was the title for a comix she published in 1976.[99] Also like their male counterparts, feminist underground comic book artists more or less completely rejected mainstream or what at the time they called "straight" comic books. This first generation of female comic book rebels unquestionably laid the groundwork for future generations of women artists to intervene and attempt to transform the field of comic books.

Underground women artists, of course, were expressing the very principles of autonomy espoused by male underground artists. Trina Robbins remembers the drive for free self-expression in the movement:

> So, a lot of folks coalesced around New York and later on, San Francisco, and began feeling like they wanted to tell their own stories. A lot of the stories they wanted to tell were, for a majority of the people in the United States, disgusting, pornographic, too sexual, too revolutionary, too detailed, too confusing, too violent, too just about everything—which was what, of course, we enjoyed doing . . . you began to run into other folks who seemed to have a similar twisted attitude toward self-expression . . . But the kind of self-expression, no matter who didn't like it or who sued us or who threatened to take us to jail or anything else, was really a fierce, very strong kind of feeling for self-expression, for commenting on what we really thought was going on in the United States.[100]

While the most successful underground artist, Robert Crumb, did not have any art school training and never attended college, quite a few underground artists attended college or art schools in the early 1960s to study art. These underground artists brought the high art ideology of authentic self-expression to comics for the first time. Spain Rodriguez remembered transferring the ideology found in the high arts to comic books: "I mean, here you have an art tradition that I was put in contact with going to art school—the idea of the unbridled artist, the artist who could do anything he wanted, and here you have this whole area open for exploration, I mean, you had literature being apprised here, you had artwork being apprised, why aren't they apprised when they're put together?"[101]

Underground artists, however, did not feel part of the high art world of visual arts. Many remembered how marginal they felt in art classes as their "realistic" drawing was rejected. The reigning artistic approach at the time was abstract expressionism, realism was out. The Pop Art movement eventually challenged abstract expressionism, but even this movement was first rejected by the high art world.[102] Joe Schenkman remembered the attitudes reigning in these early art schools: "I soon realized that, hot-shot art school that Pratt was s'posed to be, I was one of a rare breed there that could actually *draw*. And the dream of cartooning hadn't left me, though most of my instructors thought I had to be joking."[103] Spain Rodriguez remembered how his comic art drawings at art school "were kind of sneered at." And like most underground artists, he still believes that art schools reject comic art. "In art school, there's a very subtle form of brainwashing, where if you know how to draw, they don't actually say drawing is bad, but they give you the idea. They insinuate it into you. If you really work on your drawing skills, that's not a good thing."[104] This sense of the low status and marginality of comic art in relation to the high art field of the visual arts was another legacy that the underground comix movement passed on to future generations of alternative comic book artists.

By 1973, underground artists saw their ideology based on the belief in autonomous self-expression and the view of comic art as more than just commercial product confirmed in the booming underground market. Unfortunately, that same year the underground market crashed as a number of factors undermined what seemed like an unstoppable boom. The first major factor was the suppression of underground comix through government censorship. The general breaking of previous boundaries on sexually explicit material accompanying the countercultural rumblings of the 1960s reignited general fears of a rising demand for obscenity in the United States.[105] Underground comix quickly led to authorities seizing comix and busting individuals involved in selling or publishing comix. But according to Mark Estren, few led to actual convictions. Only two salesmen in New York City, Charles Kirkpatrick and Peter Dargis, were convicted for selling comix. The general debate around obscenity, however, led the U.S. Supreme Court to reconsider its stand on state censorship and obscenity. In a landmark case, the Supreme Court in 1973 introduced the "community standard" doctrine whereby local communities were given greater power to decide what was obscene and what was not obscene. This significantly empowered local authorities fighting against obscene material and dealt a terrible blow to the underground comix market.[106] Authorities, for example, went after Lyn Chevely and Joyce Farmer's *Tits and Clits* in 1973, arresting two store owners in Orange County,

California, for selling obscene material. Chevely and Farmer avoided publishing any other comic books for two years until the local district attorney dropped all charges in the case.[107]

Denis Kitchen remembers the collapse of the underground market:

> The underground comix industry—which had been burgeoning, mushrooming in size—ran into a couple of hurdles in 1973. First, the Supreme Court came up with a new definition of obscenity that basically threw the definition back to local communities to define. That sent a chill through all the head shops that were the base of our distribution. These retailers were already paranoid because they were selling drug paraphernalia and the authorities were looking for reasons to bust them. So they figured underground comix were where they were the most vulnerable. Overnight, a lot of our head shop accounts literally stopped buying underground comix.[108]

Gordon Wilson, the bookstore owner arrested for carrying underground comix in Orange Country, expressed the fears of shop owners: "The Supreme Court has fixed it now that any cop with a gripe can crack down on us and burden us with legal fees and loss of work."[109] For Denis Kitchen another problem was "the glut in the underground market. They had been so successful in the late 60s and early 70s, that a lot of what I called 'wannabe' publishers and artists jumped in . . . it started clogging up the racks. And these retailers—who by and large were not comics fans (remember, they were primarily selling tie-dyed shirts and bongs and beads, so they didn't necessarily know a great underground comic from a horrible underground comic), so that combination put a lot of us on the ropes."[110] The final fatal shot was a steep rise in paper costs that year that not only affected underground comix, but eventually wiped out the large network of underground newspapers.[111]

The main underground publishers were able to survive the collapse of their specialty market by shifting to a direct market that just emerged at the time to serve a growing fandom for comic books.[112] While some comic fans enjoyed underground comix, the direct market was not the same as the counterculture market, so underground publishers struggled to maintain lines of underground comix in the late 1970s. New underground comix did get published, but the market had shrunk considerably. The few remaining underground publishers relied on reprints of proven titles and remained highly selective in introducing new titles. Some artists returned to freelance in gentleman's magazines or other work. The most famous attempt to keep the movement going were Art Spiegelman and Bill Griffith's *Arcade* published between 1975 and 1976. But little else emerged in the wake of the underground comix collapse.

The underground comix movement was the first articulation of rebellion against the rules of art of the Industrial Age. Comix artists represented the first expression of principles of autonomy that focused on radically transforming the American comic book. Unfortunately this movement only enjoyed a short period of success and is mostly remembered for its transgressive world of sex and drugs. As comix artists Art Spiegelman and Françoise Mouly remembered in 1987:

> Underground comics had offered something new: comics by adults, for adults; comics that weren't under any obligation to be funny, or escapist pulp; comics unselfconsciously redefining what comics could be, by smashing formal and stylistic, as well as cultural and political, taboos. At last, there was a comics avant-garde. Comics were coming of age . . . Then, somehow, what had seemed a revolution simply deflated into a lifestyle. Underground comics were stereotyped as dealing only with Sex, Dope, and Cheap Thrills. They got stuffed into the back of the cultural closet, along with bong pipes and love beads, as Things Started to Get Ugly.[113]

The revival of the underground rebellion would have to wait as a new generation of rebel artists joined the old guard of underground comix in what would be called an "alternative comics" movement in the 1980s. This new generation, along with the old guard, would bring the new principles of autonomy and new criteria of judgment developed in the underground comix movement to a new comic book culture springing up from a direct market in comic book fandom.

Conclusion

The Late Industrial Age witnessed a steady decline in the mass market for comic books. By the mid-1980s, the future of the American comic book as a viable commercial product looked stark at best. Regardless of the dire state of the industry, however, the mainstream comic book had moved in a new direction that presaged future transformations in this art form. Ironically, while the anti–comic book crusade and the 1955 Comics Code had seemingly framed the American comic book as purely a child's medium, the commercial logic of the industry during the Late Industrial Age sent it scrambling for some form of stability in the market that it found in comic books geared to older adolescents and college-age male readers. And as the general press and the culture industries perceived this new generation as "hipper" and more "sophisticated" than previous generations, the comic book industry in its own fashion moved toward more "adult" content in its comic books. This transformation also was aided by a new generation of fan-artists just entering the field in the 1970s and early 1980s. These fan-artists would become the vanguard of a mainstream rebellion in the comic book field in the coming Heroic Age of comic books. This rebellion would not only develop the mainstream comic book further as an art form, but also transform the status of artists in the comic book field.

While the social and political currents of the 1960s led to the perception of a new, more sophisticated mass culture consumer, these currents also created a counterculture movement that significantly intervened in the evolution of the American comic book. The introduction of cheap offset printing created a new *social space* for this counterculture movement to challenge the mainstream press and eventually the "straight" comic book industry. While the underground comix movement was a short-lived charismatic moment in comic book history, its impact would be long lasting. At a time when the comic book industry was contracting, relying on a few old proven pulp genres, the underground comix movement was a radical intervention in reconceptualizing the potential of the American comic book. The new principles of autonomy and criteria of judgment that emerged in this movement would become the foundation of both mainstream and alternative rebellions during the Heroic Age of comic books. Similar to Pierre Bourdieu's analysis of the Heroic Age in French literature, however, while the charismatic movement of comix provided an alternative set of rules of art, what was still needed was a more coherent and sustainable subfield of art for a heroic age to appear.[114]

The mid-1980s marked the end of the Industrial Age of the American comic book. Although this marks the end of the Industrial Age, the comic book field was actually entering its healthiest period since before the collapse of the boom market in the mid-1950s. But the field would have significantly changed. Publishers would no longer serve an anonymous mass audience with quickly assembled products by anonymous craftsmen churning out comic art like an industrial product. A new comic book culture of fanzines, comic shops, and conventions would become the new nexus in which fans, artists, and publishers would interact and communicate in ways unimaginable during the Industrial Age. The new field would be dominated by fan-readers who knew and discussed the history and aesthetics of the medium; and shaped their preferences on not only characters, but on star writers and graphic artists. With their newfound recognition, mainstream artists would begin to approach the comic book as a medium of self-expression in popular fiction. Meanwhile an alternative comics movement would pick up where the underground comix movement left off, continuing the rebellion for autonomy and moving the comic book medium toward new "literary" heights. Both mainstream and alternative artists in the field now would approach, albeit differently, comic art as an art form capable of expressing their unique talents and visions. The new network of distributors and shops would open up the field to independent publishers to move the comic book in new and challenging directions. All these changes were leading to a new Heroic Age of the American comic book—a time in which the practice and meaning of comic art would undergo a radical transformation in America.

4

From the Late Industrial to the Heroic Age

*Comic Book Fandom and the
Mainstream Pulp Rebellion*

In the Late Industrial Age, a comic book fandom emerged that over time significantly changed the comic book field. While not necessarily their original intention, which was simply to express their love for old comic books, ardent fans from the 1960s to early 1980s created a subculture of fanzines, conventions, sellers, distributors, and specialty shops that in the eyes of most observers saved the comic book industry from complete collapse. What emerged from this early fandom was a new direct market where shop owners could preorder comic books for their local specialty comic book shop. As mainstream publishers struggled with a declining mass market they discovered that the high demand from the direct market might be the solution to their problems. By the late 1980s, most comic book publishers had moved to this direct market as the main focus of their publishing efforts, supported by what had become a vibrant, but marginal, subculture of comic book fans.

Comic book fandom, like underground comix, represented another *charismatic* movement in the comic book field that brought its own set of principles of autonomy and criteria of judgment to the *mainstream* of the field. This is most evident in early fandom transforming the status of comic book artists. It recognized them as the true creators of the great American comic book. Early fandom also became a breeding ground for a new generation of "fan-artists" who approached this medium as an art form worthy of respect and expecting a similar respect toward themselves as artists. These artists would become the vanguard of rebel artists who would take comic books seriously as a form of popular fiction. But the Late Industrial Age was not particularly kind to comic book artists. Most of the new generation of artists would become disenchanted from the lack of respect, poor treatment, and even worse compensation they received for all their hard labor and creative work.

Artists from comic book fandom represented the first *mainstream* expressions of revolt leading into the new Heroic Age in comic books. Fan-artists, guided by their own principles of autonomy, approached comic books as an artist's medium of self-expression whether refashioning old comic book characters and series or fashioning new ones. Marvel and DC would eventually acknowledge fan-artists as "auteurs" of the medium, placing them front and center in the marketing of comic book series, and in the process increasing their sales. But many fan-artists continued to view Marvel and DC as still stuck in the Industrial Age in terms of creativity and their treatment of artists. So when the Heroic Age began in the 1980s they would strike out on their own to challenge even more the boundaries of mainstream comic books.

The Heroic Age of comic books is also marked by the direct market transforming the core of comic book readers into a "comic book culture" of specialized fans. The main readership in this new subculture was predominantly males in their teens and twenties, and some even older. The comic book field was no longer a mass market targeting anonymous readers, but a specialized market targeting readers familiar with the history of comic books and intimately engaged in contemporary comic book series. Comic book readers developed their own criteria of judgment and forms of appreciation in a collective dialogue found in fanzines, conventions, and comic book shops. Publishers would respond to this new form of appreciation and expert knowledge. They would move to serial story lines complicating the universes of mainstream characters. Comic books also contained self-reflective moments on the history and nature of superhero and other genres.

The rise of comic book fandom also signaled a significant change from the simple consumption of comic books to a subculture focused on collecting comic books. As the field moved solidly into a direct market supported by this comic book culture it was struck by a speculative collector's boom in comics that led to an explosion in circulation and sales. This speculative frenzy led to individual issues actually selling more than the most popular titles during the Industrial Age. But the speculative market simultaneously changed the old commercial logic of the field. Publishers suddenly focused on comic books not as products to be consumed for their entertainment value alone, if at all, but as collectables to be saved for their future market value. A deluge of new titles, multiple titles for a single character, multiple covers for a single issue, and additional gimmicks to generate more sales among speculating fans and nonfans led to a bubble in circulation and sales that suddenly burst in the early 1990s. By the end of the 1990s, as the market continued to plummet, the old question of the economic viability of the American comic book once again was on the minds of everyone in the comic book field.

Comic Fandom, the Direct Market, and Comic Book Artists

The Late Industrial Age was a period in which a dedicated fandom for comic books emerged. While fans always existed for comic books—writing letters to their favorite comic book publishers or joining special Superman, Captain Marvel, or EC clubs—a comic book fandom was not established until the 1960s. One best characterizes a fandom as an *organized social network* of fans. Usually fans connect through fanzines, conventions, and other group activities. And this certainly was the case for comic book fandom beginning in the 1960s. These fans began as simply lovers and collectors of old comic books or avid fans of the superhero revival of the 1960s. What is striking about comic book fandom, however, was the major impact it eventually had in transforming the field of the American comic book. The early pioneers certainly had no idea they would create the foundations for a revolution in the comic book field. Early comic book fandom has its own dedicated historian, Bill Schelly. Schelly has published books and fanzine articles as well as organized panels at comic book conventions. His work as well as press coverage of the time inform my discussion of these early pioneering fans in the 1960s.

While fanzines existed before the 1960s, the wave of fanzines that appeared during this decade became the foundation of a new comic book fandom. These fanzines were first produced by somewhat older fans of comic books interested in collecting their favorite comic books from the Early Industrial Age. Collectors ranged from college-educated fans to working-class fans. They were virtually all white males, but several women were early pioneers as well. In 1961 two fanzines dedicated to comic books appeared: *Alter Ego* and *Comic Art*. Fan-publisher Jerry Bails followed *Alter Ego* with two more specialized fanzines in 1961. *The Comicollector* was dedicated to collecting and selling old comic books, and *The Comic Reader* presented news on the comics industry and upcoming superhero releases. While fan-art appeared in most fanzines, fanzines specially dedicated to fan-art appeared quickly with *Komix Illustrated* in 1962 and *Fighting Hero Comics* in 1963. According to Bill Schelly, starting in 1965 there was a boom in comic book fanzines. By the end of the decade around six hundred comic book fanzines had appeared over the last ten years amounting to a total of about two thousand issues.[1] These fanzines ranged from general interest to more specialized fanzines for collectors, fan-art, industry news, and fanzines dedicated to specific publishers like Marvel.[2] "Pro-zines" also appeared in the late 1960s. These magazines were published for fans but featured the work of professional comic book artists. While they cost more than nonprofessional fanzines, their high quality and use of top professional artists, according to Bill Schelly, eventually undermined the demand for less-slick fanzines.[3]

The early 1960s also witnessed the first comic book fan organization. First named The Academy of Comic-Book Arts and Sciences in 1962, it became The Academy of Comic-Book Fans and Collectors when the charter was ratified by ninety-two fans in 1963. Under the charter the academy supported the annual Alley Awards for comic books. It published *The Comic Reader* and a directory of fans. The academy also supported a Code of Fair Practices in the collectors market, and committed itself to establishing an annual comic book convention. By 1965, the organization boasted a membership of two thousand, made up of some adults, but mostly teenage and younger fans.[4] This organization lasted until 1969 when the last Alley Awards were presented.

Comic book fans also hoped to emulate the popular science fiction conventions of the time to create a place to meet other fans as well as comic book professionals. The first national convention dedicated solely to comic books was the New York City Comicon held in 1964. In 1965, New York City once again hosted a Comicon with two hundred attendees. By 1968 the attendance at this convention reached around five hundred "teen-agers, collectors, dealers, editors, cartoonists and would-be cartoonists."[5] Other regional conventions began convening across the country. Detroit hosted a successful multifan convention in 1965. Other cities hosting conventions in the late 1960s and early 1970s included Dallas, Houston, Oklahoma City, Tulsa, Chicago, St. Louis, Phoenix, Los Angeles, and Boston.[6] San Diego hosted its first comic book convention in 1970. In 1972, the San Diego convention was attended by nearly one thousand people who "gathered to talk about, admire, sell, buy and trade old comic books in furtherance of what has become a growing—and expensive—new avocation."[7]

By the first convention in New York City, the press began to notice that people were collecting old comic books. *The New York Times* noted in December 1964 that "old 10-cent comic books that tidy parents either threw away or sold by the hundred weight to the junk dealer are now being sold, individually, for prices ranging from $2 to $25."[8] One month later the paper noted the fandom busy buying old comic books. "Whatever happened to Captain Marvel, Batman, the Golden Arrow and the Flash? . . . Today some are gone—but not forgotten by thousands of comic-book fans throughout the country. These fans and collectors have their own clubs, a national academy and a widespread interest in preserving the stories about their fictional superheroes."[9] In *Newsday* in 1965, reporter David Zinman visited Comicon organizer David Kaler's Greenwich Village apartment noting he was part of "a close-knit, bustling group. Collectors correspond, publish at least 30 fan magazines, hold national conventions and costume parties, swap back issues, and buy and sell old magazines . . . Collectors even have their own language."[10] *The New Yorker* reported on the 1965 New York Comicon. "[W]e were present to learn what we could about the assemblage, made up of adults and adolescents—unhip and outside the pop-culture movement— who rather solemnly treasure vintage issues of *Action Comics* and *Detective Comics*, in the same way a bibliophile would prize a first addition of 'Paradise Lost.'"[11]

Not quite sure how to handle the enthusiasm of comic book fans, journalists suggested a certain fanaticism on the part of these fans. The least subtle suggestion was referring to fans as cultists, a more subtle suggestion was referring to their fascination with obscure details of comic book history. David Zinman in his *Newsday* article referred to fan David Kaler as a "board member of a cult of vintage comic book aficionados, who grandiosely call themselves the Academy of Comic Book Fans and Collectors. Is all this for real?"[12] That same year *Newsweek* informed readers, "With the enthusiasm of rare-stamp collectors, the comic cultists buy, sell, and swap vintage issues through the two dozen or so publications devoted to their four-color heroes." The article went on to explain how fans "studiously traced the lineage" of superheroes. Fan's dedicated themselves to knowing when Superman gained X-ray vision or when Clark Kent first made a failed pass at Lois Lane. "The Batmanians are also painstaking scholars; one, in fact, made comic-book history by discovering that a panel on page 6 of Detective Comics No. 36 depicted Batman with six fingers on his right hand."[13] It is clear that the press had a difficult time taking comic book fandom as a serious endeavor.

By the early 1970s, however, the press was discovering a veritable industry in comic book collecting. In 1972, *Newsweek* reported, "Comic books have been big business for a long time, but the bull market now is in 'antique' issues. Prices for vintage comics range from the original dime to $1,200 . . . Other collectors, however, readily admit that their primary interest is in the money they can make from comics . . . The vast majority of comic-book collectors, of course, are perfectly ordinary people who get into the game simply for the fun of it. Their interest has spawned more than 100 national conventions (4,000 fans attended a recent convention in New York), many mail-order houses and more than 75 publications."[14] *The New York Times* in 1973 also was reporting about a new lucrative market in collectables. "Comic book collecting has been growing slowly but steadily since the series of nostalgia waves began in the middle 1960s. Today, serious—not to say obsessive—collectors who analyze stories, criticize artwork and even examine the staples have created a full-fledged market, with all the trimmings: conventions where buyers and sellers meet, numerous trade journals (called 'fanzines') and hundreds of dealers."[15]

It is probably not surprising that the press focused mostly on the monetary value or simple fun of collecting. Given the low regard for comic books, the idea of collecting as a serious intellectual endeavor was difficult to imagine. Fans did try to convey to the press that their efforts were serious. As *Newsweek* commented, "Collectors, of course, find cosmic reasons to justify the hobby and its high cost. According to their fans, comics constitute a unique art form and also mirror historic changes in U.S. culture."[16] But for older fans the reasons were not cosmic, but central to their efforts as fans. Commenting on the early days of collecting, fan Shel Dorf remembered how "in the early days, nobody talked about price value. It was all about the art and story."[17] In the first issue of *Comic Art* in 1961 Dick Lupoff expressed a similar feeling in pointing to fans preserving what they considered a unique art form. "Yes, I enjoy old comics, but it's a lot more than that. I care about old comics. Old comics *matter*—they *count*. And anyone planning projects to save them can count on me."[18] Lupoff also edited, with Don Thompson, the first fan-published book on comic book history, *All in Color for a Dime* (1970).

Fans' recognition of the creators of comic books had a long-term impact on the field of comic books. Fans collected old and new comic books often because of the artists associated with the specific issue. Fans also were well aware of the invisibility of comic book creators and made it their mission to credit these artists and interview them about the world of comic books. Fan Maggie Thompson, editor of the early fanzine *Comic Art*, later commented on the role fans played in elevating comic book creators to their rightful place in the comic book field. "Another contribution of fandom was the recognition finally given professional writers and artists in the medium who had previously toiled in anonymity."[19] In both fan articles and fan news about the industry, artists were regularly cited for their work. And the fans' Alley Awards provided important recognition for writers and graphic artists. Writer John Broome wrote a thank-you letter to *Alter Ego* for receiving a 1961

Alley Award. "First, I am all for your fan organization. I feel it is the only way we comic writers (and artists) can become known by name and thus receive greater recognition (to say nothing of higher rates) . . . Some day we may attain certain legitimacy and if we do we will know who was responsible for our change in station."[20]

Another contribution of fandom's elevation of comic book artists was transforming the art of comic books. By the late 1960s, fan-artists began to enter the field in significant numbers, replacing the old guard of artists who had no particular love for comic books. The new generation of fan-artists was different. As a member of this new generation, Frank Miller noted the enthusiasm of fan-artists and their love of comic books, "That next generation charged into the field, full of love and anger and talent, ready to take comics in new directions . . . the first of what could have been a long line of kids who grew up on comics and were ready to give them their all."[21] These artists would eventually become the most successful in the field, including John Byrne, Dave Cockrum, Steve Gerber, Frank Miller, Jim Starlin, Len Wein, Marv Wolfman, and John Workman.[22]

This new vanguard of fan-artists represented a new generation of comic book artists made up of both working-class and middle-class men, many with college educations.[23] The first generation of comic book artists was young working-class men, a few never finishing high school, who approached their work mostly as an opportunity to earn a living. This generation dominated the field of comic books until the end of the 1960s. The new generation of comic book artists combined the new fan appreciation of comic books as "art" with the greater disposition stemming from a college education to take their positions as professional artists more seriously. This involved both a challenge to the Industrial Age working conditions of the comic book field as well as a whole new approach to their role as artists. This new generation did not view themselves as merely craftsmen creating an industrial product, but artists fashioning a popular art form that could be appreciated as art. While the greater level of education among this new generation certainly had an impact, given the collective development of this new appreciation of comic books, all in this new generation of fan-artists would approach their profession and art far differently than the first generation of comic book artists.

The first impact of the new generation of mostly fan-artists was a revitalization of mainstream comic books. As Frank Miller suggests, these artists viewed themselves as mavericks ready to push this art form in new directions. They also were influential in the wave of socially relevant and later more mature comic books of this period. Fan-artist Rich Buckler remembered "a renaissance going on in the comics (though none of us knew this at the time it was happening). It was the arrival of a new generation of artists and writers."[24] Many brought with them their generational attitudes about the potential of comic books as a popular art form. One of the young fan-artists Steve Mitchell remembers himself as:

> [A] member of what I call the "blue-jean generation." All the guys that preceded us were the "suit-and-tie generation" . . . all those guys were commercial artists—they weren't comic book guys—they used to wear sports jackets, and ties and suits, and they looked like grown-ups. Then, all of us guys came in, and we were wearing blue jeans, and stripped shirts, and we had long hair, and we were fans. We were really polar opposite of what the expected professional in that business had been for 20–30 years . . . We were fans. That's the other thing: We were really devoted to the form, and wanted to be part of it. It wasn't just a job.[25]

While this new generation still worked within the creative constraints of editors and the limits of the superhero and other mainstream genres, members of this generation would be the first self-conscious and recognized "auteurs" in the field of comic books—creators who viewed their work as an expression of themselves as artists and serving an audience of fans who shared a similar view of their work. It became increasingly clear that for fans, writers and graphic artists were as crucial to a series' success as the popularity of its characters. Of course, mainstream publishers by the next decade realized how the "star" power of fan-artists was a great marketing tool. While still peddling old properties like Superman or Spider-Man, now DC and Marvel could use popular fan-artists to ratchet up the symbolic value of these properties and increase sales. The assembly-line production of mainstream comic books would simply integrate these fan-artists' talents into the service of tried-and-true properties in the mass production process.

It's clear, however, that the driving force in comic fandom in its first decades was collecting. Collecting at first focused on Early Industrial Age comic books, but quickly led to building comic collections with contemporary comic books as well. In the 1960s, the average fanzine circulation was one hundred to two hundred copies, but what became the main collector's advertising fanzine in the 1960s, *The Rocket Blast—Comicollector*, far surpassed its fellow fanzines with a circulation of over one thousand by 1967 and reaching its peak of 2,500 at the end of the decade.[26] The new market for comic books led fans toward becoming serious dealers of comic books. Many of these dealers were only teenagers when they began. By the late 1960s, there was a sudden boom in guides and dealers when Marvel began featuring ads for comic book price guides and handbooks for collecting.[27] The boom in dealers and guides was capped off with the first "comprehensive" price guide, *The Comic Book Price Guide*, published in 1970 by longtime collector Bob Overstreet. With its sixth edition in 1976, the guide was over 550 pages and sales had soared to forty-one thousand copies.[28]

Given the interest of fans in not only old comic books, but also contemporary comic books, the fortunes of comics publishers should have blossomed in the late 1960s and early 1970s. But as we saw in the previous chapter, the old distribution system was breaking down and sales were falling for publishers. Ironically, part of the blame fell on the frenzied efforts of fan-dealers. Fan-dealer Robert L. Beerbohm remembers how fan-dealers quickly took advantage of this collector's market by buying up as many issues of potential moneymakers from corrupt independent distributors: "A growing number inside comics fandom figured early on that certain artists sold well in a growing after-market . . . we and other dealers around the country were buying out local ID's entire allotments of these hot items . . . When they realized that we could buy out certain titles, it was easy for them to continue claiming to the national distributor that the issues in question had been shredded. The back-door money never got back to the publisher, and the sales figures that were reported surely were bogus."[29] The fan-dealer turned speculator was further undermining a distribution system already faltering from the low demand for comic books. In a strange twist of fate, the new comic book series that suffered the most from siphoning off into an underground fan-dealer economy were by fan-artists. According to Beerbohm, dealers were making 500 to 1,000 percent markups in such top favorites in the underground economy of mail-order and convention sales.[30]

The old distribution system of comic books was in chaos. It was left to high school teacher, fan-dealer, and convention organizer Phil Seuling to come up with a solution. In 1973, Seuling approached comics publishers with the idea of a "direct market." With his intimate knowledge of the tastes of comic fans, he offered to take comic books at the same discount of national distributors, but keep every comic book with no returns. He could easily sell unsold comic books later as "back issues." Every comic book distributed in this new system was a guaranteed sale and publishers would not have to deal with a return system that was ripe with corruption.[31] But for this idea to work, the direct market needed not only a distributor familiar with the more specialized fan market, but a broader network of specialty comic book shops that could gauge more closely the demand of the new comic book fan-consumer.

While early fan-dealers worked through mail-order or sales at conventions, the new specialized market began to spawn specialty comic book shops. When Beerbohm opened his specialty comic book shop in 1972 in Berkeley, he and co-owners Bud Plant and John Barrett estimated that there were twenty-two other similar shops in the United States. Steve Schanes at fifteen and Bill Schanes at thirteen began dealing comic books in 1970 and opened their own shop in 1974. Another new shop owner in 1974, Chuck Rozanski, who opened his shop at age nineteen, later remembered at that time somewhere around thirty specialty shops with one hundred other shops featuring comic books.[32] The initial years of the direct market saw a gradual growth in the market with Marvel moving from 1.5 million dollars in direct market sales in 1976 to 3.5 million dollars in 1979.[33] The floodgate opened, however, when legal actions around Phil Seuling's exclusive arrangement with publishers led to an opening for new distributors in the direct market in 1979. With new distributors entering the market, a boom in comic shops quickly followed. Rozanski remembered the post-1979 boom, "I knew opening up to more distributors would cause growth, but I didn't realize how much it would be. It went from 7-or-800 shops to 3,000 in just three years. That was growth no one anticipated."[34]

The boom in the direct market did not go unnoticed by the major publishers Marvel and DC. Marvel was the first to see the future potential of the direct market when within the first year of the post-1979 boom it saw its direct market sales reaching approximately 30 percent of its total sales. It introduced *The Dazzler* in 1981; the first comic book exclusively published for the direct market. It sold four hundred thousand copies, twice the average sales of a Marvel comic book at the time. Marvel also reissued special editions of previously published comic books for just the direct market. By 1982 the direct market was accounting for around half of Marvel sales.[35] DC released its first exclusive direct market comic book in 1982. And recognizing the direct market power of fan-artists, DC presented one of the first marquee-name comic books in 1983, *Frank Miller's Ronin*. Both DC and Marvel, in response to the more refined tastes of fans and their direct market, also began a series of improvements in graphic and print quality that would continue into the 1990s.[36] Even Archie Comics recognized the new direct market and revamped some of their old superheroes and published eight superhero titles in 1983.[37]

While underground comix publishers and a few independent comic titles appeared in the early direct market, the post-1979 boom brought more independent publishers into the market to directly compete with mainstream publishers such as Pacific Comics' *Captain Victory and his Galactic Rangers* (1981), Capital Comics' *Nexus* (1981), First Comics' *American Flagg!!* (1983), and Vortex's *Mister X* (1984). The British publisher Eagle also imported comics for the new direct market including *Judge Dredd* (1983). While these new publishers focused on mainstream genres, fanzine publisher Gary Groth created Fantagraphics Books in 1981 in order to publish "alternative" comics, the next generation of underground comix. Publishing without the seal of the Comics Code, these publications further pushed the boundaries of content in comic books catering to a more adult audience. Independent publishers were setting the groundwork for reconceptualizing the readership for comic books.

New independent publishers would have another effect on the comic book field: better treatment of comic book artists. In the 1960s, publishers relied on the old guard of writers and artists, many who began their careers in the late 1930s and 1940s. This old guard accepted the basic working conditions inherited from the Early Industrial Age. Unlike the old guard, however, the new generation of fan-artists who began entering the field in the 1970s had different expectations about their careers as comic book artists. Many young artists were surprised at both the attitudes of older artists and the conditions of their employment. As next generation artist Mark Evanier remembers, "[T]hey all told me that, no matter how successful you were, there was no way to ever make decent money in comics and that depressed them . . . and me . . . When I got into comics around 1970 and I started hanging out with people who did comics or who'd done them all their lives. I found that the only thing most of them wanted from the field was out. Some of them hated the field."[38]

While many artists were in-house "staff" in the bull pens of publishers, virtually all writers and artists were treated like "work-for-hire" freelancers; paid per page with no company benefits. And publishers continued to claim all rights to the work of writers and artists. While National had contractual agreements, Marvel continued the old practice of stamping the back of paychecks with a waiver of all rights to ones' work. Since the 1950s, pay rates had barely increased. In the fanzine *Mediascene* in 1978, fan Ken Bruzenak complained about the compensation and benefits afforded comic book artists. "An artist who drew comic books in 1952 for, say DC, made $35 to $50 per page, pencil and ink. Now that same artist may make $75 per page. Workers have unemployment compensation. Freelancers have none . . . Most employees at both Cadence [Marvel Corporate Owner] and DC have retirement benefits. Freelancers have none . . . Describe these conditions to any other professional and the response is one of horror. In every respect, we're years behind them and losing ground."[39]

There were some efforts by artists to change their working conditions. In 1969, the Academy of Comic Book Artists (ACBA) was formed. Unfortunately, some members wanted this organization simply to act as a promotional organization instead of a union. It only lasted until 1975. It accomplished very little to change the working conditions of artists.

Publishers did acknowledge the right of return of original artwork to artists and also hiked page rates for certain artists. Publishers also began to initiate payments for reprints.[40] Artists' anger was reignited, however, when a new copyright act went into effect in January 1978. The U.S. Congress designed the act to improve the rights of artists. Unfortunately, a loophole in the act exempted "work-for-hire" artists from these rights. DC and Marvel immediately made up new contracts and release forms that designated artists as work-for-hire artists. Angered artists formed the Comic Book Creators Guild that same year. Fanzine *Mediascene* lambasted the industry in support of the guild. "The past (and present) system of doing business in comics is feudal in design, right down to its class distinctions between wealthy publishing 'barons' and powerless working 'serfs.'"[41] But like the ACBA, the guild faltered from lack of solidarity among independent freelance artists. Most artists signed the new contracts.[42]

While the market for popular fan-artists significantly increased their page rates, it was only when Marvel and DC's economic interests were challenged by independent publishers that they significantly changed their treatment of artists. The new independent publishers needed to attract top talent from the major publishers, so they offered deals never imagined by artists in the field. Pacific Comics publisher Steve Schanes remembered, "We were the first to introduce better paper in comics, the first to offer royalties and creator-owned comics. . . . Eventually, we forced Marvel and DC to match our terms."[43] By 1982 Marvel and DC had significantly changed their treatment of artists. Fan-artist Frank Miller, in the fanzine *Comics Scene*, noted this major change. Marvel offered creators of graphic novels new rights to their work. Both DC and Marvel also instituted profit-sharing policies. "All of a sudden, it's a brand-new ball game. Writers and artists of established titles can look forward to sharing in the profits made from their work. It is conceivable that a comics artist could make more money next year than he has in the last five years combined . . . For all the sweat and blood of the generations of talent who built this peculiar industry of ours, this is the payoff. I'm grateful to be part of it."[44] DC and Marvel increased the page rates and profit sharing of writers and illustrators. But inkers, letterers, and other minor artists remained on a strict lower-end page-rate system. And all artists remained under a "work-for-hire" contract, unlike the "creator-owned" policies of independents.[45] For the moment, however, artists felt that the industry had at least moved out of the dark ages.

By the early 1980s, fandom and the direct market had set the stage for a major transformation in the comic book field. What once was a market of large commercial publishers, trade-craftsmen, and a mass audience, was being transformed into a specialty market of commercial and independent publishers, well-paid auteur comics artists, and committed fan-readers. The limits of the Late Industrial Age comic book were being challenged in a variety of ways, setting the stage for the Heroic Age of comic books. The stage was set, therefore, for artists to see comic books as a medium of self-expression, not simply an industrial product they crafted for a mass market. Artists and fans also treated comic books more seriously and looked to expand comic books toward broader and more mature content. The comic book was beginning to be viewed as an art form with a history, an aesthetic, a potential to be as "mature" as other forms of popular entertainment. What was emerging was a new North American subculture of comic books that would become the foundation for a new revolution in this medium.

Comic Book Culture

The boom in the direct market depended on a large comic book culture that developed out of the early comic book fandom of the 1960s and 1970s. The boom also helped create this comic book culture of fans, artists, publishers, shops, conventions, fanzines, Internet electronic bulletin boards, and Web sites. Matthew Pustz uses the term "comic book culture" instead of "comic book fandom" to emphasize two aspects of this fandom. The first is the marginal state of both comic book fans and the art form they love. By the 1980s, comic books were virtually limited to comic book fandom with very few people outside of this subculture actually reading comic books. Unlike most fandoms revolving around popular art, comic book culture revolved around an entire medium of expression that survived both aesthetically and commercially on a specialized direct market of fans. This market was structured in ways that marginalized fans and comic books into a more or less insular subculture. This led to the second aspect of what makes comic book fandom a unique subculture for Pustz. Only individuals in comic book culture had what Pustz called "comics literacy": the ability to enjoy and understand the unique formal aesthetics of comic books. By this time in North America, a vast majority of people were not only unfamiliar with contemporary comic books, but if they actually were to read a comic book Pustz argues that they would have a difficult time appreciating it.[46]

By the end of the 1980s, almost anyone interested in actual comic books likely engaged in some way with this subculture. While commercial interests still dominated the comic book field, particularly the interests of Marvel and DC, comic book culture determined to a large degree the meanings and practices associated with this medium. Comic fandom was dominated by a large community of committed "fanboys" who collected contemporary as well as older mainstream comic books. This community was joined by an old guard of collectors mostly interested in Industrial Age comic books and artists. These two communities determined to a large degree the field of comic books. Marginal to these two communities were hard-core "alts" dedicated to the alternative comics movement that developed out of the earlier underground comix movement. This movement will be discussed in the next chapter. While remaining marginal in the field of comic books, the alt community relied on the strength of the other two communities to maintain a comic book culture and direct market that allowed this medium to survive with the collapse of a mass market for comic books.

Comic book culture during the direct market boom was a decidedly teen and adult male culture of fanboys. The rise of the direct market and comic book culture accelerated the process that began during the Late Industrial Age of comic books: a declining readership among all females and also among male child readers. Estimates of females participating in comic book culture, for example, ranged from 5 to 10 percent.[47] A number of accounts are given for this decline: the disappearance of female-oriented and child-oriented genres like the romance and kid comic books; the dominance of the superhero genre; the increasing hypermasculinity of this genre; and the less than female- and child-friendly nature of the comics industry, comic shops, and conventions. Fanboys in comic fandom also were on average older than the average readership during the Industrial Age; a trend first appearing in the 1960s and continuing with the rise of comic book culture. The average fanboy was in his teens or twenties.[48] Fanboys avidly read and collected comic books. They hung out at comic shops and attended conventions. And they participated in other fan activities like fanzines and eventually webzines.

While early fandom was a more personalized small community of around five hundred committed fans, comic book culture was a far larger subculture of fans. Estimates of the size of the dedicated fandom, or even the overall readership for comics, were difficult to gauge.[49] This was particularly the case because buying multiple copies of comic books was a standard practice in the direct market as consumers collected comic books as financial investments. Fan Don Thompson, editor of *Comic Buyer's Guide*, told *Esquire* in 1985 that fifty thousand Americans collected comic books. One analysis of the market put the total readership of comics in 1991 at 1.25 million.[50] A marketing agent specializing in comic books told *The Comics Journal* in 1992 that the total number of consumers of comic books ranged from eight hundred thousand to one million.[51] *The New York Times* was told by the *Comics Buyer's Guide* in 1993, the peak of the direct market boom, that the overall readership for comics was 2.2 million.[52]

The best indication of the size of comic fandom was probably the circulation of fan and industry magazines. The main catalogs for preordering new comics in the direct market, *Previews* and *Advance*, had circulations of around ninety thousand in 1993, while the most popular fanzine during the boom, *Wizard*, claimed a circulation of roughly four hundred thousand that year. Other fanzines had much lower circulations in 1993, but still far greater than the old fanzines of early fandom. Another glossy fanzine, *Comics Scene*, had an every-other-month circulation of 160,000. The longest running general interest fanzine, *Comics Buyer's Guide*, had a circulation of twenty-one thousand, while its collectors price guide, *Comic Buyer's Guide Price Guide*, had a circulation of seventy thousand. The main fanzine for alternative comics fans, but a fanzine that also covered the comics industry and other aspects of mainstream comic books, was *The Comics Journal*, which had a circulation of eight thousand.[53]

The longest running fanzine, *The Comics Buyer's Guide*—its original title *Guide to Comic Fandom* (1971) was changed in 1983—covered the comics industry and comic fandom. It featured news, market and industry analysis, and special columns. This publication reflected the views of mainstream collectors from early fandom. The top-selling fanzines, *Wizard* and the *Comics Scene*, served a younger readership of fanboys. They focused on both the contemporary comic book scene and collecting. The old guard of early fandom also introduced the fanzines *Alter Ego* and *Comic Book Artist* in 1998, specializing in the history of the Industrial Age of comic books. *The Comics Journal* (1977) provided news, articles, interviews, and reviews related to the past and contemporary field of comic books. But *The Comics Journal* was also a boisterous advocate of the alternative comics movement and positioned itself as the "art" magazine of comic books with "literary" interviews, criticism, and reviews. The publisher of *The Comics Journal*, Fantagraphics, also published a companion fanzine dedicated to mainstream comics and fanboys, *Amazing Heroes* (1981), with content more like mainstream fanzines. While these more professionally made fanzines dominated comic book culture, smaller circulating fanzines with interviews, articles, columns, and art existed as well, although not in the overall numbers found in early fandom. These fanzines ranged from a focus on mainstream comics, to underground comix, to alternative comics.[54]

Comic fandom also produced books in the 1980s and 1990s geared to the interests of this subculture. A number of history books were published like *Women and the Comics* (1985) and *The Comic Book in America* (1989).[55] DC and Marvel also commissioned books promoting their history. Books appeared with biographies and interviews of past and present artists such as *The New Comics* (1988), *Comic Book Superstars* (1994), and *Comic Book Rebels*

(1993). Books also appeared related to collecting comic books, to the comic book industry, and to the craft of mainstream comics. For collectors there were *Comic Book Collecting for Fun and Profit* (1985) and *Start Collecting Comics* (1990). Robert Overstreet continued his price guide, *The Comic Book Price Guide*, while the fanzine *Comics Buyer's Guide* came out with a new book-sized price guide in 1994. Books about getting into the industry and the craft of mainstream comics also appeared like *How to Become a Comic Book Artist* (1986) and *Getting into the Business of Comics* (1994).[56]

Matthew Pustz and Jeffrey A. Brown, in their analyses of comic book culture, both point to the importance of the early Internet in comic book culture from electronic bulletin boards, online communities, to early web pages. Brown points to early electronic bulletin boards and chat rooms as important ways for fans to "virtually" interact with other fans and industry professionals. Pustz emphasizes how earlier online communities tended to separate fans more clearly into more specific "interpretive communities" from mainstream to alternative; and later, the importance of early Web home pages and fan Web sites exponentially expanding the interaction of fans and artists.[57] The greatest contribution of the early Internet, therefore, was extending the social networking of fans through message boards, online communities, and web pages. In Chapter Six I will present a longer discussion of the impact of the Web on not only comic book fandom, but also the comic book industry and comic books as an art form.

Awards also became an important way comic book culture recognized comics artists. There were two types of awards: professional-based awards and fan-based awards. In 1974, the San Diego Comic-Con introduced the Inkspot Awards, which were awarded to people active mostly in comic books, but also people active in other genres. The *Comics Buyer's Guide* introduced the fan-based Comic Buyer's Guide Fan Awards in 1982. *Wizard* introduced a similar fan-based award, Wizard Fan Awards, in 1993. Both awards are still active in comic fandom. These awards centered on the fanboy territory of mainstream comics. In response to the fanboy bias of these awards, Fantagraphics established a professional-based Jack Kirby Awards in 1985. Over a dispute on ownership, the Kirbys were split into two professional-based annual awards in 1988 named after the two biggest icons in comic book history, Will Eisner and Harvey Kurtzman. These awards, still active today, have recognized both past and contemporary artists in the comic book field.

The direct market boom led to a similar boom in comic book conventions and shows in the 1980s and 1990s.[58] Conventions ranged from multi-genre "supercons," to large regional conventions, to city "mini" conventions, to local dealers' shows. These events were located in large convention centers, top hotels, motor inns, to shows at local fire stations. While "supercon" conventions such as in San Diego were the main national conventions, there were large regional conventions like the Mid-Ohio-Con as well as hundreds of comic conventions in cities around the country. While many smaller mini-cons, some hosted monthly, had attendances of five hundred in the early 1990s, the San Diego Comic-Con became the largest convention and went from an attendance of five thousand in 1983 to twenty-eight thousand in 1993 to forty-two thousand in 1998.[59] Comic conventions were a big business.[60] In 1997 the fanzine *Wizard* bought the Chicago Comicon and started *Wizard World*, which eventually became the biggest convention producer in the country. Comic fans were also interested in collecting superhero and science fiction toys and cards, so there were virtually hundreds of local cards and comic dealer shows each year as well.[61]

Many comic book conventions, but even more so the supercons, were concerned with not only comic books, but also trading cards, video games, game-playing, film, and television; any medium that featured elements of the popular genres found in mainstream comic books. In terms of comic books, the main activity at these conventions remained the large area for selling and buying comic books. Another major activity was the mainstream publishers' hall where publishers marketed their goods, fans could meet creators to talk and get autographs, and models paraded around as popular superheroes. These conventions also featured artist galleries where fans could meet their favorite artists and maybe show them their portfolios of comic art. Conventions also featured panel discussions, lectures, workshops, and seminars ranging from the frivolous and fun to serious discussions on comic books, comic book art, and the industry. Special "spotlight" panels also featured industry professionals past and present. There were movie previews and costume contests. While most events focused on mainstream comic books and the mainstream comic book industry, conventions occasionally had events related to the underground comix and alternative comics movement. Conventions involved serious commerce, serious interaction between professionals and fans, and simple fun as fans reveled in the world of comic books and met other fans.

Fangirl journalist Susan Pierce informed readers of the *Arkansas Democrat-Gazette* of the importance of conventions in comic book culture in her report on the 1995 San Diego Comic-Con:

> For fans, it's a chance to approach a favorite creator to get an autograph or mumble shyly how much you love his stories; to attend panels exploring myriad facets of things called comics; to buy mass quantities of the books; and to tote a portfolio of drawings around in

the hopes that an editor will faint dead away at the glory of obvious genius . . . There's something magic about the San Diego edition . . . maybe it's simply that seeing 35,000 comic book fans milling about a cavernous convention center floor forcefully reminds any fan or creator that they are not alone, nor a weirdo—no matter what their co-workers, friends or family might think. What's immediately obvious is how seriously most fans take their favorite reading material . . . We compare notes about what we like and dislike, speculate on what might happen, or trade gossip as though we were discussing close friends and relatives.[62]

The press, however, still had a hard time dealing with the seriousness fans displayed at comic book conventions in the 1980s and 1990s. *The Boston Globe* coverage of the San Diego Convention is a good example of the stigma still associated with comic fandom:

For every Imperial Stormtrooper, there is a Spider-man, for each Klingon an Aquaman. They come from galaxies—OK, towns—far, far away for a chance to mingle with others of their subspecies: comic book geeks . . . In his other life—his more mundane life—Michael Sandeffer is a 58-year-old college professor. In his divergent one, he is Admiral K-Tek, a member of the Klingon warrior race from "Star Trek," from the bottom of his spiked black boots to the top of his ridged nose and forehead. "A trekkie, which I'm not, is a fanatic," he explained, ignoring his long wig. "A trekker, which I am, is interested in other things. I have a real life" . . . At Comic-Con, no one has to be abashed or ashamed—a revelation for many adult comic book and sci-fi fans. Theirs is a culture of outsiders, but for 3 1/2 days a year at least they have somewhere to belong.[63]

Comic book fans always carried a certain stigma because of their commitment to comic books since the early days of comic book fandom. Like other fans of popular culture, comics fans commitment to what was considered a lowbrow form of popular culture challenged prevailing official views of the nature of popular entertainment. As Henry Jenkins shows with fans of *Star Trek*, comics fans were stigmatized for not only the way they treated comic books as serious art to be collected, discussed, and written about in detailed histories, interviews, and reviews; but also for the amount of time dedicated to comic books and the immersion into the comic book universe with fan art, collectables, and costumes.[64] With the rise of the direct market the increasing marginality of both the subculture and the art form increased fans' sense of this stigma. For fans, outsiders carried the old stereotype of comic books as subliterate art for young children, but certainly not for adults. Even young teenagers felt the stigma of reading what nonbelievers thought was a children's medium. A young teenage fan wrote *Wizard* asking for help with his disapproving mother. "I am a 16-year-old sophomore in high school. My favorite thing to do is collect comics. Whenever I ask my mom for a ride to the comic store (which isn't very often) she goes nuts. She says I'm too old to collect comics . . . Please publish this letter and help me explain to her and other mothers nationwide why I and other kids my age like to collect comics. *Help me!!*"[65]

Ironically, the term "fanboy" was generated within comic book culture to describe, in a derogatory way, the most avid collectors and fans of mainstream comic books. The fanboy stereotype was of an asocial young male who pays little attention to his personal appearance and devotes considerable time and devotion to certain mainstream comic books. And as fanboys get older they have the additional stereotype of suffering from arrested development. Eventually the tag "fanboy" or "fangirl" became more a badge of self-identity. As comics fan discourse evolved, it filled up with double meanings, constant irony, and terms of group identification as fans in general grappled with the stigma of their shared commitment. This is most evident in the common self-identification of a fan as a "geek," "nerd," or "dork" as a reference to their relationship to nonfans. This discourse is even evident in comic books that deal with various issues in comics fandom in humorous and self-reflexive fashion, such as John Kovalic's *Dork Tower* (1997). This self-reference was so strong by the end of the 1990s, the press began using the term "geek" in covering comic conventions.

All comic book fans, however, whatever stigma they may have felt, or whatever label they may have worn as a badge of group identity, took comic books seriously. While official culture might not have understood the efforts fans made to enjoy the collective celebration of comic books, comic book culture was a vibrant subculture that saved the medium of comic books from extinction. Some alternative fans and artists might look askance at my characterization of comic book culture in the 1980s and 1990s as being innovative, as a tension emerged in this subculture between the large majority of fans committed to mainstream comics and those who wanted to move beyond what they viewed as an old and limited paradigm in the field of comic books. But as we will see, comic book culture in general created the necessary support for a direct market that actually allowed more "independent" and "alternative" minds in the field of comic books to rebel against the old ways of the industry and test the potential of the American comic book as an art form.

The Direct Market Boom, Mainstream
Comics, and the Pulp Auteur

The comic book industry in the mid-1980s entered a boom period in an expanding direct market of comic book shops. While roughly three thousand comic book shops existed in 1983, the number doubled by the end of the decade. The number of comic book shops reached a peak of around eighty-five hundred to ten thousand shops in 1993. In 1983 the industry had reached a nadir in annual sales estimated at around fifty million dollars. By 1987 annual sales had rejuvenated to around 350 million dollars and continued to grow for another six years until they peaked at around nine hundred million dollars to one billion dollars. The annual sales in 1993 equaled in constant dollars the estimates made at the peak of the first comic book boom back in 1954. In 1974 only six publishers were active in the comic book field, fifteen years later over fifty publishers were active. The number of publishers peaked in the early 1990s at well over one hundred. By the early 1990s anywhere from eight hundred to over one thousand titles were released monthly. It seemed leading into 1993 that the comic book field had miraculously recovered to become a vibrant and healthy industry.

Publishers and shop owners constantly recounted to the press that the new direct market was serving an older, almost exclusively male consumer base. *BusinessWeek* noted in 1985 that "young executives and Harvard graduate students now mix with 12-year-olds in search of cheap thrills . . . Just when all seemed lost, specialty shops came to the rescue. Such stores attract older and wealthier clientele."[66] And these new consumers were dedicated purchasers. Jeff Morris of Wilson's Book Store told the *St. Petersburg Times* in Florida in 1987 that "three-fourths of my customers are over 20 . . . I have some people who get one of everything at a cost of more than $400 each month."[67] As *The New York Times* reported in 1987, "[E]veryone in the industry—from publishers to distributors to retailers—agrees that the future of comic books lies in the adult market . . . Typical of the adult aficionado is Jason A. Kinchen, a 26-year-old engineer in Boston. 'I'm somebody who collects comic books for fun,' he said of his collection of 3,000 comics. 'I tend to buy based on characters that I like. A lot of other people follow writers and artists around to different comic books.'"[68]

The success during the direct market boom of Marvel, DC, and independent mainstream publishers reflected the preferences of a vast majority of fans in comic book culture. And their preference was for the pulp genres of superheroes, sword and fantasy, science fiction, horror, vigilante-crime, and war. This new fan base was older and more knowledgeable about comic series, comic artists, and comic history than previous generations of comic book readers. Joe Queenan, in *The New York Times*, noted in 1989 how DC and Marvel had retreated from the mass audience, "zeroing in on a cult of perhaps 500,000 dedicated readers who would zealously buy their products month in and month out. The causal fan was shown the door."[69] Marvel, DC, and independent publishers provided better quality graphics, multi-issue stories, multiple story lines, crossover between series, intertextual references, and extended stories in graphic novels. In general, readers were finding a more complicated form of storytelling than in earlier mainstream comic books. The new adult demographic also moved comic books even more to "mature" storytelling involving not only dark, violent, and sexual content, but also moral, political, and social elements as well.[70]

In the direct market boom, a new generation of artists was setting the stage for one of the major strategies of rebellion in the Heroic Age of comic books. These rebels employed a "pulp strategy" of rebellion against the strictures of the Comics Code and the narrative and graphic limitations found in traditional mainstream comic books. Following Ken Gelder's work on pulp fiction, the pulp strategy of mainstream rebels involved exploring the genre boundaries of traditional pulp fiction in comic book form.[71] However, this meant more than just expressing personal visions through more sophisticated and diverse pulp narratives, but also "playing off the grain" of the graphic tradition of realism found in mainstream comic books leading into the Heroic Age. Many rebel artists expressed their autonomy in making their graphic art stand out more clearly as personal styles reflecting their talents and visions as graphic artists while still remaining wedded to the basic aspects of the mainstream realist tradition. Mainstream rebel artists, however, also focused almost exclusively on male-oriented pulp genres of action, adventure, crime, science fiction, and fantasy geared to the male-dominated mainstream of comic book culture. As the direct market expanded artists with the "Big Two" and mainstream independent publishers would apply this strategy in making the American comic book a more diverse and serious *popular* art form.

The first major press article on the new pulp sensibility of comic books appeared in *Psychology Today* in 1984 just before the direct market boom. Benjamin DeMott's "Darkness at the Mall" attacked a slew of mostly independent adult comic books. "The world of adult comics is full of downers; the tone aimed at, in general, is knowing cynicism, and the feelings evoked are, more often than not, grim, self-taunting and hopeless."[72] The following year, freelance writer Mark Perigard, in a guest editorial for *Newsweek*, also was wary of this new trend:

Comic books have changed dramatically over the last few years. Appealing to an older, more literate crowd, comics have become glossier and more artistically detailed. The stories are larger in scope and darker in substance . . . A hero these days is more likely to emerge from battle with severe emotional wounds, if not physical scars . . . The code of honor in comics nowadays seems to be an eye for an eye. Today's heroes will kill if they have to, without compunction . . . The artwork has improved, the depth of characterization is more sophisticated and today's comics, reflecting the diversity of the world, feature growing numbers of women and minorities in important roles . . . Perhaps comic books are more mature, but in presenting a world view closer to today's gray realities, our own ideals are being sacrificed.[73]

While these early articles were critical of the pulp trend in comic books, most press reports framed this change as comic books "growing up" to an adult audience. In 1987, for example, the *St. Petersburg Times* noted the more complex, dark stories found in the graphic novels *The One*, *Watchmen*, and *Ronin*. "At its best the graphic novel can create and sustain effects impossible in simple prose . . . In this context, mainstream comic book publishing (DC, Marvel) has discovered the concept of the closed-end 'mini-series' . . . These are all intelligent, well-crafted comics with adult themes, as far away from standard pow-biff-sock comics as Masterpiece Theater is from Gilligan's Island."[74] Or as *The New York Times* put it in 1988, "the adventures of these new heroes have changed to meet the tastes of a more sophisticated and cynical time."[75] The most discussed mainstream graphic novels were Frank Miller's *Batman: The Dark Knight Returns* and Alan Moore's *Watchmen*. Both works were published as graphic novels in 1986 and presented dark and violent musings on the vigilante subtext of the superhero genre mixed with intertextual references to comic book history and critical takes on American politics.

While the new "adult" mainstream comic book already was evident by 1986, the success of *Dark Knight* and *Watchmen* accelerated and consolidated the rise of the mainstream adult comic book. Marvel's dominance of the market led it to remain more wedded to its successful superhero line, simply relying on more complex plots and the creative talents of top fan-artists to attract the new fan readership. But its Epic Comics line, established in 1982, was a more creator-friendly line of comics. This line dropped the Comics Code in order to publish more mature adult comics. DC, however, saw adult comics as a possible strategy in competing with Marvel as well as independent publishers who were threatening its second position in the market. Starting in 1987,

DC introduced a number of adult comics without the Comics Code by new mainstream rebels in serial and graphic novel form. These series included *Sandman, Hellblazer,* and *Animal Man.* In 1992, DC officially launched a Vertigo Imprint for mature readers, citing "reader interest in more challenging and controversial stories."[76] During the nineties Vertigo was the principal mainstream publishing line for the pulp strategy with such titles as *The Last One, The Invisibles,* and *Transmetropolitan.* Independent publishers, like First Comics, Dark Horse, Comico, Eclipse, and others, also published adult, pulp-strategy mainstream comics in the late 1980s and 1990s.

But publishers by the late 1980s were feeling some pressure from distributors, retailers, and others about the increased violence and sexuality in comic books. Publishers occasionally had used labels in the past like "For Mature Readers," but DC announced guidelines for implementing a systematic labeling system in early 1987. A large outcry from DC's most popular artists, like Alan Moore and Frank Miller, led to DC never implementing the policy. But reports and exposés continued to appear in the press. *Forbes* editor Joe Queenan wrote a savage attack on comic book violence and sadistic sex in his article "Drawing on the Dark Side" in the *New York Times Magazine* in 1989. *The Comics Journal* noted the bad press following Queenan's article in "Violent Comics Draw Unfavorable Spotlight," including exposés on CNN's *Larry King Live* and NBC's *Today Show.* While the question of violence and sex in mainstream comics held press attention for a short period, it never led to a concerted attack against mainstream comic books, or any concerted effort at self-censorship by mainstream publishers.[77]

The top-selling issues during the boom also indicated that fan-artists were the biggest draw among fans. And the new generation of fan-artists in the North American comic book field included artists from the United States, Canada, and Britain. The success of a title was far more dependent on the reputation of the artists working on it. Joe Queenan interviewed fan-artist John Byrne for *The New York Times,* "'We're treated better than we used to be; we're not just hired hands,' concedes Byrne. In 1986, he helped revamp and simplify the Superman legend. One reason his name is on the cover, he notes, is because a Superman story drawn by John Byrne will sell a lot more copies than one drawn by one of DC's less-gifted artists. 'I have my faithful 50,' says Byrne. 'That's 50,000 people who follow me wherever I go. My name on the cover usually means a 20 percent increase in sales.'" Writers and artists in general saw their fortunes rise during the boom. Joe Queenan noted, "Artists and writers are certainly earning more money than they ever did in the past. Journeyman artists can now earn $50,000 a year, while top guns receive $200,000 to $300,000. After years of bitter wrangling, comic-book creators now earn royalties that start once titles pass 75,000 in sales, plus certain copyright privileges."[78] Page rates for writers and artists, for example, rose to an average of two hundred dollars per page during the boom.[79] Todd McFarlane reportedly made one million dollars from his Marvel Spider-Man series. But the success of mainstream artists, particularly the top stars, empowered them to reconsider their relationship to the Big Two. Marvel and DC still maintained a basic "work-for-hire" arrangement with royalties, but no creator-owned rights. And as artists began to feel like "auteurs" of a maturing medium, they resented the creative limitations imposed by the "dinosaurs" at the Big Two.

So many mainstream auteurs left the Big Two during the boom to find greater financial rewards and greater artistic freedom. This independence helped expand the "pulp strategy" of rebellion during the Heroic Age—comic artists stretched the boundaries of genre comic books in even more complex and creative directions. The biggest auteurs in the field, Frank Miller and Alan Moore, went independent in 1988. Alan Moore in 1992 expressed his need for independence. "My main interest in comics is aesthetic rather than commercial, so I'm not at all interested in the comics industry. I'm interested in the art form . . . I'm still hoping that I could establish, along with all the other people who are out there, some sort of basis for worthwhile comics that is separate to that superhero circus."[80] The biggest revolt was the creation of Image Comics in 1992 by seven top artists from Marvel. Image artist Chris Claremont told *The Comics Journal*, "Image is also proof of the other side of the pudding, which is an awareness on the part of a lot of us that market conditions and forces now exist that will enable us—and I mean 'us' in a very general sense of all comic book creators—to make our fortunes on our own. To create properties that we own, that we can shape and craft and market according to our own individual vision."[81]

Mainstream rebels believed in the potential of comic books as a popular art form. Their pulp strategy of rebellion was not only a strike against the constraints of the Big Two and the dominance of the superhero genre, but also a rebellion against official culture's view of comic books as simply lowbrow, subliterate, adolescent fantasy. "My idea was always that comics was an art," commented artist Eddie Campbell in the 1993 book *Comic Book Rebels*. "An art like any other form of entertainment that should be out there, competing in the marketplace with every other form of art."[82] Rebel writer Neil Gaiman expressed a similar view in a 1996 interview with *The Comics Journal*. "My thesis was that it was possible that you could write comics with as much intelligence, as much power, as much life, as you could find in any other medium. That you could write comics that had as much weight behind them, as much substance to them, as you'd find in a novel, in good poetry, in films and television."[83]

Comic book culture provided the foundation for mainstream artists to claim legitimacy as artists, never imaginable during the Industrial Age. Now many of these artists were auteurs applying their personal vision and talents to mainstream comic books; whether Todd McFarlane's unmistakable personal vision in reimagining Spider-Man, Frank Miller's dark deconstruction of Batman, Neil Gaiman's complex fantasy-horror *Sandman*, or Alan Moore's sophisticated retelling of Jack the Ripper in *From Hell*. The pulp strategy of comic artists was moving comic books in new innovative directions. The old rules of art in the comic field were being challenged as mainstream fan-artists claimed autonomy and applied a different set of criteria in judging comic books, one that was more similar to pulp literature and pulp film than old Industrial Age comic books.

While fans were enjoying more complex and mature comic books, the direct market boom was more clearly the result of a speculators' boom in comic books in the late 1980s than a response to changes in comic book content. While everyone noted the "suits" who would wander in to purchase plastic-sealed mint-fresh comic books, it seemed like every fanboy also was busy building his portfolio for early retirement. The press previously had noted comic book cultists collecting comic books, but by the mid-1980s the press was noting and celebrating a boom in comic books as financial investments. *The Globe and Mail* in Toronto noted the rise of a speculator's market in 1986. "Comic book collecting is a hobby in the midst of (as an illustrator would put it) a ka-boom market . . . Two years ago a 'pristine mint' copy of Marvel #1 went for $35,000 (U.S.) in a private sale. Though prices are a concern, most collectors are unapologetic comics fans. They might not read them on the bus, but they have sparked an explosion in the number of titles being created . . . the market for new titles are as volatile as penny stocks."[84]

The impact of speculation was most obvious in the unprecedented sales for the industry for certain issues and series. The highest circulation comic book before the direct market boom was *Captain Marvel* in the 1940s with a top circulation of 1.4 million. Fan-artist Todd McFarlane was given his own Spider-Man series in 1990 and his *Spider-Man #1* sold over 2.5 million copies and the series continued to sell eight hundred thousand to one million copies a month. The following year fan-artist Rob Liefeld's *X-Force #1* sold 3.7 million copies and fan-artists Chris Claremont and Jim Lee's *X-Men #1* sold eight million copies. The most popular titles were selling two hundred thousand to three hundred thousand copies monthly. Publishers boosted sales with a number of strategies and gimmicks. Titles appeared with multiple covers, such as five different covers for *X-Men #1*, while popular characters carried multiple titles, such as Spider-Man eventually sporting nine separate titles in 1993 with annual sales of fifty million copies. Multiple titles of Superman and Batman alone gave DC annual sales of twenty million copies.[85] The final big event of the boom was DC's "Death of Superman." *Superman* #75 in 1993 generated three million in sales in its first week of release.

Independent publishers publishing mainstream comic books of either new series or repurposed material from other media also succeeded in the speculator-driven direct market. The publisher Dark Horse in 1990 saw *Alien and Predator #1* sell four hundred thousand copies, *Aliens: Earth War #1* sell two hundred thousand, and fan-artists Frank Miller and Dave Gibbons *Give Me Liberty* sell 120,000. That year Dark Horse saw its overall sales at five million dollars. In 1992, Image Comics published its first comic books; Rob Liefeld's *Youngblood #1* sold 325,000 copies, while Todd McFarlane's *Spawn #1* sold 1.2 million copies. The success of these independent publishers slowly took some of the market share from Marvel and DC. For a brief period in 1992 Malibu Graphics became the second largest publisher, passing DC in overall sales.[86] In 1992, *Wizard* told fanboy readers, "The investment opportunities have multiplied recently by intriguing offers from some of the independents—mainly Valiant, Dark Horse, and Image. The increased output and strong product lines from these companies has resulted in the emergence of some new talent, which in turn can of course lead to some good long-term investment opportunities."[87]

Publishers in the early 1990s were glutting the market with titles, increasing prices, and accelerating the use of gimmicks like enclosing trading cards, holographic covers, limited editions, and other items. Even mainstream fans and professionals were lamenting the lack of concern over story line and artwork as publishers fed the growing frenzy. Eclipse's Beau Smith later complained about "the trading card—foil embossed—look at me—I glow in the dark—scratch me—feel me—smell me—make the buyer feel like he or she is getting a limited edition—send your kid through medical school era of raccoon marketing . . . By raccoon marketing, I mean that some publishers feel that, if they offer the comic book reader a bright, shiny object in the form of a comic book, they will kiss it, caress it, think that it is worth far more than it really is."[88] *The Washington Post*, covering the frenzy in 1993, lamented:

> Remember when your best-beloved comics were well-worn from being stuffed in back pockets, stashed under pillows and between mattresses, and hidden behind textbooks during class? Now comics are stored in expensive, chemically inert containers to preserve collectibility and value. Comics used to be considered unique if they

had a cover, now they come with flashy scratch 'n' sniff, die-cut, holographic covers. Comic books used to be a cheap source of escapist entertainment. Now comics are thought of as issue-oriented educational supplements, and as a source of financial investment.[89]

With the press celebrating the boom market in comic books, suddenly the direct market was hit with a recession in late 1993. Unfortunately, the market continued to plummet. Almost immediately fault was placed on frenzied speculators who left the market, but other problems plagued the industry such as a glut of titles, delayed publication of preordered comic books, distribution wars, Marvel and DC hemorrhaging, and increased printing costs. John Miller, editor of the industry magazine *Comics Retailer*, remembered, "It was like a wildfire. And like a wildfire, it wound up burning all our houses."[90] *Business and Industry* in 1996 reported:

> Industry experts estimate the comic book sales in 1995 were $500 mil, down from 1993's $1 bil . . . Zowie! Distribution snafus, boring story lines and higher prices (the average price for a comic book was $2.50 last year, almost double from 1991) . . . Kerpow! A glut of speculators, disappointed by comics' potential as lucrative collectibles, have recently exited the market. Powee! Newsprint prices have skyrocketed. Bif! Powerhouse publisher Marvel Entertainment Group, home of X-Men, Amazing Spider-man and others, has undergone massive restructuring, cutting back titles, laying off 275 staffers and, last summer, instigating its own distribution system, the immediate result of which was chaos. Blam![91]

The industry was unquestionably facing a crisis. DC's Superman/Batman monthly circulation by 1996 had dropped 72 percent; and by the end of the same year Marvel filed for Chapter 11 bankruptcy protection and fired another 143 employees. The market continued to fall precipitously. Over half of comic shops folded by 1998, with Marvel releasing fifty-six titles compared to the average of two hundred titles during the boom, and sales were falling below four hundred million dollars annually. By 2001, profits had plummeted to an estimated 260 million dollars and the number of comic shops was hovering around thirty-five hundred.[92] In such desperate straits, Marvel announced that it was leaving the Comics Code Authority and creating its own ratings system.[93] While not as terrible as the depression of the early 1980s, many in the industry and comic book culture by the end of the century were once again asking if the American comic book was doomed to disappear.

Conclusion

While the frenzy of speculation eventually led to the collapse of the direct market, the short-lived boom it created provided the opportunity for mainstream rebel artists and independent publishers to expand the boundaries of popular fiction in the comic book medium. The power of fanboys' commitment to the most celebrated artists allowed those fan-artists to transform the superhero genre as well as expand the genre boundaries of this medium, whether in the special DC imprint Vertigo or with independent publishers. As we will see in a later chapter, it was many of these rebel artists' work during the boom that eventually brought comic book culture back into the mainstream of North American culture in the next century. And the top independent publishers who first established themselves during this speculative boom, and survived the bust, would become important publishers in the revitalization of this medium in the next century.

The rebellion of a new generation of mainstream fan-artists marked one major starting point for the Heroic Age in American comic books. Supported by a comic book culture steeped in appreciation for the art form and its artists, mainstream rebel artists by the 1980s were expressing what Pierre Bourdieu calls principles of autonomy in heroic ages of art.[94] Within this new restricted subfield of art, they asserted an independence from the old rules of art practiced by Marvel and DC, which included an autonomy expressed in creating comic books as expressions of their own personal talents and visions. While Marvel and DC clearly remained dominant in the direct market, comic book fans and artists had developed independently a new set of criteria of judgment that the Big Two had to adapt to in some measure, while independent publishers took even more advantage of these new criteria and the desire of rebel artists for more autonomy. This rebellion of artists, however, remained wedded to a pulp fiction strategy that reflected the tastes, affections, and disposition of the core of comic book culture. The direct market boom would provide another major starting point for the Heroic Age in American comic books by presenting an opportunity for an alternative comics movement to establish a foothold in the field of comic books in the 1980s and 1990s. This is the topic of the next chapter.

While the direct market collapsed, comic book culture survived. Certainly the remaining comic book shops struggled with industry magazines like *Comics and Games Retailer* promoting the concept of "diversification" as their best strategy of survival. But the fan base remained, many celebrating the exodus of speculators who they viewed as destroying the creative core of mainstream comic books as well as the affective core of comic book fandom and its love of the medium as an art form, not as a financial investment. While certainly worried about the future of the American comic book, constantly debating what was wrong with the industry and what would be its salvation, comic book fandom continued to thrive, invading the World Wide Web with Web-based fanzines, online communities, and eventually social networks on the new Web 2.0. And the main comic book conventions would continue to thrive with increasing attendance as well. But the collapse of the direct market certainly for many only reemphasized the marginal status of comic book culture and its fans. They would never have imagined at the end of the 1990s that only five or six years later, they would suddenly enter the mainstream of American culture as the new arbiters of popular entertainment as "geek" culture was discovered by mainstream mass media.

5

The Heroic Age II

*Alternative Comics and a Rebellion
from the Margins*

For Pierre Bourdieu the most defining feature of heroic ages is how artists, critics, publishers, and audiences reject market-imposed rules of art; when they lay claim to principles of autonomy and their own criteria of judgment of what constitutes the best and brightest in the field.[1] While the last chapter showed how "mainstream" artists and independent publishers challenged the old rules of art of the Industrial Age, the rise of "alternative" comics best exemplifies this aspect of heroic ages in art. Artists, critics, publishers, and readers of alternative comics staked claim to a radical rejection of the dominant aesthetics, practices, and meanings in the comic book field. Given how narrow the mainstream in comic books had become by the 1980s, the alternative comics movement entailed quite a diverse array of comic art as well as criticism and discourse about comic books. One can point to two overarching ideas that defined this movement regardless of its diversity. The first idea was the commitment to the complete freedom of artists to express themselves and control their creative work. And the second idea was that the comic book had a broad potential as an art form that had yet to be fully explored.

Out on the margins of the comic book field emerged another challenge mounted by women, gays, and minorities against not only the rules of art in the field, but also against the barriers they confronted in comic book culture. The fictional world of American mainstream comic books by the 1970s was mostly a white, male, heterosexual universe. For women and gays, the rebellion in the Heroic Age occurred parallel to the feminist and gay rights movements in which assumptions about gender, femininity, sexuality, and queerness were being challenged. For minorities, the same period occurred when questions about representation and artistic independence in the mass media industry moved center stage. Women and gay fans would begin to challenge the hypermasculinity in mainstream comic books. Black artists would mount a campaign to diversify mainstream and alternative comic book content to include more multicultural, socially relevant, and political content. In the alternative comics movement both women and gays would become critically acclaimed artists in the movement. This rebellion from the margins during the Heroic Age would find success in some areas of the field and unfortunate failure in others.

All these rebellions during the Heroic Age faced the mundane realities of the structural and ideological limits posed by the direct market and comic book culture. The American comic book in many ways was saved by a comic fandom whose interests lay with commercial mainstream comic books. This fandom also was not a particularly diverse community, as white heterosexual males from their teens to early thirties made up a vast majority of this subculture. While fans certainly could enjoy the pulp rebellion of white male mainstream artists, more radical attempts to transform the field did not necessarily resonate with their particular love of comic books or their self-identity as comic book readers. But comic book culture and the direct market were the only game in town for anyone interested in creating and selling comic books. There was no viable alternative market. For a brief period in the late 1980s there seemed to be an opening back to a mass market for comic books in the form of graphic novels in the trade book market. But this opportunity quickly fizzled out as a commercial failure. The ultimate irony of the rebellions from the margins of the comic book field is that the direct market and comic book culture in certain ways made such rebellions possible, yet in other ways severely limited their potential to transform the American comic book.

Alternative Comics and Rejecting the Mainstream

The alternative comics movement positioned itself as distinctly not mainstream. And artists and publishers in the alternative comics movement had a rather large playing field in which to be "outside" the mainstream. This was not only in terms of writing and graphic art, but also in terms of artists and readers who mostly remained on either side of the alternative–mainstream divide in the comic book field. Crossover did occur for some artists, publishers, and readers. But the alternative comics movement was on a radical mission: to reshape the comic book field to incorporate the broadest array of aesthetics, artists, and readers as possible. The movement wanted to transform this field to replicate the diversity of narrative art found in other major media like books or film.

The alternative comics movement's roots were in the underground comix movement. Following the underground comix market crash of 1973, however, few new artists could get published by commercial publishers. In this wake, a new generation of artists began to self-publish what were quickly called "alternative" or "newave" comics. Old underground publisher Jay Kennedy noted that "the new selectivity of the underground publishing houses meant that in 1974, beginning artists couldn't find publishers . . . some of these new cartoonists would come full circle and publish their own newave comix. A second generation of underground cartoonists had emerged alongside the first . . . At first newave cartoonists sold their comix locally, to friends, or through nearby comic shops that by the mid-1970s had replaced head shops as the major retail outlet for comix . . . newave comix have become a mail order phenomenon. They are sold almost exclusively through the mails." These black-and-white mini-comics of four or eight pages were exchanged among fans with the help of fanzines like *Comix World* and *the Buyer's Guide for Comic Fandom*.[2]

In 1982, newave artist G. Erling remembered the energy of this new self-publishing movement. "By 1976 new alternative titles were popping up from all over the country. More artists were getting involved . . . Gradually the alternative scene became organized. We passed ideas and information around to help one another. Many times when someone published a new comix he would list other alternatives inside to boost their sales . . . New alternative titles and cartoonists continued to appear even though it was apparent that there wasn't any money to be made . . . it is an almost impossible feat to keep track of all the alternative comix titles being published. There are more people involved now than ever before."[3] In 1985, Dale Luciano informed readers of *The Comics Journal* that the term *newave* "is best regarded as a catch-all term referring to hundreds of mostly self-published comix being sold, traded, or otherwise exchanged through the mails by a surprisingly diverse group of artists." Newave artist Bob Conway explained the spirit of the movement, "As an art form, comics can reflect an individual's hopes, dreams, losses, and failures as well as any other media. There is complete individual artistic freedom in these comics."[4]

Some self-publishers became spokespersons for the movement by writing articles and touring conventions in North America. One major spokesperson for alternative comics was the successful self-publisher of *Cerebus the Aardvark* (1977) Dave Sim. Sim, in *The Comics Journal* in 1986, wrote about the new freedom to escape the "inverted pyramid"—the top-down editorship at major publishers:

> Those with something to say not in tune with the traditional bureaucratic thinking of the inverted pyramid now have the option to pursue their vision as long as their finances and stamina allow. The means are at hand ... As the truly independent comics—mini-comics, self-published ventures, and cottage industries—turn the pyramid upright, the medium takes its first faltering steps into the sunlight ... we are in a position to be one of the very few media to make regularly available untrammeled, single-expressions of creativity which will sink or swim on their own merits—unhampered by dim bulbs, hype, market surveys, and all the other garbage that infects movies, television, novels, plays and what-have-you ... And failing some momentous calamity, this trend will not be eradicated, or seriously hindered, as it gains balance, strength, and direction. Free at last, free at last. Thank almighty God we are free at last.[5]

While most self-publishers in mini-comics were not looking for financial rewards,[6] a number of self-published artists found financial success in the direct market. The early self-publishing successes of comic books like *Cerebus the Aardvark* and Wendy and Richard Pini's *Elfquest* (1978) pointed to a possible bright commercial future. *Cerebus* enjoyed circulations of around twenty thousand to thirty thousand copies. The biggest success unquestionably was Kevin Eastman and Peter Laird's self-published black-and-white *Teenage Mutant Ninja Turtles* (TMNT), first published in 1984. By 1986 *TMNT* had a circulation of over 125,000 and had a licensing arrangement that quickly brought an animated *TMNT*. By 1988, *TMNT* was generating twenty-three million dollars just in the sale of plastic toys.[7] The success of *TMNT* led to a short-lived "black-and-white" boom and bust in the late 1980s. While no one replicated the level of success of *TMNT*, self-publishing successes in the early 1990s more similar to the circulation of *Cerebus* included Jeff Smith's *Bone*, Colleen Doran's *A Distant Soil*, and Terry Moore's *Strangers in Paradise*.

But self-publishing for a profit was hard work and a long shot.[8] Publisher Gary Reed in his Self-Publishing Guide in 1993 estimated that 8 to 15 percent of comic shop owners might show interest in self-published comic books. But the challenges were daunting given the flood of titles from over a hundred small publishers competing for the small percentage of the market not controlled by the top five publishers in the field.[9] Even the professional Image Comics had problems supplying their work on time. Most self-publishing artists interested in deriving greater income from their art eventually published for commercial independent publishers in the 1980s and 1990s. The market crash in 1993 also devastated the commercially oriented self-publishers with even more self-publishing artists moving to the few commercial independent publishers still active in the field.[10] But the self-publishing movement remained strong regardless of the economic difficulties in the direct market.

Old underground commercial publishers continued to publish in the 1980s and 1990s. They published anthologies and solo works of mostly underground artists. The two major commercial publishers of alternative comics were Fantagraphics (1976) in Seattle and Drawn and Quarterly (1990) in Toronto. Other commercial publishers supporting the alternative movement included Vortex (1982), Renegade (1984), Slave Labor Graphics (1986), Tundra (1990), Alternative Comics (1993), Conundrum (1995), Highwater (1997), Top Shelf (1997), and Oni (1997). While the direct market provided opportunities to publish alternative comics, the alternative niche market was small with top titles garnering usually around ten thousand in circulation.[11] Most comic shop owners had limited interest in alternatives, so only around 10 to 15 percent of comic shops ordered alternative titles.[12] A few underground and alternative publishers also published erotic or pornographic comic books, which boomed beginning in the 1990s.[13] In the initial years following the 1993 crash, alternative publishers and titles did not see the same decline as mainstream publishers and titles.[14] But as the market continued to fall and comic shops continued to close up, alternative publishers confronted tougher times.

The artistic breadth of alternative comics makes it difficult to characterize them beyond their position against mainstream comic books. While new alternative artists inherited the rebel spirit of the undergrounds, most artists were less interested in transgressing mainstream tastes, morals, and politics. They were more interested in exploring the creative potential of comic books in terms of stories and graphic art. The most important shared characteristic of alternative comics was the emphasis on a single artist's vision. Alternative artists almost always created their work in its entirety, unlike mainstream rebel artists who usually worked with other artists to collectively produce a comic book. This in part was possible because virtually all alternative comics were "black-and-white" comics, based on the expediency and lower cost of making them.

Rebels in the alternative comics movement followed two basic strategies of rebellion: a pulp-strategy and an alt-strategy. In the previous chapter we saw how mainstream rebels followed a restricted pulp-strategy of rebellion that focused mostly on a narrow set of action-oriented genres and played off the grain of the traditional aesthetics of mainstream comic books. The alternative pulp-strategy also remained wedded to exploring the boundaries of traditional pulp fiction, but rejected any commitment to the narrow genres or aesthetic realism of mainstream rebels. The alternative alt-strategy, on the other hand, was wedded to what Ken Gelder calls the "literary" in fiction.[15] This alt-strategy rejected the pulp genre tradition and followed a path similar to what we call "fine literature" as opposed to "popular literature." Artists in the alt-strategy also were far more interested in experimenting with the graphic-art tradition in comic books as well. Alternative rebels, both pulp and alt, also were defined by their position in the field outside the Big Two and mainstream independent publishers.

From the outset it should be made clear that for any given alternative comic book, artist, or publisher, the line between these two strategies was not necessarily clearly defined. These strategies should be seen as part of a continuum of possible positions from a purely popular aesthetic to a purely avant-garde aesthetic in which alternative rebels articulated their own unique approach. This breadth and diversity reflected a void in the comic book field created by the large dominance of superhero and other fanboy genres in the direct market. Alternative comics artists and publishers were simply attempting to extend the field to the diversity found, for example, in the field of trade books. As Randy Reynaldo argued in 1985 in *The Comics Journal*, "the comics industry merely exploited a trendy market and sucked it creatively dry. As this historical sequence of events indicates, a major failure of the industry has been its repeated inability to adequately exploit interest in the comics medium so as to diversify and expand the field."[16]

The alternative pulp-strategy explored a diverse array of pulp genres, often creatively mixing genres as well. This strategy included mystery-crime in Dean Motter's *Mister X* (1984) and horror in the anthology *Taboo* (1988). The horror genre was mixed with other genres like the goth-horror of Dame Darcy's *Meat Cakes* (1990) and Roman Dirge's *Lenore, the Cute Little Dead Girl* (1998). Colleen Doran's *A Distant Soil* (1991) and Linda Medley's *Castle Waiting* (1996) were fantasies, while Jill Thompson's *Scary Godmother* (1995) was a witchcraft comic book. And the strategy was clearly evident in Carla Speed McNeil's science fiction comic *Finder* (1996). The biggest pulp genre in alternatives, however, was humor. These titles ranged from the simple comic exploits of slackers to more surreal and transgressive comic books, so these comic books were a mix of the pulp- and alt-strategies. Humor alternative comic books included Chester Brown's *Yummy Fur* (1986), Gary Panter's *Jimbo: Adventures in Paradise* (1989), Peter Bagge's *Hate* (1990), Dan Clowes's *Eightball* (1990), and Roberta Gregory's *Naughty Bits* (1991).

The alt-strategy was clear in the avant-garde work found in the anthologies *Raw* (1980) and *Drawn and Quarterly* (1990). Historical works also were part of the alt-strategy such as Art Spiegelman's *Maus* (1980), Jason Lute's *Berlin* (1998), or Ben Katchor's historical-fiction *Cheap Novelties: The Pleasures of Urban Decay* (1991). Alternative artists also created political agitprop like the anthology *Real War Stories* (1987) and journalism in Joe Sacco's *Palestine* (1993). This strategy also led to boundary-breaking surreal work such as Chris Ware's *Acme Novelty Company* (1993). The predominant approach in the alt-strategy was the autobiographical or slice-of-life alternative comics that focused on the complexities, absurdities, and problems of everyday life. But like the diversity found in alt-humor comic books, these comic books represented a mix of the alt- and pulp-strategies. Harvey Pekar's *American Splendor* (1976) stands out as the first of this "literary" genre in alternative comics. Others include Adrian Tomine's *Optic Nerve* (1991), Seth's *Palookaville* (1991), Jessica Abel's *Art Babe* (1992), Terry Moore's *Strangers in Paradise* (1993), and Ed Brubaker's *At the Seams* (1997).

The constant lament of alternative rebels was the inability to expand their readership. And the two main culprits usually presented were fanboys and the low regard toward comics outside comic book culture. The main pulpit for alternative comics was the fanzine *The Comics Journal*. In 1983 publisher Gary Groth lambasted the foolish idea that the direct market would lead to a comic book renaissance. "The very idea that the extension of a fan cult into an exploitable market would bring about a renaissance of comic art is lunatic. The fan cult represents the most fanatical and inbred comics readers in the medium's history; what hope is there to expand the expressive possibilities in a world in which *The X-Men* are king?"[17] In terms of a readership outside comic book culture, Randy Reynaldo, in *The Comics Journal*, complained in 1985, "comics as a medium of expression possesses a potential far beyond what super-heroes have ever achieved. Despite this expressive potential, the super-hero has become comics most popular and marketable genre . . . The superhero genre is, after all, an inherently ridiculous form, antithetical to real profundity . . . Adding to this already long list of stifling qualities with the genre is the general public's preconception of comics, often justifiable, as semi-literate."[18]

Matthew Pustz, in his work on comic book culture, points to the tensions between members of the alternative comics movement and fans of mainstream comic books.[19] Brian Hibbs, owner of the comic shop Comix Experience, in 1991 discounted the possibilities of fanboys reading alternative comics. "The average *X-Men* reader, who by inference is the average comic book reader, has no interest whatsoever in any item that Fantagraphics (or Kitchen Sink, or . . .) releases. They are a closed set, interested in super-heroes nearly exclusively; trying to persuade them to buy *Eightball* is absurd."[20] Dave Sim pointed to the divide in comic book culture:

> I came back in 1992 to do essentially a year-long fact-finding mission . . . the biggest thing I noticed in the first couple of months of my tour, which kept getting reinforced from that time forward, is that there's a 90–10 split in the direct market. And that's among creators, distributors, retailers, fans, collectors and investors. Ninety percent of the people are very happy with the way things are going, or at least are very much adjusted to the fact that this is how things are today . . . Then there is this newly vocal ten percent who are interested in change, who are no longer content to sit back and say that "Quality material doesn't sell. Only crap sells."[21]

Fans of mainstream comic books were not too pleased with the criticism and often elitist views expressed by members of the alternative comics movement. Fangirl-journalist Susan Pierce, in her coverage of the San Diego Comic-Con for the *Arkansas Democrat-Gazette* in 1995, noticed the tension between fanboys and alts. "Those who disdain the superhero books sit around sneering about how creatively moribund those titles are and wail—sometimes rather pretentiously—about what a shame it is that the more creative books that actually tell a story don't have massive sales . . . Despairing critics point to independent and self-publishers as the salvation of the industry, perhaps over-praising worthy titles that emphasize story over art. Superheroes aren't my first choice, but I hardly think they're creative wastelands."[22]

The alternative comics movement struggled with its marginality in comic book culture. Besides the small hold alternatives had in the direct market, alternative artists and fans felt marginalized at large comic book conventions. In response to this marginality, Slave Labor Graphics publisher Dan Vado founded the Alternative Press Expo (APE) in 1994 as a convention dedicated to self-publishing, alternative comics, and independent publishers. That same year saw the first annual Small Press Expo (SPX) in Bethesda, Maryland, which carried a similar mission as APE. In 1997, SPX introduced the Ignatz Awards for alternative comics. Another support for alternative artists was the Xeric Foundation established by Peter Laird in 1992 from the profits generated by his successful *TMNT*. This foundation provided grants to help artists self-publish their work. Many of the successful artists in the alternative comics movement received Xeric grants in their early years as self-publishers.

While remaining marginal in the comic book field, the alternative comics movement during the Heroic Age did establish a new artistic paradigm. It established principles of autonomy that rejected the market forces in the comic book field that allowed comics artists to radically reshape the comic book as an art form. And even with the plummeting market for comic books, the alternative comics movement remained strong leading into the next century. Young artists were still entering the field, self-publishing remained an active field of creativity, and regardless of the financial troubles of independent publishers, alternative comics artists continued to create innovative and challenging work. The question remained, however, about whether alternative comic books would ever be taken seriously as a truly legitimate form of art both within and outside comic book culture.

Taking Comic Books Seriously: The Direct Market Boom and Bust

Alternative rebels certainly tried to transform the perception of comic books as just lowbrow entertainment. These rebels attempted to develop a new "literary" appreciation for comic books and position comic art as Art. They attempted to generate a new criticism for comic art for hopefully a new connoisseur of the medium. And artists and others discussed the potential of comic art to rival the legitimate fine arts as well as fine literature. But the other main question daunting alternative comics rebels was whether official culture would ever take comic books seriously. Advances made in transforming official culture's view of comic books were essential if rebels transforming this medium into a serious art form were to find a broader audience and market.

Alternative artists published books on the unique aesthetics of the comic book medium. These books were not like the "how-to" books published for aspiring mainstream artists. These books approached comic art as Art. They discussed the formal aesthetics and general craft of comic art instead of simply the craft of creating superhero, adventure, or other mainstream comic books. Golden Age artist Will Eisner published *Comics and Sequential Art* in 1985 and *Graphic Story Telling and Visual Narrative* in 1995. In the forward to *Comics and Sequential Art*, Eisner informed his readers that his work was "intended to consider and examine the unique aesthetics of Sequential Art as a means of creative expression, a distinct discipline, an art and literary form that deals with the arrangement of pictures or images and words to narrate a story or dramatize an idea . . . The premise of this book is that the special nature of Sequential Art is deserving of serious consideration by both critic and practitioner."[23]

Alternative artist Scott McCloud published *Understanding Comics* in 1993, a comic book that celebrated the great potential of comic books and explored the aesthetics of the medium. "As comics grows into the next century, creators will aspire to many higher goals than appealing to the 'LOWEST COMMON DENOMINATOR.' Ignorance and short-sighted business practices will no doubt OBSCURE the possibilities of comics from time to time as they always have. But the TRUTH about comics can't stay hidden from view FOREVER and sooner or later the truth will SHINE THROUGH."[24] *Understanding Comics* was a huge success in comic book culture. McCloud quickly became a major voice in advocating for expanding the potential of comic art as Art. His next book was even more of a manifesto of this agenda. McCloud begins *Reinventing Comics* (2000) with a brief introduction to his work:

> [C]omics remains relegated to non-art status by *conventional wisdom.* A status some try to *combat,* (though some in the community *relish* it). Comics' place in society is *vital,* though, as one of the few forms of *personal communication*—in a world of *committee-built automatons* and corporate *mass-marketing.* Comics offers a medium of *enormous breadth* and *control* for the author—a *unique, intimate relationship* with its *audience*—and a *potential* so *great,* so *inspiring,* yet so brutally *squandered,* it could bring a tear to the eye.[25]

Another major advocate for comics as Art was underground artist Art Spiegelman. Spiegelman expressed his hopes for the comic art medium to the *Toronto Star* in 1986. "What it really comes down to is comics are just one more language. And as more people read them, enjoy them and recognize their potential, the body of comics literature will begin to change."[26] Spiegelman was a bit less sanguine by 1995 on both comics fans and the general public:

> There was a kind of breadth of possibility of expression that justified work that wasn't necessarily as fully realized as a great work in another medium, but that implied greatness around the corner . . . And that changed. It began to seem that maybe we were stuck with a bunch of freakish, gawky adolescents that were actually fully grown creatures and wouldn't develop further . . . But it seems to me that comics have already shifted from being an icon of illiteracy

to becoming one of our last bastions of literacy. If comics have any problem now, it's that people don't even have the patience to decode comics at this point . . . Sometimes I feel like comics are post-literate literature, in a world that doesn't have any need for literature, post-literature or anything remotely like literature because it doesn't move and it's not on the screen.[27]

Others still hoped for a better future for comic books. Several comics critics in a special issue of *The Comics Journal* on the "State of the Art Form" in 1996 stressed the crucial role of critics and criticism in advancing the potential of comic books as Art. Kent Worcester was hopeful that "the ideas of Scott McCloud, Will Eisner, and Art Spiegelman and other powerhouse organic-intellectuals have helped generate the foundations of a comics discourse that can transcend the limitations of mere fanboy empiricism."[28] Critic Ray Mescallado noted the role of critics as special cognoscenti of the form. "This is true for most any other medium—think of William Gaddis' novels, or Jim Jarmusch's films, or the music of Borbetomagus. For every great artist who is recognized as such by critics *and* sales, there are a dozen others who are appreciated only by the culturati, the aesthetic-minded who're the market's exceptions rather than the norm."[29] And critic Charles Hatfield remained optimistic about the future of comic books as Art:

Despite the parochialism of the direct market, many comic readers have made the effort to become more knowledgeable . . . a concurrent increase in criticism which treats comics as a form worthy of intrinsic study rather than simply a naïve reflection of popular taste and prejudices. . . . we've seen a growing formal awareness in comics creators themselves—from cartoonists like Spiegelman and the Hernandez Brothers, who woke a lot of people up, to an explosion of form-conscious cartoonists today, such as Chris Ware, Dylan Horrocks, Mary Fleener, Jason Lutes, and Jeremy Eaton . . . So the growing awareness of comics as a form goes hand in hand with more diversity in content. It's a revolution in both critical reception and practice.[30]

Worcester, Mescallado, and Hatfield were part of a group of mostly male critics in the alternative comics movement attempting to elevate comic art in the pages of *The Comics Journal*. These new critics hoped to create a new criticism that approached comic books as a serious "literary" art form. At times, however, these critics were rather harsh in their criticism, gaining the journal a reputation as acrimonious and elitist. And given the reputation and circulation of *The Comics Journal*, unfortunately, these critics were writing for the small minority of the already converted connoisseurs in comic book culture.

A major hope for alt rebels in the Heroic Age was to build a bridge to the outside world. In the late 1980s, their dreams seemed to have turned into a reality. With the critical success in 1986 of Frank Miller's *Dark Knight*, Alan Moore's *Watchmen*, and Art Spiegelman's *Maus*, trade publishers, bookstores, and the press began to take comic books seriously in the form of graphic novels. Trade publishers like Pantheon, Penguin, and Doubleday, as well as comics publishers, quickly released graphic novels into the trade market. As the *Christian Science Monitor* noted in 1988, "a new genre of comics is coming to the fore in the U.S.: graphic novels . . . Adult consumers are reading the entire range of graphic novels: superhero, adventure, science fiction, satire, historical drama, fantasy . . . Graphic novels have won a niche in *Publishers Weekly*, which earlier this year introduced a review category for them. And bookstores are testing the waters."[31]

Publishers Weekly noted the new trend in graphic novels in 1987. "They're not traditional novels, and they're not traditional comic books. They go by the catch-all phrase of 'graphic novels' because not even the people who write and/or publish them can agree on just what they are . . . Now major publishers such as Ballantine, Berkeley, Pocket Books and Simon and Schuster are diving in with graphic novel series and imprints . . . Art Spiegelman, author of the acclaimed *Maus*, feels that graphic novels aren't just another genre, but a separate medium of artistic expression."[32] *Adweek* also noted the rise of adult graphic novels, "comics are gaining respectability as publishers bring out 'graphic novels,' which look like trade paperbacks and cost around $12 apiece. Pantheon's *Maus*, in which Art Spiegelman tells the story of a concentration-camp survivor, has sold 90,000 copies since it came out in 1986 . . . 'The comic-book medium is expanding to include more complicated, more adult themes,' says Kevin McDonald, manager of Forbidden Planet, a sci-fi store in New York. 'Some publishers have been taking hints from Europe, where comics are an art form.'"[33]

Suddenly the rebellion in comic book culture was catching the attention of the press. Bart Bull noted in *Spin* what he, somewhat tongue in cheek, called the New Brass Age in comics:

> There is certainly no end in sight . . . there's no reason to believe that anybody's going to give up the freedom that the new comics have granted themselves. There's no reason to believe they *could*—now that the fences have been kicked over, nobody can seem to remember why they were there in the first place . . . As the comics embrace more and more of the world, more and more of the world seems ready to—well,

not to embrace them, actually, but at least to admit their existence . . . what matters most about the Brass Age is its diversity, its multiplicity, its incredibly amazing over-goddamn-abundance.[34]

Will Eisner, in *The New York Times* in 1990, celebrated the new status of comic books. "Everything has changed now; comic books are the arena for some of the most inventive expressions of literature . . . It is the promised land for a reading medium with humble origins . . . But I feel that my original sense of the potential of comics is about to be realized and that the medium can finally lay claim to legitimacy . . . The future for the comic book as worthwhile reading is so much brighter than it was before . . . The walls of the comics ghetto have been breached. The comic book is free."[35]

While Spiegelman's *Maus* received wide attention and acclaim, and articles appeared noting the new renaissance in comics and graphic novels, the trade market test was a bust. As publisher Gary Groth complained in 1991, "Despite all the hoopla in the mass media over the last three or four years that may have led you to believe that comics was finding acceptance among a culturally mature, adult readership, there is little or no evidence of this . . . no mainstream book publishers who jumped on the comic bandwagon lasted long."[36] By the early 1990s the major trade publishers published only a few titles, while independent comics publishers returned to the direct market. But ten years after the initial fanfare over graphic novels, *Publishers Weekly* was still hoping for better times. "Comics publishers necessarily look longingly at the vast number of chain and independent bookstores and can't help seeing the promised land. But that doesn't mean it will be easy."[37]

A few articles in the late 1980s and 1990s also noted the respect comic art was receiving from the world of high art. *U.S. News and World Report* informed readers:

Remember the comic books of your youth? They've grown up . . . And that's not all. The comics are also winning new respect: literary honors, respectful reviews, museum exhibits—even academic attention . . . The work of RAW stars like Sue Coe and Gary Panter now hangs in galleries in New York, Baltimore and elsewhere. Comics from the publication have been showcased in a show at New York's Whitney Museum, and some will be featured in exhibits planned for the Museum of Modern Art and in "The Great American Comic Strip," offered by the Smithsonian Institution's Traveling Exhibition Service, scheduled for 1989. Even scholars are getting into the act . . . there's no doubt that there is audience aplenty for today's mature comics . . . the comics can be regarded as serious art.[38]

But comic art in the late 1980s and 1990s only had a few exhibits at legitimate galleries and art museums. It was not invading the sacrosanct world of fine art anytime soon. *U.S. News and World Report* noted the resistance in the fine art world to comic art. "Some critics are still skeptical, Hilton Kramer, editor of the New Criterion arts magazine, dismisses out of hand any effort to elevate comics to the level of high art. That, he says, is 'non-sense' aimed at 'people who don't want to tax their mind and yet still want to be regarded as cultivated.'"[39] In response to this resistance, enthusiasts of comic art created their own museums. In 1987, the Comic Art Museum opened in San Francisco. And in 1992, rebel artist Kevin Eastman founded the Words and Pictures Museum in Northampton, Massachusetts.

While the fine art world mostly ignored comic art, comic artists did gain recognition from art foundations and prestigious literary awards. Art Spiegelman was awarded a Guggenheim Fellowship in 1990. In 1992, he received an American Book Award and a special Pulitzer Prize for the second volume of his graphic novel on the holocaust *Maus II*. In 1994 comics artist Eric Drooker won an American Book Award for *Flood: A Novel in Pictures,* a wordless graphic novel about surviving in the urban dystopia of New York City. Artist Joe Sacco also won an American Book Award in 1996 for his jarring journalistic ethnography *Palestine*. Unfortunately, none of these prestigious recognitions of the seriousness of graphic novels and the artistic accomplishments of comics artists seemed to have any effect on bringing a general readership to graphic novels.

Alternative comic books in the 1980s and 1990s also received serious attention in quite another way. The direct market allowed alternative publishers to publish material of a sexual nature. This elicited some attempts at censorship. Several retailers and artists were prosecuted for obscenity in the late 1980s and 1990s. The first major case was the prosecution of comic book retailer Frank Mangiaracina in 1986.[40] This case sparked the formation of the Comic Book Legal Defense Fund (CBLDF) in 1986, organized to support retailers and artists arrested for selling comic books. A few retailers in the United States and Canada were prosecuted for selling alternative comics containing what authorities considered obscene material. Most retailers simply paid fines, although in the most covered case, artist Mike Diana served three-years probation after his conviction on obscenity charges in Florida in 1994.[41] The biggest effort at censorship was actually through customs authorities in Canada, Britain, New Zealand, and other countries.[42] In Canada hundreds of alternative comic books were confiscated, banned, or destroyed by customs authorities.[43] In 2000, the Canadian Supreme Court ruled that the burden of proof that expressive material was obscene lay with customs. Problems, however, persisted with Canadian customs even after the court ruling. In support of efforts against censorship in Canada, artists in 2002 contributed to the comics anthology *What Right? Graphic Interpretations Against Censorship.*

By the end of the 1990s, the original optimism of gaining a new and viable readership outside of comic book culture had lost its luster—a mass market for comic books failed to materialize. And the future did not look much brighter. Tom De Haven, in 1998 in *The New York Times*, lamented the failure to attract new readers for adult comic books:

> Whatever happened to the legitimacy—to the hip cachet, even—that serious comics enjoyed only a few years ago? Following the great success of Art Spiegelman's "Maus," major book publishers actively sought out narrative cartoonists, and bookstores promised to make room for "graphic novels." The art form seemed primed for unfeigned respect, if not wholesale acceptance. For the first time, "comics" (an unfortunate, as well as an ineradicable, name) were being recognized as simply an umbrella designation like "movies." . . . by the late 1980s and early 90s there was an interested, aware and growing new audience for serious comic art. But those palmy days were astoundingly short-lived.[44]

At the Margins: Gender, Sexuality, and Race

Efforts to expand the field in terms of gender, sexuality, and race were a significant part of the Heroic Age in comic books. This rebellion not only included strategies to transform comic book content, but also efforts to break barriers for readers, artists, and others producing comic books. Comic book culture was a predominantly white, heterosexual, male subculture whose fictional universe reflected its readership, artists, and publishers. The direct market boom, however, provided opportunities to reshape the field in terms of gender, sexuality, and race, but significant barriers had to be overcome. Given the invisibility of women, minorities, and gays in the mainstream of this subculture, the mere act of someone from these marginal groups creating a comic book whose content broke away in some manner from the narrow universe of mainstream comic books was itself a violation of the rules of art in the field. Yet this rebellion from the margins also articulated a broader politics around gender, sexuality, and race in America. The general rebellion in the comic book field, therefore, became a social space in which women, gays, and minorities not only challenged the status quo in comic book culture, but explored the broader identity politics occurring beyond this subculture.

The largest rebellion from the margins of comic book culture was females challenging the male-dominated field of comic books. For some female artists this meant exploring questions related to the social and political construction of gender, femininity, and sexuality. For others, it was simply the opportunity to create comic art based on their own artistic vision. Female underground comix artists from the 1970s continued to produce comic art in the 1980s and 1990s. Most of their work was published by old underground publishers. Their more directly political and in-your-face approach continued among the next generation of female alternative comic book artists such as Julie Doucet, Roberta Gregory, Debbie Drechsler, and Ellen Forney. But like the alternative comics movement more generally, women artists explored a diverse array of artistic paths in challenging the field. As first-generation female underground comix artist Trina Robbins argues, these "post second-wave-feminism" women artists pushed female-created comic art in radically new directions.[45]

Since the 1980s, women artists have created a large number of comic books, almost exclusively in the alternative comics movement. These artists presented an assertion of previously absent identities, perspectives, tastes, and representations in the world of comic books. These interventions were through content and genre following both the pulp- and alt-strategies of the alternative comics movement. Intervention by content involved both new narrative conventions and prominent female characters; and images of females far removed from the gender representation characteristic of mainstream comic books. Intervention by genre was the attempt to introduce women's genres such as fantasy, witchcraft, and romance into the comic book market. While autobiographical or semiautobiographical comic books were one of the more popular genres among female artists, Trina Robbins argues "as many women cartoonists break the mold as fit into it, with as many different styles as there are artists."[46]

A very popular genre among female artists was the autobiographical, semiautobiographical, or fictional slice-of-life comic book. Julie Doucet's *Dirty Plotte* (1989) presented a scathing and surreal critique of a misogynist world. Ariel Schrag's self-published comic books *Award, Definition,* and *Potential* were autobiographical musings in the mid-1990s on a lesbian teenager's years in high school. A more humorous example of autobiography was Ellen Forney's *Monkey Food* (1999). Fictional comic books included the jarring looks of child abuse in Debbie Drechsler's *Daddy's Girl* (1996) to the everyday quandaries of young urbanites in Jessica Abel's *Artbabe* (1997). The importance of this work by women is seen in this comment by female comic artist Megan Kelso on reading *Dirty Plotte*. "I was struck by this totally female voice . . . being able to read women artist's work where I could relate on that really intense level definitely inspired me to want to do comics."[47]

A popular strategy among female artists was creating pulp genres viewed as more attractive to female readers. Linda Medley's *Castle Waiting* (1996) was an example of the fantasy genre. Witchcraft was also popular with Elizabeth Watasin's *Charm School* (2002) and *Scary Godmother* (1995) by Jill Thompson. You had romances like Oni Press's *Cheat* (2003) by Christine Norrie or the self-published *Eternal Romance* (1997) by Janet Hetherington. You had teen comic books featuring female protagonists like *Blue Monday* (2000) by Chynna Clugston-Major and *Bohos* (1998) written by Maggie Whorf. Also different genres could overlap as in the gothic fantasy *Gloomcookie* (1999), written by Serena Valentino, while Lea Hernandez's *Cathedral Child* (1998) was a science fiction romance. Female artists even tweaked the superhero genre like *Girlhero* (1993) by Megan Kelso. All-women anthologies also were published geared to female readers. *Action Girl* (1994), a comic book "girl positive and female-friendly" was edited by Sarah Dyer and published by Slave Labor Graphics.

Female artists have created erotic comic books as well. T. M. Lowe discussed female-created erotica for *The Comics Journal* in 2001. She noted that "the variety of tone, subject and quality of work is just as wide as the number of women doing the work." But she also noted that female-created erotica seems "more concerned with story and relationship."[48] Female artist Molly Kiely agreed, "Women's erotic work usually has feelings, storyline and compassion."[49] Kiely's *Tales of a Dominatrix* (1994) and *Saucy Little Tart* (1995) explored the world of S and M without the nonconsensual violent scenes characteristic of male artists in this subgenre. Pornography is a lucrative market in comic books and male artists dominate this genre, but then again they dominate the field in general. But women have intervened in a variety of ways, from twisted sister mode to camp mode to lesbian mode, to transform this male-centered genre in comic books.

What about comic books published by Marvel, DC, and mainstream independent publishers? There were a few attempts by these publishers to publish romances or other female-oriented comic books in the 1980s and 1990s, but they eventually abandoned any thought of publishing mainstream comic books for female readers.[50] Only the old mainstream Archie Comics maintained a line of female-oriented comic books for adolescents including *Veronica* and *Sabrina: The Teenage Witch*. Overall the one clear lack of change was in the continued dominance of the traditional-figured female comic book character, even with the introduction of strong positive female protagonists. Not only did Marvel and DC remain wedded to this tradition, even successful independent publishers like CrossGen, which specialized in the fantasy genre, remained in this tradition.

Scholar Sherrie A. Inness points to how in the mid-1990s the "bad girl" comic was a successful genre with some fifty series. Examples of what Inness calls "tough girls" included *Lady Death* (1994) and *Elektra* (1996). The most successful bad girl, however, was *Vampirella*, in publication since 1968. Inness points to how "tough girls" in mainstream comic books exhibited strength, intelligence, and other positive qualities, but still confronted the opposition of these qualities to being feminine.[51] And these tough girls remained wedded to the traditional representation of women in mainstream comic books. Inness's arguments pertained to virtually all mainstream comic books with female characters. Only in a few comic book series in the more "adult" imprints such as DC's Vertigo could one find female characters outside the traditional mold, such as Vertigo's *Transmetropolitan* (1997). While more female protagonists existed in contemporary mainstream comic books than in the past, this intervention in mainstream comic books obviously remained mostly trapped in traditional comic book imagery and narrative.

Women artists were to gradually find a small place among editors, writers, and artists in the mainstream comic book market. In 1974, only two women artists worked in the industry.[52] In the 1980s and 1990s, some women artists did work for the Big Two. Before *Castle Waiting*, Linda Medley worked on DC's *Doom Patrol* and *Justice League of America*. While Jill Thompson created the female-friendly alternative comic book *Scary Godmother*, she previously worked on *Wonder Woman* and *Sandman* among other mainstream comic books. Colleen Doran, while struggling to publish her fantasy *A Distant Soil*, worked as an illustrator on such mainstream series as *Wonder Woman* and *The Amazing Spider-Man*. What's striking in all three examples is how given the opportunity to create their own comic books these female artists used graphic styles, characters, and images strikingly different than what they created for mainstream publishers.

The biggest problem female artists faced was the barrier to reaching female readers. Critics argued that the content of mainstream comic books, and the perception outside comic book culture that they represented all comic books, kept female readers from discovering alternative comics. Critics also pointed to the uninviting nature of comic book culture at conventions and comic book shops for female readers. Rebel artist Megan Kelso complained in 1996, "The women customers thing is frustrating in and of itself because women don't buy comics as much as men do, and a lot of it has to do with the typical comic book store experience, and the history of comics—how there's so little out there that appeals to women, I feel like there's a lot of women out there who would probably really dig my comic, but it's just invisible to them because they don't go to comic book stores, and my comic isn't in book stores. That's continually frustrating me."[53]

In 1994, the nonprofit organization Friends of Lulu (FOL) was established to support women in the industry and bring female readers back to comic books.[54] A major strategy of FOL was targeting young girls, since it was believed that comic book reading was more likely to become a regular activity if picked up at an early age. Junior Lulus was established where young members would receive comic books on a regular basis. Eventually FOL published anthologies geared to young female readers like *Broad Appeal*. And in 1997, FOL published *How to Get Girls (Into Your Store)*, a guidebook for retailers to help make their shops female friendly. Deni Loubert informed retailers, "The reality is that as long as shops don't perceive themselves as places where women can buy comics, women and girls will never walk into those shops . . . We love this medium, this art form—and we all want to see it prosper . . . Let's face it: You are on the front lines. You are the one who takes all our hopes and dreams and puts them out there for the world to see. You are our key."[55]

While comic book culture was a male preserve often uninviting to female fans and artists, there were "fangirls" who enjoyed mainstream comic books and comic book fandom. *Wizard*, a fanzine that was steeped in this hypermasculine world of comics, quickly found some rather irate women who found this magazine offensive. But other fangirls wrote letters supporting *Wizard* as well. As one fangirl wrote, however, "I think I am well-adjusted to the male view of women in comics, movies and magazines. I realize that more males buy comics than do females, and that the comic book industry must cater to those readers . . . But every month, we're surrounded by females with erect nipples, breast implants, thong costumes and legs everywhere. I want to let people in the industry know that there *are* women readers out there, and we'd like to even out the field."[56]

Besides female artists and readers striking from the margins of comic book culture, gay artists and fans also confronted the boundaries of a heterosexual subculture. It should probably not come as a surprise that no gay characters appeared in comic books during the Industrial Age. Gay characters in mainstream comic books only began to appear in the 1980s. Unfortunately, they replicated stereotypes of homosexuals. But following another revamping of the Comics Code in 1989, homosexuals were required to be portrayed in a positive way, so more gay characters appeared in mainstream comics. The most famous "outing" in mainstream comic books was the mutant superhero Northstar in 1992, a member of the Marvel Canadian super-team Alpha Flight and later a member of X-Men.

But the few gay characters in mainstream comic books in the 1990s mostly were with DC or independent publishers like Malibu and Image.

Gay, lesbian, and bisexual superheroes included the Pied Piper, Spectral, Turbo Charge, Rainmaker, and Ice Maiden. Outside of the superhero genre, Neil Gaiman introduced gay characters in his successful DC-Vertigo *Sandman* fantasy series in 1991. DC-Vertigo also published an autobiographical graphic novel by gay artist David Wojnarowicz. And the comic book *Star Trek* had a lesbian character introduced in 1997 and a male gay character in 1998.[57] But gay characters and gay themes in mainstream comics remained a rarity, although usually arousing media attention. Mainstream publishers' fears of parents' and fanboys' reactions to gay characters were partly to blame for their failure to introduce more gay characters.[58] DC titles did receive awards from the Gay and Lesbian Alliance Against Defamation (GLAAD). The first GLAAD media award for comics was given to DC's *The Flash* in 1992. But gay creators and fans debated whether the awards for mainstream comics were more about media hype than the actual substance of the comic's stories.[59]

Unquestionably, however, the alternative comics movement was where radical change in gay representation in comics, and rich opportunities for gay artists, occurred. Some of the most popular and critically recognized artists in alternative comics have been gay. We have already seen how female underground artists paved the way for lesbian characters and themes in the 1970s. But male underground artists also paved the way for gay characters as well. Howard Cruse had his character Headrack come out in *Barefootz Funnies* in 1976. The first all gay-male comic *Gay Heart Throbs* was published that same year. At the end of the decade the most important gay anthology in the alternative comics movement appeared. Kitchen Sink's *Gay Comix* (1980) was first edited by Howard Cruse and featured some of the best gay and lesbian artists in the field. Fan Joe Palmer remembered the impact of *Gay Comix* #1: "The book was still fascinating for me simply because of the idea behind it: gays and lesbians telling stories about themselves . . . the most important and empowering aspect for me of GAY COMIX #1 was the potential for gay people to use this medium to tell stories about themselves."[60]

Gay artists would employ both the alt- and pulp-strategies of the alternative comics movement. Alternative anthologies included *Naughty Bits* (1991) and *Boy Trouble* (1994). Gay alternative artists published slice-of-life and semi-autobiographical comic books and graphic novels like Ivan Velez Jr.'s *Tales of the Closet* (1987) about gay and lesbian teens and Howard Cruse's *Stuck Rubber Baby* (1995), a graphic novel based on his young years in the south. The alt-humor genre included Diane DiMassa's popular *Hothead Paisan, Homicidal Lesbian Terrorist* (1991). In terms of the pulp-strategy, the superhero genre included Neil Johnston's *Go-Go Boy* (1994) and Jennifer Camper's *SubGurlz* (1999). Jimmie Robinson's *Cyberzone* (1994) was a cyberpunk adventure featuring an African American lesbian character named Amanda Shane. Elizabeth Watasin's witchcraft comic *Charm School* (2000) featured the lesbian main character Bunny. Gay artists also published a wide range of erotica comics. One of the earliest successful erotic anthologies was *Meatmen* (1986). There were female artists doing lesbian erotica such as Petra Waldron and Jennifer Finch's *The Adventures of a Lesbian College Girl* (1998) and Colleen Coover's *Small Favors* (2000).

Gay activism in comic book culture began during the direct market boom. The first major fanzine article to appear addressing gays in comics was Andy Mangels's two-part series, "Out of the Closet and into the Comics," in *Amazing Heroes* in 1988. A critical review of the poor state of gay representation in mainstream comics, the series also addressed the industry's attitudes toward gay writers and artists. As one artist told Mangels, "I think that the fact that we are anonymous, and choose to remain anonymous at this time—in this article—is in itself, the strongest indication of where society is at right now, and how homophobic comics and the industry is, and can be."[61] Gay presence in the mainstream of comic book culture gained a major victory in 1988 when the first of the annual "Gays in Comics" panel was inaugurated at the San Diego Comic-Con. Two amateur press associations (APAs) were formed to distribute comic art by gay artists: Northstar was established in 1989 and The APA That Dare Not Speak Its Name was established later that year. Gay artist and activist Andy Mangels published "Out in Comics" in 1999; a guidebook of openly gay comics creators. In 2002, gay comics activists incorporated the nonprofit Prism Comics, dedicated to promoting LGBT creators in the field.

In 2004 activist Rich Thigpen pointed to the importance of Prism Comics for gay artists and gay representation in both mainstream and alternative comics. "Prism is important in a couple of ways. One, it helps promote the independent creators who are producing non-traditional fare. Two, it works to educate the general public both about LGBT themes in comics and the number of LGBT professionals in the industry. With the state of the comics industry today, both of these facets can only be good for the industry as a whole . . . having LGBT characters and creators in the comics industry diminishes the traditional stigma . . . Currently, characters in the comics industry still don't represent the full diversity of humans seen in the real world."[62]

Gay alternative artists continue to create challenging queer-themed comic art. Activists and fans also continue to promote gay artists and gay representation in mainstream comics. Over the last few years the Big Two have introduced more gay characters and even attempted titles featuring main gay characters like Marvel's *Rawhide Kid* (2003) and DC's *Midnighter* (2006). But efforts by the Big Two continue to receive mix responses from gay artists and fans. Positive portrayals of gay characters are still mixed with other gay characters experiencing violent acts toward them or simply dying off. And it is almost guaranteed that new titles featuring main gay characters end up as mini-series with very short runs.[63] The heterosexual male world in mainstream comics continues to marginalize gay fans and gay representation.

How have minorities fared in comic book culture? DC and Marvel made faint efforts to increase minority representation during the short-lived "socially relevant" phase of the early 1970s. Of the minority superheroes appearing during the 1970s, only two remained active and playing prominent roles into the 1980s and 1990s: the black superheroes Storm and Green Lantern. As the direct market expanded in the early 1990s diversity was not a major concern of mainstream publishers. Some failed attempts at black superheroes carrying their own titles were made. The few minority characters that appeared in the mainstream superhero universe usually were found in superhero teams like X-Men, Teen Mutants, Alpha Flight, Justice League, or All-Star Squadron. There were two successful black superheroes carrying individual titles. Marvel's *Blade*, first introduced in 1973, was reintroduced in 1992 and became a very successful property, while Todd McFarlane's *Spawn*, introduced that same year, became a mega-property for this rebel fan-artist.

Beginning in the early 1990s black publishers and black artists mounted a campaign to transform what they considered a superhero universe poorly representing African Americans and other minorities. Popular culture scholar Jeffrey A. Brown presents a detailed analysis of these efforts of black publishers and artists to transform the comic book field. He points to two strategies of rebellion. One followed a more radical political and aesthetic agenda. Brown views the first strategy as an extension of the Black Arts Movement that emerged in the 1960s. This movement promoted a distinct black aesthetic in art as best representing and speaking to the black community. The other strategy attempted to assimilate into the mainstream of comic book culture. These publishers and artists created mainstream comic books featuring black and other minority superheroes.[64]

A number of independent black publishers and artists followed the more radical strategy. They promoted what they believed was a more authentic Afrocentric approach to comic books. Publisher Eric Griffin brought black independent publishers together under an umbrella collective called ANIA— Swahili for "protect" or "defend"—to promote the new movement. In his 1993 review of this movement for *The Comics Journal*, Jeffrey Winbush introduced readers to the "The New Black Age of Comics." "Both ANIA and other independent black comic makers are fighting limited budgets and resources to reach their audiences. Black comic books with Afrocentric themes will be confusing to readers, both white and black, who are unfamiliar with the philosophy. But just as the emergence of rap as a popular music form challenged previously held beliefs and forced critical reappraisal of its legitimacy and durability, the same principle will be applied to this new group of comics."[65]

Most radical artist-publishers focused on a separate distribution system of African American distributors and African American–owned bookstores. Others like Nabile Hage of Dark Zulu Lies hoped to enter the comic book direct market. Hage told *The Comics Journal* in 1993, "The main reason that I got into publishing comics as an independent was there are no blacks in this field who owned their own company . . . Of course, there were other African-American publishers out there whose work appeared in the African American bookstores, the African American trade shows. They appeared in the mainstream, only carried by one or two [comics] distributors, got low orders, and subsequently quit. I decided to come in here and help integrate this particular system, because there were *no* black-owned publishers."[66] These publishers did release several titles into the comic book direct market, including Turtel Onli's *Malcolm 10* and *Sustah Girl*. Other Afrocentric titles included Eric Griffin's *Ebony Warrior*; Roger Barnes's *Heru, Son of Ausar,* and Nabile Hage's *Zwanna, Son of Zulu*. Comic books less wedded to an Afrocentric theme, but emphasizing a radical black politics included Guy Sims and Dawud Anyabwile's (David Sims) superhero comic *Brotherman* and Christopher Clarke's social-message comic *Inner-City Products*.

But comic book culture was not particularly receptive to a radical black perspective. Jason Sims, president of Big City Comics, argued in 1993, "There's a resistance going on, and there has been since we started . . . But it doesn't stop us, and I think it is becoming more noticeable to the public."[67] Nabile Hage complained that same year about resistance to this new rebellion. "But I know I get a lot of criticism in the comic-book press, with retailers writing in who've never even seen the book. Just because Zwanna is coming from the left, I get all this criticism. They're calling me racist. It hasn't come out yet, and it's already being condemned as a racist book! But if they took the time to read that book, cover to cover, they would see that book as the most anti-racist book in the world!"[68] Hage's dream of integrating these more radical comic books never materialized. This more radical strategy of intervention into comic book culture was a failure. Brown notes that none of the Afrocentric titles went past a single issue in the direct market.[69]

Independent publishers or studios also created mainstream superhero comic books with central black or other minority characters. They distributed their titles through top mainstream publishers. The most successful was publisher Milestone Comics. It found success with a distribution agreement with DC Comics in 1993. Dwayne McDuffie, Denys Cowan, Michael Davis, and Derek Dingle started the publishing enterprise. McDuffie, Cowan, and Davis were all veteran artists in the industry. In *The New York Times,* Cowan told reporter Veronica Byrd that the company would produce a line of comic books with not only black superheroes but "a whole segment of the population in comics that has never been represented before, including women, Hispanics and Asians."[70] The Milestone team also was interviewed in 1993 in *The Comics Journal.* In the interview, Cowan pointed to the need for Milestone to break the stereotyping in mainstream comic books. "The key is, if they had already done minority characters in a non-stereotypical way successfully, there would be no need for Milestone. Milestone is fulfilling a need." McDuffie agreed, "I think the demographics of this country and the growth of this industry dictates a breaking down of the status quo . . . How can we have more of a balance of images, how can we have more images out there? Milestone presents one of the answers. You have an independent group of creators who form a company to preserve their vision and to ensure that it goes to the widest possible audience." Dingle expressed the mission of Milestone. "Our mission is to create a truly multicultural universe and to have multicultural talent develop it, which we've done."[71]

The most successful of Milestone's line of superhero comic books were *Hardware* (1993), *Static* (1993), *Blood Syndicate* (1993), and *Icon* (1993). Hardware, Static, and Icon were black male superheroes, while the Blood Syndicate was made up of a multicultural superpowered street gang. In the early years of Milestone, the company touted its immediate success as an independent publisher. In *Black Enterprise* it was reported that Milestone in 1993 sold 3.5 million copies of its first seven titles earning five million dollars. A crossover miniseries featuring both DC and Milestone superheroes, *Worlds Collide* (1993), sold 1.8 million copies. The magazine informed its readers, "There is a revolution going on in a Manhattan high-rise on 23rd street near the Avenue of Americas. On the fourth floor, a small army is busy creating a new universe . . . The denizens of this world are made in the image of their creators—a band of artists, editors and writers of backgrounds not limited by race, age or gender. It's a strange new world, one you may not have heard of yet, largely because its universe is the comic book industry."[72]

Unfortunately, after its initial success, Milestone failed to produce other successful titles or increase the circulation of its first titles. Milestone folded its comic book line in 1997. Brown attributes the problems faced by Milestone to resistance on the part of comic book retailers. In interviews with retailers, Brown found that they held the view that their white male customers would not be interested in black, political superhero comic books, even though Milestone had virtually a 100 percent sell-through for their comics.[73] Milestone's Denys Cowan told the fanzine *Wizard,* "I have been completely surprised by the resistance our books have received from the direct market. I thought there would be some resistance, but I also thought that our idea would have appeal. I didn't expect the scale of resistance we've seen. I've been in the comics field for 20 years, it's frustrating." Milestone editor Dwayne McDuffie expressed his frustration to Wizard, too. "I was blindsided, I was shocked."[74] Another black independent studio, Brent Dorian Carpenter's Foundation Studio, tried a similar strategy as Milestone, working with the major independent publisher Caliber's Gauntlet imprint in 1993. The Studio's *UN Force* (1993) initially received attention from the press and good sales. But none of the Foundation's superhero comic books for Caliber succeeded beyond six issues. This mainstream strategy of rebellion in the 1990s failed to create a more multicultural superhero universe.

DC and Marvel in 2006 publicized a concerted effort on their part to make the superhero universe a more multicultural universe. *The New York Times* reported on this new strategy of the Big Two. "Comic books have featured minorities before, but the latest push is intended to be a sustained one, taking place in an alternate world that nevertheless reflects American society in general and comic readers in particular, in much the same way that the multicultural casts of television shows like ABC's 'Lost' and 'Grey's Anatomy' mirror their audiences."[75] DC planned on resurrecting old characters like Blue Beetle as a young Hispanic man and Batwoman as a lesbian. Marvel had maintained its Black Panther superhero in some fashion since his introduction in the 1970s, but introduced a new *Black Panther* series in 2005 written by black artist Reginald Hudlin. Marvel also reintroduced the black character Luke Cage. Overall, however, this effort by the Big Two has not really remade mainstream comics into a multicultural universe.

Brad Mackay of the *Toronto Star* investigated the continued lack of black and minority representation in 2007. "Of the 300 comics published monthly by Marvel, DC and a clutch of other companies, only a half-dozen or so titles feature a black hero in a starring role." Reginald Hudlin was perplexed. "In every other medium, the most successful concept or product is black. Whether it's music, movies, TV shows: out of the top 10, four of them are black . . . Only in comics are blacks so underrepresented. Somehow, in this medium people are so out of touch with popular culture that they don't understand that black culture is popular culture." Toronto comic shop retailer Peter Birkemore answered Mackay's question on "the mainstream industry's pitiable, and even outright embarrassing, track record on diversity . . . 'Everything that these companies do is in complete isolation from true market forces . . . Companies run by fans with comics drawn by fans rarely think of catering to anyone but themselves.'"[76]

The response of some fans to a more diverse comic book universe shocked Marvel editor Axel Alonso. He oversaw two critically acclaimed series. The first was *Rawhide Kid* (2003), featuring a gay cowboy. The second series was *Truth: Red, White and Black*, which revolved around the early experiments done on black soldiers, in Tuskegee-like fashion, for the drug that eventually created Captain America. According to Brad MacKay in the *Toronto Star* "both series were praised by many outside the comic industry, yet Marvel weathered intense—and often racially charged—criticism from fans." Alonso also oversaw Reginald Hudlin's reintroduction of Marvel's Black Panther in 2005. It landed in the top-thirty best sellers with its debut. But over the next two years, sales dropped 50 percent. MacKay reported that "Hudlin has been the target of venomous criticism. One early scene that depicted Black Panther beating Captain America in a fight provoked online critics to accuse him of 'shameless race-card playing' and 'promoting an exaggerated super Negro.' It got so bad last fall that the website Comic Book Resources temporarily suspended all discussion of the comic on its message board, citing an 'unacceptable level of vitriol.' 'I won't lie,' says Alonso. 'This is a title that we need to fight to keep alive. I mean, I've yet to see a writer take more hits from the right people than Reggie.'"[77]

Comic book culture has been a direct market catering to a specific subculture. While minority readers have existed in this market, they have not existed in numbers sufficient to convince mainstream publishers and retailers that their economic interests could be served by catering to such a niche market. And publishers and retailers believed, and continue to believe, that white fanboys are not interested in any major multicultural transformation. While Brown argues that in the early 1990s it was probably a self-fulfilling prophecy as retailers prevented Milestone from attracting a larger readership, the later experience of Marvel editor Alex Alonso and artist Reginald Hudlin would suggest otherwise. Multiculturalism has confronted an apparent investment on the part of white fanboys in their cherished world of white male fantasy. Such successful characters like Blade and Spawn might suggest otherwise, but the exceptions do not make the rule. Both also are very ambivalent and violent superheroes; one a vampire vigilante and the other the spawn of the devil. But one cannot simply discount the experiences and views of publishers and artists like Alonso and Hudlin.

While the mainstream fictional universe has failed to significantly diversify, minority artists have gained a larger presence in the field compared to the Industrial Age. During the Late Industrial Age minority artists also rose to prominence in the North American comics field, such as George Perez.

And we've seen how African American artists Dwayne McDuffie, Denys Cowan, and Michael Davis worked for the Big Two before they started Milestone in 1991. Other African Americans in the field in the 1980s included editor Christopher Priest and artist Kyle Baker. Early Asian American comic artists included Larry Hama, a veteran from the 1970s, and entering the field in the 1980s were highly acclaimed artists Whilce Portacio, Jim Lee, and Ron Lim. In the 1990s, more minority artists, writers, and editors began to enter the field. The influx of minority comics professionals, however, has only translated into some minor changes in the diversity found in the mainstream comic book universe of superheroes.

In the early 1990s even the alternative comics movement was overwhelmingly white. Successful early minority alternative artists included Gilbert, Jaime, Lea and Javier Hernandez, and Stan Sakai. And most of the radical black artists in the early 1990s did not really identify with this movement. The editorial by Carole Sobocinski to the special 1993 issue "Black Comics Artists" of *The Comics Journal* spoke to the present state of the alt movement in terms of its lack of multicultural diversity. "THERE'S A TRANSFORMATION occurring in comics which is being reflected here at *The Comics Journal*. There was a time when this magazine provided a safe haven for white guys to debate the relative merits of each other's works . . . But as the comics art medium matures and expands to include a more representative sampling of the world at large, we're beginning to see that comics aren't just for white guys anymore. There are some in the comics community who welcome the broadening influence while others view this as an intrusion on their world."[78] While the alternative comics movement still remains predominately white, a number of minority artists also have entered the world of alternative comics.

While the Heroic Age inspired women, gays, and minority artists to rebel for greater representation and participation in comic books, the political economy of comic books has presented structural impediments that have reinforced the white-, heterosexual-, and male-defined world of mainstream comic books. Women and gay artists were certainly successful in finding greater opportunities in the alternative comics movement, but the mainstream of the comic book field remained difficult to fundamentally change. Herman Gray shows how the political economy of television at a crucial moment in the 1990s opened up this mass market to niche programming of all-black shows.[79] And Ron Becker has made a similar argument on the rise of gay representation in prime-time television programs in the 1990s.[80] It was, however, the economic interests of the culture industries that led to such critical junctures, not the liberal politics of media executives or audiences. But the comic book industry has not faced structural changes that could open up possibilities for considering new niche markets or catering to new demographics. The direct market of comic books has served a very narrow demographic of readers invested in an interpretive community based on what became a limited set of genres. Like the alternative comics movement, these rebels from the margins confronted a comic book culture not particularly interested in radically changing the superhero and pulp universes they had come to enjoy. And they confronted a readership whose interests and prejudices were not particularly conducive to the identity politics of gender, race, and sexual orientation of the 1990s.

Conclusion

The Heroic Age of the American comic book witnessed a diverse array of challenges to the rules of art in the comic book field inherited from the old Industrial Age. Like mainstream rebels, alternative rebel artists and publishers claimed principles of autonomy from these old rules of art and staked claims to creating comic books fashioned by their own visions of the greater potential for this medium. For alternative rebels the direct market boom signaled even greater possibilities for expanding the field. But the direct market and comic book culture were not very receptive to alternative rebels and their art. The Big Two and the most successful independents remained wedded to the tried-and-true superhero genre, taking advantage of the fan-celebrated talents of mainstream rebels to bring a more "sophisticated" rendering of their commercial properties, or occasionally promoting new pulp genres by mainstream rebels.

Unfortunately for alternative rebels, the superhero and pulp-strategies in mainstream comics resonated with the core fan base of retailers, collectors, and readers in comic book culture. This fan base was not interested in the various transformations alternative rebel artists were attempting during the boom or after. A few alternative artists did attract fans' interests, even fans' interest in speculating with comic books. But overall the alternative rebellion of the Heroic Age faced a structural barrier in which alternative rebels survived at the margins of this direct market. But regardless of their marginality, alternative rebel artists and publishers were able to maintain a presence in the field and develop their own network of support. And they did set the foundation for approaching comic books in new and radical ways.

Alternative rebels also faced the contradiction of reproducing the type of status hierarchy that had stigmatized comic books for so long. Those committed particularly to the alt-strategy of framing comic books as legitimate as any other high art simply reproduced the popular art versus high art dichotomy that in many ways comic book culture worked hard to escape. And ironically for certain high art elite outside comic book culture claiming that a subliterate medium like comic books could be high art undermined this very status hierarchy. The long history of disrespect for comic books placed such a high art strategy in a double bind of insulting both the majority of fans in comic book culture and many cognoscenti in official culture. The alternative comics movement in many ways faced the same problem Pierre Bourdieu claimed for any popular art holding pretensions to high art status—you alienate popular audiences at the same time as you fail in the eyes of legitimate institutionalized arbiters of high art.[81] One audience views you as a snob, the other as a middlebrow pretender to high art status.

The story of the alternative comics movement also points to a fascinating coalescence of rebellion in the Heroic Age of the American comic book. The generation of principles of autonomy in the comic book field was driven by developments both within and outside this field. The mainstream rebellion of fan-artists discussed in the previous chapter evolved within this field as comic book fans developed their own criteria of judgment that elevated comic book artists as artists with unique talents and visions. Mainstream rebels embraced these new criteria and applied a pulp-strategy to transform mainstream comic books. The alternative comics movement was the child of the underground comix movement. And the comix movement first emerged in the counterculture movement of the 1960s outside the comic book field. But with the collapse of an independent comix market, this movement found a new home in the emerging direct market of comic books supported by comic book fandom. Alternative rebels would bring a more "radical" agenda in transforming the American comic book that applied both a pulp- and alt-strategy to expand this art form even further than mainstream rebels. And while the mainstream and alternative rebellions by the end of the twentieth century both faced a collapse in the direct market and a failure to find an audience beyond comic book culture, they both set the stage in their transformation of the American comic book for an unexpected resurgence of this art form in the twenty-first century.

Unfortunately, the overall problem of marginality of women, minorities, and gays in mainstream comic books remained mostly unchanged. Certainly such marginality in some fashion—gender, sexual orientation, or race—exists in other media, but not to the extent that it exists in the mainstream comic book universe and culture. While the direct market boom provided a new social space for interventions in the politics of gender, sexual, and race representation in popular culture, these interventions confronted significant obstacles for success. Whether a question of the political economy of the comic book field or the resistance found in comic book culture, the comparative marginality in comic books is unmistakable. When it comes to diversity, while more previously marginal artists and fans have appeared in the comic book field, mainstream comic books have failed to truly diversity their universe. Like alternative rebels, the rebels from the margins greatest hopes lie outside comic book culture. Finding a bridge back into a mass market for comic books presents the greatest opportunities for alternative, women, gay, and minority rebel artists. Luckily such a bridge suddenly began to materialize only a few short years into the twenty-first century.

6
The Heroic Age III

*New Movements, Winning Respect,
and the Rise of the Graphic Novel*

The decade of the 1990s ended with the failed materialization of a mass market for graphic novels and some people questioning the vitality of the comic book direct market. And many still felt that official culture simply did not take comic books seriously. When all looked dark and foreboding, however, something unexpected happened to comic books in North America. Suddenly the fastest growing publishing market became Japanese comic books, *manga*, sweeping young female and male readers into a reading frenzy. Then a movement among librarians and teachers emerged, promoting graphic novel collections in libraries and comic books as wonderful educational tools. Serious graphic novels and their artists suddenly had their reputations vastly improve with greater critical recognition from official culture. In less than ten years, graphic novels actually became one of the fastest growing publishing markets in North America. Maybe there was a bright future for comic books after all.

There was other good news in the comic book field: the revitalization of the Big Two through the licensing of properties. Superheroes invaded Hollywood film like never before. And they generated top box office revenue. Many hoped America's reintroduction to the superhero universe would revitalize the comic book market. Of course, some lamented the dominance of licensed product as the profit centers for the Big Two with comic books merely acting to keep licensed characters active. And others complained about the superhero once again defining comic art in the popular imagination. Audiences flooding movie theatres to watch Spider-Man probably knew he came from a comic book, even if they never actually read one. But how many audience members for *Road to Perdition* or *A History of Violence* actually knew these films were taken from graphic novels?

Comic books' low status in official culture as a subliterate art also seemed to have been overcome. Something surely had changed if librarians and teachers had become major advocates for the power and depth of comic books, or *The New York Times* had regular reviews of graphic novels. More importantly, the revitalization of comic books was not in the direct market, but in the trade market. Comic books were reaching new readers! And some alternative comics artists had best-selling graphic novels. It was clear that the field was in a transformation as significant as the rise of the direct market in the 1980s.

Part of the new changes in the world of comic books was the invasion of the Web by comic book culture and comic art. The most significant contribution of the Web was providing a new social space for comic book fandom. The Web was an ideal space for the participatory nature of comic book fandom, creating greater opportunities for networking and other activities. Unfortunately for those who hoped the Web would become a new revolutionary social space for the commercial as well as aesthetic growth of comic books, such dreams never truly materialized. The unpredictable nature of the impact of new media was evident in the Web's greatest effect on comic art not being in comic books, but in comic strips.

The Manga Revolution: Girl Power and Transforming the Comic Book Field

Comic books are a widely popular form of reading in Japan. Manga cater to young and old alike, female and male readers, and cover every subject matter imaginable. They are published in magazine anthologies and in paperback series. The major categories for manga are based on their target readership. *Shonen* cater to young boys, while *Shojo* cater to young girls. These two genres were the foundation of the boom in manga in Japan from the late 1940s to the 1960s. *Seinen* manga target adult males; and *Josei* are for adult females. These genres became widely popular in Japan in the 1970s and 1980s. But within these demographic-based genres one can find a wide variety of content-based genres. Sales of manga magazines and books in Japan peaked in 1995 at 2.3 billion copies, but have remained at around 40 percent of the Japanese publishing market.[1] And as Paul Gravett, in his history of manga, points out, while the vast majority of the millions of Japanese who read manga are "causal consumers" enjoying "cheap, disposable, mass literature," there are also the *otaku*, "obsessive fans, who make manga a lifestyle."[2]

An important aspect of manga in Japan, and an important part of the story of manga's success in North America, is its intimate relationship to Japanese animation, *anime*. Anime developed out of manga, and since early anime the two have evolved together as popular forms of entertainment. The Japanese national icon Osamu Tezuka is considered the father of both modern manga and modern anime. In the early 1960s, Tezuka transformed two of his popular manga series "Astro Boy" and "Jungle Emperor" into some of the first animated television shows produced in Japan. But the real boom in anime in Japan did not occur until the 1980s. And by the late 1990s, animation was Japan's most successful export of popular culture. While the international market for anime far surpassed the international market for manga—in 2003 the U.S. market for anime alone was 4.2 billion dollars compared to one hundred million dollars for manga—*Publishers Weekly* noted in 2004 that Japan had been enjoying "an international pop cultural phenomenon—two forms of Japanese visual storytelling linked by a distinctive visual style and offering a wide range of material for girls and boys as well as adults."[3]

In North America a fandom for anime emerged in the early 1990s. They discovered anime via videotapes and discussed them avidly in fan clubs and on the Internet. *The New York Times* noted this new fandom in 1995. "Even in the United States, where there is more competition, Japanese animation, or Japanimation, has developed a cult following . . . Numerous American colleges have anime clubs, and there are conventions for American fans. But the place fanatics really meet is on the Internet computer network."[4] While a few anime conventions were held in the 1980s, the longest running anime convention began in 1991 with AnimeCon in San Jose, California. Its name was changed to Anime Expo the following year and the convention moved to Southern California in 1994. Anime fandom began to significantly grow beginning in 1997 when fourteen conventions or shows were held in North America. Anime conventions were just as equally manga conventions and mixed with other popular culture and events revolving around "cosplay," costume playing. The eventual recognition of manga and anime by comic book culture and other fandoms meant *otaku* could find over ninety conventions and shows in North America featuring anime and manga by 2003.[5] In 2003, the two largest anime conventions were the Anime Expo with seventeen thousand attendees and Baltimore's Otakon with 17,388.[6]

English-language manga were introduced in North America during the direct market boom. In 1986, Studio Proteus formed in San Francisco, specializing in translating manga for independent comics publishers in North

America. The Japanese publisher Shogakukan established Viz Communications in San Francisco in 1987 to translate manga for the North American market. Viz Communications became the biggest publisher of translated manga. Dark Horse Comics became the major promoter of translated manga among North American independent publishers. In the direct market, manga never reached the level of circulation of mainstream American comic books. The more popular manga sold around thirty to fifty thousand copies per series. In 1997, Viz was publishing forty graphic novels and Dark Horse was publishing around a dozen manga.[7] During this early phase of translating manga, publishers feared that the right-to-left reading and the unique visual representations of action in Japanese manga would confuse English-language readers. So manga during this period were "flipped" left-to-right and more familiar textual representations of action were used. This was a time-consuming and expensive endeavor that limited the potential of manga in North America.[8]

In the late 1990s, the rising popularity of anime on television soon spurred a boom in manga. Three anime series pointed to the potential of manga in North America: *Sailor Moon* (1995), *Dragon Ball Z* (1996), and *Pokémon* (1998). A new company, Mixx Entertainment, introduced *Sailor Moon* in 1997 in its manga anthology and attracted a cult following among female *otaku*. Mixx publisher Stuart Levy made the decision to publish this translated manga in its traditional format, rejecting the "flipping" of previous translated manga. *Dragon Ball Z* (1998) also remained in its traditional format at the request of its artist Akira Toriyama. But the Pokémon phenomenon truly pointed to the future of manga when in 1998 its manga title sold millions of copies outside the direct market and newsstand distribution.[9]

While manga was finding success in the U.S. market, it was Stuart Levy's publishing company Tokyopop that truly sparked a boom in manga. Following his earlier philosophy with Mixx, he released translated manga in traditional format into the trade book market in 2001. While in the first wave of English-language manga publishers targeted young male readers with shonen manga, Levy published English-language manga in the young female shojo genre as well. He also expanded his line by translating Korean *manhwa*, which are traditionally read left-to-right like English-language comics. Also, by avoiding the costs of "flipping" manga, Levy was able to produce graphic novels of translated manga at a reduced price of ten dollars. *Publishers Weekly* quickly noted the success of Tokyopop and the new manga boom:

> Some of the best selling graphic novels in America are actually Asian: Japanese manga and their close relatives from Korea and Hong Kong. As young American readers grow accustomed to the story-telling

conventions of Asian comics—and as American media outlets like Cartoon Network show Asian anime, or animated cartoon TV series, about the same characters—they've become dedicated fans and repeat customers of manga in English translation . . . The most prolific American manga publisher, though, is Tokyopop—and the biggest thing on its docket right now is the "100% Authentic Manga" line—graphic novels meant to be read right to left and back to front, rather than photographically "flipped" to read left to right in English translation. *Cowboy Bebop* is the sales leader—it's based on the anime series that Cartoon Network is airing . . . the publisher has launched 18 new series this year, for a total of 33 active manga titles.

By 2003 manga publishers were facing a boom in market sales. "Manga releases dominate BookScan's reporting on the best-selling graphic novels. Manga's dynamic artwork and its science fiction, supernatural and action-oriented plots are attracting hordes of teenagers as well as older readers to the medium . . . The popularity of manga has led to a jump in the number of titles in the marketplace and more investment by Japanese publishing and entertainment firms in the American market. There are already hundreds of titles being released annually in the still relatively small U.S. market, and that number is likely to increase." In this enthusiastic appraisal of the manga market, *Publishers Weekly* pointed to small publishers like Comics-One releasing nearly one hundred titles, while Tokyopop released more than two hundred titles and Viz Communications more than one hundred titles.[10] Manga in 2003 would bring in about one hundred million dollars in sales with Tokyopop leading the pack with thirty-five million dollars in sales.[11] Tokyopop was now outselling Marvel and DC in the trade book market.[12] By the end of 2004, *Publishers Weekly* reported estimates of one thousand manga titles released for the year and major publishers like Penguin with plans to enter the market.[13]

Otaku fandom continued to rise with the largest anime convention in North America, Anime Expo, gathering forty-four thousand attendees in 2007.[14] The main marketing source for graphic novels in North America, ICv2, reported 1,224 manga and manhwa titles in this market in 2006. ICv2 predicted 1,461 titles for 2007. *Publishers Weekly* reported that manga represented 43 percent of graphic novel titles in 2006 with estimated manga sales of 170 to 200 million dollars.[15] Manga sales were overwhelmingly in the trade book market, so the only obstacle to even more phenomenal growth was the limited shelf space in bookstores and mass-market retailers. While manga during their boom represented the fastest growing publishing market in North America, they remained a minor niche market. Manga competed for shelf space in 2006 with 8.3 billion dollars in hardbound and paperbound trade books and 1.1 billion dollars in mass-market paperbacks.[16] The question remained how publishers, distributors, and retailers would handle the continued growth and demand for manga in the future.

Most observers of the manga boom noted the dominance of young and adult females among manga readers.[17] Estimates suggested that females comprised roughly 60 percent of manga readers. As the *Edmonton Journal* noted in 2002 in an interview with a female fan, "the 20-year-old is among a legion of young women who've turned their backs on western comics in favour of expensive, stylized imports coming from Japan . . . Japanese manga (print comics) and anime (animated cartoons) have long boasted women-friendly storylines and fleshed-out character development."[18] In 2004, *The New York Times* observed the important role of female readers in the manga boom in "Girl Power Fuels Manga Boom in U.S." "Sales of Japanese comics—more familiarly known as manga (pronounced MAHN-gah)—are exploding in the United States, and much of the boom is due to efforts by comic book publishers to extend their reach beyond young male readers. Beyond all males, in fact . . . Manga often celebrates strong female characters in adventure yarns or stories focusing on love and relationships."[19]

But the revolutionary impact of manga was not only about creating comic books for young female readers. Women artists also dominated the field of shojo manga. While originally created by male artists, in the 1960s shojo manga were captured by a new generation of female artists who revolutionized the genre. By the 1970s, female *mangaka* dominated the field of shojo manga.[20] And female artists were integral to the success of manga in North America. As *The New York Times* reported in 2006, "Many of the most popular manga on both sides of the Pacific are written and drawn by women, including Rumiko Takahashi . . . Hirmu Arakawa . . . and Clamp." As Dallas Middaugh, associate publisher of Del Rey Manga told the *Times*, the female artist group Clamp was "an integral part of the manga explosion that's occurred in the U.S. over the last several years. Their fluid, dramatic artwork and storytelling style struck a strong chord with male and female manga readers."[21]

The manga boom also broke the old paradigm that only superhero comics had mass appeal. Manga were outcompeting superhero comic books in the trade market. As *Publishers Weekly* noted in 2003, "manga is unquestionably king (or perhaps queen) of comic sales in the book trade, in particular national chains. Led by the books of Tokyopop, manga is driving the sale of graphic novels."[22] Manga dominated the top-ten best-selling graphic novels every month. Another refrain, however, was how the manga boom was helping non-manga graphic novels reenter the trade market and gain once again the attention of trade book publishers. As *Publishers Weekly* reported in 2003, "Sales of manga graphic novels are driving sales of all graphic novels in the bookstore market."[23] The radical impact of the manga boom on the North American comic book field was obvious to *Publishers Weekly*'s regular comic book beat reporter Calvin Reid. "Since the late 1990s American sales of licensed Japanese comics in English translation, better known as manga, have grown at such a phenomenal rate that they are transforming the land-scape of American comics publishing . . . This remarkable boom in interest is changing the prevailing understanding of who reads book-length comics and transforming publishing strategies about how to produce, market and sell comics . . . Indeed, girls and women are going to bookstores to buy manga in numbers that are unheard of in the U.S. comics industry."[24]

The manga boom also highlighted the true failure of the American comic book industry to revitalize comic books as a mass medium. In part, this resided in the Big Two having no incentive, or imagination, to move beyond their limited core of superhero properties. The path to making comic books once again a mass medium depended on the commercial success of popular fiction in comic art form, but the Big Two and major independents remained wedded to serving mostly a fanboy base and its favorite genres. It is certainly ironic that it was forces mostly external to the comic book field that inevitably succeeded in establishing a bridge to the trade book market for comic art. The success of manga also undermines the constant refrain in comic book culture that the failure to reach a mass audience was because of readers' unfamiliarity with the formal elements of sequential art—what Matthew Pustz calls "comics literacy."[25] The fact that millions of North American readers had no problem reading not only sequential art, but sequential art created in the right-to-left style of manga, points to how the failure of the North American comic book field had more to do with the commercial and fan interests dominating the field than any formal aesthetic constraints. Manga truly represented a poten-tial radical transformation in comic art in North America.

Getting Respect: Pop Mainstream and Alternative Rebels

Other factors besides the manga revolution played a part in reinvigorating the comic book market. The popular entertainment industry suddenly redis-covered mainstream comic books and their fans. Alternative comics also gained even more attention and respect from the press and official culture. For many observers, comic art seemed to be invading every corner of culture in North America from film theatres, to television screens, to newspapers, to magazines, to bookstores, to museums, and even to the most prestigious university presses. And with the solid bridge built by the popularity of manga, mainstream and alternative comics discovered a growing graphic novel market outside the old direct market. What had once seemed an impossible dream was suddenly becoming a reality, although many in comic book culture were well aware of past dashed hopes. But by the end of 2007, the future of American comic books was looking far brighter.

In terms of mainstream comic books, the biggest boost was Hollywood's financial success with mainstream comic book franchises. Marvel led the charge to recapture the interest of Hollywood. In 2001 the *Los Angeles Times* reported on the successful new strategy and the rebounding of Marvel under the leadership of Avi Arad. "Arad has been the driving force in trying to revive the fortunes of the troubled Marvel Enterprises, which filed bankruptcy in 1998 and appeared dead in the water after years of management turmoil and a series of ugly Wall Street legal battles. After the success of 'X-Men,' the Marvel comic-based film that did $157 million at the box office last year and is one of the top-selling DVDs of all time, Marvel is back in a big way."[26] Marvel's Spider-Man in 2002 was a box office success. A slew of sequels and new franchises of Marvel properties quickly followed. The success of Marvel films and merchandising unquestionably revitalized the old publishing house. Besides the millions earned through film, Marvel earned four billion dollars in 2004 in licensing arrangements, becoming one of the top five licensing companies in the world.[27] DC also courted Hollywood and continued to generate large profits from licensing. As part of AOL Time Warner, DC, according to *Forbes* in 2001, was "a lucrative R & D tool for Warner Brothers. Even if the books were bringing in paltry sales, hit films like Batman and Superman series have grossed $1 billion in the U.S., excluding video rentals and sales of an endless parade of merchandise."[28]

Hollywood also discovered the work of rebel artists working either for independent publishers or the special DC imprint Vertigo. Independent film companies supported alternative rebels with movies based on Dan Clowes's *Ghost World* in 2001 and Harvey Pekar's *American Splendor* in 2003. Stylistic renditions of crime pulp graphic novels included movies based on Max Allan Collins's *Road to Perdition* in 2002 and John Wagner and Vince Locke's *History of Violence* in 2005. The biggest push was adopting mainstream artists' graphic novels. These included movies based on Alan Moore's *From Hell* in 2001, *League of Extraordinary Gentlemen* in 2003, and *V for Vendetta* in 2005. Auteur Frank Miller had films made of his graphic novels *Sin City* and *300* in 2005 and 2007. The importance of film adaptations on graphic novel sales was clear with graphic novels such as *Sin City* and *300* rising to the top of the graphic novel best-sellers list. The astounding sales of *300* took the industry by surprise. The thirty-dollar hardcover edition earned 1.5 million dollars in sales in the trade book market in the first half of 2007.[29]

Clearly, comic book characters and stories had captured the popular imagination and successfully altered the entertainment industry's view of their potential. Covering the convention Wizard World Chicago in 2002, the *Chicago Sun-Times* noted the rising commercial importance of comic books. "Going to the movies or turning on the TV, you can't help but notice that wealth of material being generated by the comic book industry . . . Clearly comics have moved out of hobby shops and specialty stores to take film and television by storm . . . This has led some pop cultural analysts to refer to recent successes as a second coming for the comic book industry."[30] *New York Times* film critic A. O. Scott in 2005 recognized comic books' new clout:

> Their ascendancy in Hollywood is a triumphal chapter in a 70-year epic during which comic books have moved from disreputable, juvenile margins of pop culture to its center . . . The cachet of comics—and I mean the old, cheap, pulpy kind, not "comix" or "graphic novels"—is all the more remarkable given that most of their history, they could count on provoking the disdain of literary intellectuals, the panic of moralists and the condescension of mainstream show business, which saw them as fodder for cartoons and campy kid shows . . . The superheroes demand to be taken seriously as they have always taken themselves. For one thing, they command some very serious money.[31]

The clearest evidence of comic books and their fans new cachet was the transformation of the San Diego Comic-Con into a national media event and magnet for the entertainment industry.[32] The Comic-Con was seen as the clearest way to make film and television deals and especially to spread the word about any new popular entertainment product. In 2001, the convention hosted fifty thousand attendees as the largest multigenre convention in North America. But by 2005 over one hundred thousand people were attending the four-day event; and newspapers and magazines were touting the age of the geek or nerd. The *San Diego Union-Tribune* touted the new age in its 2006 article "Around Here, the Geeks Decide What's Cool." "With media companies devoting more money and talent to projects based on comic books, science-fiction and fantasy, Comic-Con and its 100,000 plus attendees have become some of the biggest, most vital cogs in the Hollywood promotion machine . . . Comic-Con is the center of the entertainment universe, and it got there by connecting the media giants with the memorabilia-collecting, chat-room lurking, blog-generating little people who can spread the word in a very big way."[33]

While the press heavily used terms like "geek" and "nerd" in its coverage, this mostly stemmed from the self-referencing of the fans themselves. As fan Brad Meltzer told *Entertainment Weekly* in 2007, "It's the golden age of geekdom."[34] Or as the *San Diego Union-Tribune* put it, "Comic-Con: Where 'Nerd Has Become Normal.'"[35] Manohla Dargis, in her coverage of the 2007 Comic-Con, noted how "geekdom" was part of the new mystique of comic book fandom. "The outsider identity that clings to comic books has been instrumental to the creation of what has become a multi-million-dollar industry. The cliché about fans being losers with no social skills, no friends and no clue is essential to its myths, marketing and even its most loyal readers. In the last few decades the emergence of a geek elite has helped legitimize this outsider culture and helped bring legions of 97-pound weaklings into the sightlines of the industrial entertainment complex."[36] This rise of the comic book geek reflected a general transformation in the popular entertainment industry that embraces popular art fandom as part of its marketing strategy in the age of New Media or what Henry Jenkins calls the new "convergence culture."[37]

The trade book market for North American graphic novels also was growing at unprecedented levels. By 2004, *Publishers Weekly* informed readers that:

> Every year seems to bring a new highwater mark for the graphic novel business, and 2004 saw still more explosive growth for the category in both bookstores and the comic shop market. While manga is leading the charge in bookstores, other formats and genres are beginning to find sales traction as well. With mainstream publishers like Random House, W. W. Norton, Scholastic, Penguin and Simon and Schuster jumping on the graphic novel bandwagon, 2005 should be an even more impressive year . . . One thing is clear—there is more good comics material available than ever before, with even more on the way.[38]

By 2005, *Publishers Weekly* was touting the unquestionable boom in graphic novels. "The temperature of the hot U.S. graphic novel market may be cooling a bit, bit it's still cooking. Total estimated retail sales of graphic novels in the U.S. in 2004 were between $205 million to $210 million, about a 35% increase over 2003."[39]

The future of the graphic novel market looked so promising that *Publishers Weekly* was reporting on trade publishers raiding alternative comics publishers for their talent:

> Anyone who's been keeping an eye on the independent comics world for the last year or two can't help but have noticed a certain, well,

migration. A growing number of critically acclaimed comics artists who made their literary reputations with small independent publishers or even as self-publishers—from Charles Burns to Craig Thompson to Jeff Smith—are flocking to New York trade book imprints to publish their next graphic novels . . . New York trade houses are paying close attention to graphic novel's burgeoning sales and critical acclaim. They're luring indie stars with big advances and promises of much increased distribution and promotion.[40]

Graphic novels also were receiving greater coverage and critical acclaim in the press. Once again articles in the press were reminding readers of the new "serious" comics. The Associated Press in 2002 pointed to a time when "the business of comic books seemed limited to tales of costumed superheroes, gumshoe detectives or thwarted alien invasions, the clientele an assortment of adolescents, collectors and geeks. But the industry stereotype is undergoing transformation of sorts thanks to a longer, more literary comic offshoot called the graphic novel . . . Book reviewers are devoting more space to graphic novels and treating them as serious literary works."[41] In "Graphic Novels Come of Age," the *Sacramento Bee* noted in 2003, "Although graphic novels take many forms—from stand-alone stories to hardbound collections of previously issued comics—there's been a marked increase recently in prominent titles that would fit just as well in the high-brow literary world as they would at a comic book convention . . . these sophisticated tomes feature handsome, often-edgy artwork and smart writing."[42]

More press articles appeared on the rise of the serious graphic novel in 2004. The *Houston Chronicle* told readers in "From Pulp to Pulitzer," "For years these books have been seeping out of the comic-book ghetto and into the mainstream, and now the current seems to be picking up speed."[43] The *New York Times Magazine* in 2004 had a major article on the new renaissance in alternative comics written by Charles McGrath:

Comics are also enjoying a renaissance and a newfound respectability right now. In fact, the fastest-growing section of your local bookstore these days is apt to be the one devoted to comics and so-called graphic novels . . . often in hardcover, with titles that sound just like the titles of "real" books: "Palestine," "Persepolis," "Blankets" . . . "David Chelsea in Love," "Summer Blond," "The Beauty Supply District," "The Boulevard of Broken Dreams" . . . These are the graphic novels—the equivalent of "literary novels" in the mainstream publishing world—and they are beginning to be taken seriously by the critical establishment . . . There was a minor flowering of serious comic books in the mid-80s . . . But the movement failed to take hold, in large part because there weren't enough other books on the same level. The difference this time is that there is something like a critical mass of artists, young and old, uncovering new possibilities in this once-marginal form.[44]

Graphic novels had certainly entered a new phase of recognition. Reviews of new graphic novels could be found in newspapers and magazines on a regular basis from *The New York Times* and *Village Voice's* reviews of alternative comics to *Entertainment Weekly's* reviews of mostly pulp graphic novels. In 2005, *New York Times Magazine* began a regular graphic art series called the "Funny Pages" with alt artist Chris Ware as the first featured artist, while magazines like *Esquire* and *The New Yorker* featured graphic artists as well. And the Houghton Mifflin "Best American" series in 2006 added *The Best American Comics 2006*, edited by Harvey Pekar; and followed with *The Best American Comics 2007*, edited by Chris Ware. Series editor Ann Elizabeth Moore noted the new series addition's significance. "Perhaps more significantly, the collection is a new addition to the esteemed line of distinguished titles in the Best American series that's been helping define literature since 1915. That such an honor would be bestowed upon the traditionally low-brow medium of comics is a direct violation of the laws of both comics history and literature. I just hope we can get it done before Houghton Mifflin figures this out."[45] Graphic artists were also winning fellowships and literary prizes such as Ben Katchor receiving a MacArthur "Genius" Grant in 2000 and Chris Ware winning the Guardian First Book Prize in 2001. More recently, Gene Luen Yang was the first graphic novelist to be recognized by the National Book Foundation with his children's graphic novel, *American Born Chinese,* receiving a nomination in 2006. In 2007 the book received the annual award for literary excellence in children's literature, the Michael L. Printz Award, from the Young Adult Library Services Association, a branch of the American Library Association.

Charles McGrath was right in arguing that comic art was finding some respectability in the publishing world, the general press and in certain literary journals like *McSweeney's Quarterly*. For many alternative rebels, however, Hollywood's love affair with superheroes, or blood-splattered Spartans in the film *300*, only reinforced the notion of comic art as a purely pulp world. And in the graphic novel trade market, mainstream and pulp graphic novels garnered far greater overall sales and shelf space than alternative graphic novels. But regardless of alternative rebels' reticence about serious graphic novels' place in the popular imagination, within the graphic novel market several alternative graphic novels have reached sales of one hundred thousand, some over five hundred thousand. In 2004, two alternative graphic novels were among the top-five best-selling graphic novels: Iranian artist Marjane Satrapi's *Persepolis 2* and Art Spiegelman's *In the Shadow of No Towers,* which was the number-one best-selling graphic novel of the year.[46]

Most of the new respect for graphic novels emphasized the literary quality of this new form. For comic artists, the world of art galleries, museums, and education was a whole other issue. In terms of comic art in academia, courses on comic books could be found at some colleges and universities, although not necessarily in the art departments. James Sturm wrote a scathing critique of comic art's position as "visual art" in *The Chronicle for Higher Education* in 2002. "Despite the growing critical recognition and commercial success of cartoonists' work and the fervent interest in the medium from young artists, academe does not recognize the medium's legitimacy . . . The limited number of programs at colleges and universities reflects the public's perception of comics as primarily prepubescent adventure stories or bland daily comic strips . . . Comics appear to be in the same category as graffiti: They might be talked about in a cultural-studies or sociology class, or in an art survey class, but that's about it."[47] Sturm, with Ben Towle, cofounded the National Association of Comics Art Educators (NACAE) to promote comic art education, particularly in postsecondary education. As of 2007, the NACAE only listed nine postsecondary programs in comic art in North America.[48]

A few comic art exhibits appeared in galleries and art museums, but comic art was not storming the ramparts of the fine art world. Alt rebel Chris Ware achieved the most attention. In 2000, he had an exhibit at the Smithsonian Cooper-Hewitt Design Museum in New York City, and was featured in the biennial exhibition at the Whitney Museum of American Art in 2002. He also had his own exhibit at the Museum of Contemporary Art in Chicago in 2006.[49] The most important event was the Masters of American Comics exhibit that debuted at the Hammer Museum and the Museum of Contemporary Art in Los Angeles in 2005. The exhibit featured eight comic strip and seven comic book artists as representative of the evolution of the art form. In the catalog for the exhibit, the directors of the two museums, Ann Philbin and Jeremy Strick, noted what a privilege it was to "collaborate on this ground breaking exhibition of American comic art . . . The art of comics is one of the most distinctive and important genres in the history of American art and has had an immeasurable impact on other forms of art and culture. At the same time, however, it has remained a subtext in the history of art. Certainly the subject never has been presented on such a scale in any major museum."[50] The exhibit received media attention for what the *Christian Science Monitor* called "the first national show to explore comics as a serious art form" or as the *Los Angeles Times* called it, "the first major museum show to trace the history of the medium as an art form in itself."[51] The Masters of American Comics, however, was the exception to the rule of the continued outsider status of comic art in the fine art world.

In terms of academic publications, while university presses had published a few works on the artistic merits of comic books in the 1990s, more academic books have appeared over the last seven years. Penn State Press, for example, published David Carrier's *The Aesthetics of Comics* (2000); and University Press of Mississippi published *The Language of Comics: Word and Image* (2001) and *Alternative Comics: An Emerging Literature* (2005). More prestigious university presses also began to recognize comic books as serious art. The most telling new respect for comic art was Yale University Press' commitment to add comic art to its major list of art books. In 2005 it published the catalog for the Masters of American Comics exhibit. *Publishers Weekly* touted the press' interest in comic art as a major turning point in this art's respect as a legitimate visual art. "Yale University Press is justly celebrated for its extraordinary array of titles about the visual arts, including numerous volumes done in association with the Metropolitan Museum of Art and the National Gallery, London. Nearly 100 years old, Yale University Press is now turning its attention to the comics medium as well."[52] Yale published two books in 2006. Ivan Brunetti edited *An Anthology of Graphic Fiction, Cartoons, and True Stories*, which featured the work of alternative artists, while Todd Hignite's *In the Studio: Visits with Contemporary Cartoonists* featured interviews with ten alternative artists. Besides university presses, the Smithsonian in 2004 published a new comic book anthology, *The New Smithsonian Book of Comic-Book Stories*, that focused mostly on underground and alternative artists with a slight nod to rebel pulp artists.

Other efforts have been made in comic book culture to promote taking comic books, especially alternative or adult comic books, seriously. Todd Hignite started a glossy art magazine on comic art in 2002. "From the outset, I just wanted *Comic Art* to be smart, nicely done art magazine about comics that conveyed some sense of the medium's great range of possibilities."[53] Comic artists and fans also opened another museum dedicated to comic art in 2002, the Museum of Comic and Cartoon Art (MoCCA) in New York City.[54] "It will be the mission of the museum to promote the understanding and appreciation of comic and cartoon art as well as to detail and discuss the artistic, cultural, and historical impact of what is the world's most popular art form. Comics and cartoons have been instrumental in effecting significant dialogue on issues involving society, culture, philosophy, and politics. History has shown them to be instrumental in documenting—and interpreting—historic events and social change. Artistically, comic and cartoon art is created at the highest levels by some of the world's finest graphic illustrators."[55]

MoCCA also initiated another alternative comics convention that same year, MoCCA Art Fest, that continues to the present.

The renewed interest in mainstream and alternative comic books seemed to be heading this medium toward a brighter future in terms of its commercial viability and potential to once again be a *mass medium* enjoyed by more than a marginal subculture. By 2006, overall sales for comic books and graphic novels were 640 million dollars, with manga accounting for 170 to 200 million dollars.[56] Sales of non-manga comic books in constant dollars had never been better since 1995, two years after the collapse of the direct market boom. While sales in the direct market increased, the major driving force was the sales of graphic novels outside this market. The number of comic shops has remained at around three thousand. For many the graphic novel seemed to be pointing to the future of the comic book as an art form. And this certainly pointed to a possible brighter future for the alternative comics movement. As DC President Paul Levitz told *Publishers Weekly* in 2002, the new audience for graphic novels outside the direct market was "a disgustingly literate bunch of people"[57] The future of the comic book as a mass medium seemed even brighter when one considered that one of the strongest forces behind the resurgence of the American comic book was the unlikely emergence of a movement of librarians and teachers to make graphic novels a regular reading habit of all Americans.

Librarians and Teachers to the Rescue

From the very beginning of the new boom in graphic novels, librarians and teachers were at the forefront of rejuvenating the American comic book. Activist librarians in particular were spreading the word about the power of graphic novels to activate children's and teenager's interest in reading and visiting libraries. But librarians also were touting graphic novels for adults. While graphic novels' invasion of the trade book market signaled a new audience for comic art, librarians and teachers were instrumental in interesting a whole new generation of readers in this art form. While librarians and teachers during the Industrial Age spent time debating whether comic books were harmful or benign, in more recent years they have spent time discussing how to engage young minds with graphic art, how to create collections of graphic novels in libraries, and how to categorize such a diverse array of material.

By the 1970s, the attitudes of teachers and librarians toward comic books had already changed considerably from the dark days before the Comics Code. Numerous articles appeared in this decade in professional education and library journals about comic art as a teaching tool. In 1983, James L. Thomas compiled over thirty articles from professional journals from 1971 to 1981 on the positive value of comic strips and comic books in the classroom.[58] Advocates for comic books in libraries also pointed to their popularity among young, particularly male teen, readers as a way to bring more young readers into the library. With the new graphic novels of the late 1980s and early 1990s, some articles also appeared in professional journals suggesting a new serious form of comic book had arrived and promoting the creation of graphic novel collections.[59] But there were few reviews of graphic novels appearing in library journals at the time. And there were even bigger obstacles to graphic novels entering libraries. First, it was difficult for librarians to acquire them. The book distributors for libraries were clueless about this new form of literature, so librarians were dependent mostly on local comic book shops with which they were unfamiliar.[60] And second, and a more obvious reason, the early 1990s graphic novel market was a bust, so there was no expansion of this literature for librarians to acquire. By the end of the century, graphic novels had not made significant inroads into libraries and classrooms.

All this was to drastically change in just a few years. The launch of a major movement to bring graphic novels to libraries came through the initiative of the Young Adult Library Services Association (YALSA), a branch of the American Library Association. In June 2002, the association sponsored "Getting Graphic at Your Library," a pre-conference before the annual conference of the American Library Association. That same year, YALSA also organized its fourth annual Teen Read Week with the same theme. A new movement was clearly appearing among librarians when both the *Library Journal* and *School Library Journal* that same year launched major efforts to promote graphic novels. The journals featured major articles on graphic novels and began regular reviews. Other professional journals for educators and librarians joined the movement with graphic novel articles, reviews, and columns including *Voice of Youth Advocates, Library Media Connection,* and the American Library Association's *Booklist.*

Librarians were discovering that graphic novels were perfect magnets to attract teens to libraries. Librarian Michele Gorman, in the *School Library Journal* in 2002, pointed to the new strategy. "It's not often that a teenager walks into a library seeking the latest award-winning book or critically acclaimed novel. Some despise reading, doing it only when threatened with a book report, while others adore it, devouring everything from classic literature to current popular fiction. Graphic novels, however, have proven to be a hit with kids and are flying off the library shelves."[61] That same year Stephen Weiner also informed readers of the *Library Journal* that graphic novels had gotten serious and appealed to both young and old alike. "Graphic novels have never been hotter . . . most of the attention, however, is the result of the graphic novels themselves, whose subjects have expanded beyond standard comic book material . . . many graphic novels are now concerned with conflicts often found in more accepted forms of literature."[62] Both Gorman and Weiner's extensive articles also provided advice on building graphic novel collections, on displaying and cataloging graphic novels, and provided a beginning list of graphic novels to acquire.

The movement among librarians and teachers was immediately apparent to publishers and journalists watching the new graphic novel market. *Publishers Weekly* noted the graphic novel movement appearing among librarians. "Another pleasant surprise in 2002 was the aggressive support from librarians for comic material." Comics publisher Jim Valentino told the magazine, "Librarians seem to be ahead of the curve in recognizing the enormous potential of the graphic novel for the YA and reluctant reader. They also understand that the medium covers a wide range of interests and demographics."[63] The *Chicago Daily Herald* in 2002 noted "a new outlet for the art form: the local library . . . This boom, fueled in part by high-profile movie adaptations like 'Spiderman' and 'Road to Perdition,' has focused primarily on works for teens and young adult readers, though libraries are building collections for older adult readers as well."[64] *The Washington Post* noticed the change in attitude of teachers toward comic books. "Comic books used to be serious contraband in America's public schools, covert reading that students would sneak under their textbooks and peruse during math lessons . . . Teachers today have a different philosophy. Comic books, no longer such a staple of youth, are now thought of as an old-fashioned way to encourage actual reading, drawing and writing in an age of passive, bottomless satellite-TV watching and Internet surfing."[65] *Publishers Weekly* in 2003 also noted how distributors for libraries were finally jumping on the graphic novel bandwagon.[66]

The initial boom in library acquisition focused on young adult and adult graphic novels. This in part was a reflection of how most comic book publishers had long abandoned young children as readers. But publishers began focusing on young children and "tweens" as well.[67] Papercutz was launched in 2005 with graphic novels of the Nancy Drew and Hardy Boy series. Publisher Scholastic started a special graphic novel imprint, Graphix, in 2005 geared to young children. It released a special guide, *Using Graphic Novels in the Classroom*, that same year. "Graphic novels powerfully attract kids and motivate them to read . . . School librarians and educators have reported outstanding success getting kids to read with graphic novels, citing particularly their popularity with reluctant readers, especially boys—a group traditionally difficult to reach . . . Providing young people with diverse reading materials, including graphic novels, can help them become lifelong readers."[68] Scholastic's entrance into the graphic novel movement was especially important because of its successful book club as well as its successful book fairs. The 110,000 annual Scholastic book fairs held at schools across the country reached fifty-seven-million children in 2006.[69]

Web sites and books also quickly appeared to support librarians in building collections for their libraries. The University of Buffalo Library started a Web site, *Comic Books for Young Adults,* in 2000. A major figure in the movement, librarian Robin Brenner, started a Web site, *No Flying, No Tights,* in 2002 to help readers, librarians, teachers, and others interested in graphic novels. Books for aiding librarians already had appeared before the new movement, but more books appeared once the movement gained momentum, such as *Developing and Promoting Graphic Novel Collections* (2005) and *Graphic Novels: A Genre Guide to Comic Books, Manga and More* (2007). Other books promoted graphic novels in the classroom like *Graphic Novels 101: Selecting and Using Graphic Novels to Promote Literacy for Children and Young Adults* (2003) and *Building Literacy Connections with Graphic Novels* (2007).[70]

There were certainly detractors of graphic novels as educational tools or as valued literature.[71] Advocates' fears about the old stigma of comic books as subliterate became more pronounced when graphic novels began being touted for younger children. They feared the old questions of comic books hindering the development of literacy among children. Scholastic's 2005 *Using Graphic Novels in the Classroom* acknowledged the possible resistance to graphic novels for young children. "Some parents and educators may feel that graphic novels are not the 'type of reading material' that will help young people grow as readers—many dismiss graphic novels as inferior literature or as 'not real books.' However, quality graphic novels have increasingly come to be accepted by librarians and educators as a method of storytelling on a par with novels, picture books, movies and audio books. . . . Reading graphic novels can help students develop the critical skills necessary to read more challenging works, including the classics."[72] Many of the Web sites and books promoting graphic novels also addressed the possible concerns of librarians, teachers, and parents that comic books were subliterate, junk literature that hindered the development of good reading. But unlike the old anti–comic book crusade, no major efforts have been made to challenge the appropriateness of graphic novels for young children.

From the beginning, however, librarians were aware of the possible problems with introducing adult graphic novels in public and school libraries. Michele Gorman's extensive 2002 article introducing *School Library Journal* readers to the new graphic novel warned, "Although most of you are opposed to censoring, be aware that certain genres of graphic novels will be the target of parental or community objections . . . In short, there are several critically acclaimed graphic novels essential for building a core adult collection but inappropriate for your library's children or young adult section."[73] And troubles quickly appeared as adult graphic novels with sexual content caught the attention of the wrong people. When alternative artist Phoebe Gloeckner's *A Child's Life*, a graphic novel about incest, appeared in the Stockton Public Library in 2004 it inspired the city's mayor to have the city council discuss ways of controlling certain books and materials in the library. Three national organizations—The National Coalition Against Censorship, the American Library Association, and the CBLDF—quickly responded, creating guidelines to help librarians deal with adult graphic novels.[74] Adult graphic novels, however, only elicited a few challenges. The American Library Association pointed to only fourteen such challenges between 2003 and 2006.[75]

With the booming popularity of manga, librarians also faced the problem of dealing with these graphic novels' sexual content. Manga traditionally deal more openly with intimate relationships and sexual matters. This includes manga for both adults and teenagers. Librarians were suddenly confronted with a problem when they discovered one of the more popular genres in manga among female teens is *yaoi*. Yaoi deal with intimate, and often sexual, relationships between boys. As librarians built manga and anime collections they faced potential problems with their sexual content. The *Library Journal* had a special panel at the New York Comic-Con in 2006 where one hundred librarians discussed the new problems with manga. The journal reported that the librarians attending found more problems with staff over manga than adult non-staff. But the journal defended manga, "although sex is prolific in manga and its assorted gay offshoots, the genre deals equally with the emotional side of relationships."[76] In an effort to help librarians and parents, the major manga publisher Tokyopop redesigned its age-rating system in 2007.[77] Despite these problems, libraries have not faced an onslaught of major challenges against manga and anime.

The movement among librarians and teachers to promote graphic novels has unquestionably had a major impact on the comic book field. The New York Comic-Con in 2007 had four panels especially focused on libraries with some four hundred librarians attending the convention. In terms of the new graphic novel market, purchases from libraries by 2007 accounted for 10 percent of this market.[78] And this does not take into account the purchasing of graphic novels by children and young adults through Scholastic's book club and book fairs. Besides opening up the market to comics for children and tweens, this movement, like the manga boom, also furthered the trend toward new female readers. In 2007, DC announced a new specialty imprint,

Minx, geared to teenage female readers.[79] More importantly, however, is how the movement demonstrated that the old status of the comic book as a harmful subliterate medium no longer held. This movement actually transformed comic books into magnets and aids to promoting greater literacy among children and teens. The greatest impact of this movement on the comic book field, however, remains in the future. Will this movement truly transform the reading habits of children and teens to make comic books once again a major source of reading pleasure? And will the young children and teens introduced to comic art at an early age make comic book reading a lifelong pursuit? If the answer to the last question is yes, then the future of serious adult graphic novels looks bright, very bright, indeed.

The Web and Webcomics

We have already seen in Chapter Four how the early Internet contributed to comic book culture by providing opportunities for social networking and communication between fans in message boards, online communities, and early web pages. While the Mosaic web browser in 1993 introduced web pages to the Internet, it took a number of years for the full potential of the World Wide Web as a popular and easily accessible mass medium to radically transform the Internet. The visual interface of the Web obviously made the Internet an ideal form of communication and commerce around comic books. So the role of the Web increased as access and bandwidth increased, computers' speed and memory increased, and new software for production and consumption of comic art appeared. While some in comic book culture dreamed of the revolutionary potential of the Web for comic books as an art form, it mostly remediated the activities of fans, artists, and publishers found in the non-virtual world of the comic book field and comic book fandom. The greatest impact the Web had on comic art actually was not in the field of comic books, but in the parallel field of comic strips. The Web became a social space for a new movement in webcomics dominated by artists and fans mostly from outside comic book culture. Ironically, the potential for comic art was co-opted by a movement with a far different agenda than radically transforming comic books and the comic book field.

While the older social spaces and print culture of comic book culture remained—shops, publishers, distributors, clubs, conventions, fanzines, comic books, and graphic novels—some individuals predicted that the advent of the Web would bring about a revolutionary transformation in the comic book field. While such a revolutionary change has yet to truly appear, there is no question that the Web has become a vital new social space in the Heroic

Age in comic books. But the impact of the Web has been more in its power to "remediate" the various practices and material culture of the comic book field and comic book culture onto the Internet, not to radically transform them.[80] But by transferring these practices and materials to the Internet, the Web brought such special qualities of new media as "interactivity," "hypertext," and "dispersal."[81] The Web allowed for both greater interaction between fans, artists, publishers, and activists as well as a more collaborative social space of production and consumption. Hypertext in the form of "links" also increased this interactivity by expanding the social network of connections reaching across fandom and the comic book field. And the Web aided in the dispersal of the practices and material culture of comic book culture. This dispersal included the proliferation of new points of communication, production, and consumption, and the breaking down of geographical barriers. Dispersal also included the opening up of new social spaces for marginal fans, artists, and publishers who felt constrained by the original print-based, geographically bound worlds of fandom and the comic book field.

The first major impact of the Web was on comic fandom. This is not surprising given community building became one of the most important activities on the Web, with groups sharing interests or hobbies being one of the most popular types of online communities.[82] This new social space first provided opportunities to create or disseminate new web-fanzines. The first web pages were mostly the work of one or two individuals with the knowledge necessary to construct this new medium of communication.[83] These early comics web-fanzines grew slowly, adding new features, contributors, and staff. The longest running general comics web-fanzine *Comic Book Resources* (*CBR*) first featured links pages and an online message board. But in 1998, contributors began adding original content in regular columns and *CBR* began to gradually remediate features found in print fanzines like the *Comics Buyer's Guide*. Another of the popular general comics web-fanzines, *Newsarama*, had a staff of "over a dozen writers" by 2002 and worked "with publishers, movie studios, game producers, and countless creators to bring readers news about comic books, comic book characters and issues surrounding the industry to readers."[84]

Beginning in the late 1990s, other general comics web-fanzines also appeared, including *Silver Bullet, Sequential Tart,* and *Broken Frontier,* three of the most popular of the next generation of web-fanzines. These top general and news web-fanzines remediated the quality and breadth found in the more successful print fanzines. They also emphasized collaborative efforts by many contributors to their various features and columns. Other general and news comics web-fanzines have been more the expression of a single contributor such as Tom Spurgeon's *Comic Reporter* or John Jackson Miller's the *Comics*

Chronicler. While all the main print comics fanzines launched Web sites, only *Wizard's* Wizard Entertainment eventually established a web-fanzine with the full features appearing on the competing web-only fanzines.

Along with the more popular general and news web-fanzines, thousands of more web-fanzines, fan pages, online communities, and blogs have dedicated themselves to comics, webcomics, alternative/independent comics, mainstream comics, collecting, fan art, comics artists, comics characters, comics publishers, and the universes of Marvel and DC. And this does not include the thousands of sites dedicated to manga and anime. The whole gamut of fan practices found in the earlier print-based comic book culture, including role-playing and cosplay, have remediated themselves on the Web. The web-fanzine *Comiccon.com* is actually designed to be an online comic book convention! Many web-fanzines also feature forums and message boards for visitors to interact and discuss various topics. Hundreds of sites are dedicated solely to comics or anime-manga online communities like *AOL Comics Alliance*, the *Naruto Community*, the *Comic Wire*, or the hundreds of online communities found on LiveJournal and ezboard. With the rise of Web 2.0, new comic book social network sites appeared like *Comic Space* in 2006, which eventually hosted a community of over twenty-three thousand fans and creators. In 2007, MySpace launched a "MySpace Comic Book" social network community.

One of the more interesting developments is how the Web has become a major new space for collecting and disseminating historical and contemporary information on comic books. The *Grand Comic-Book Database (GCD)* began in 1994 using e-mail for communication and floppy disks to gather information on all comic book titles ever published. The *GCD* eventually found its way to the Web continuing its efforts to index. The *GCD* by 2007 had cataloged over 325,000 comic books covering over 26,500 series published by over 3,900 publishers.[85] The biggest boost to information dissemination and the virtual writing of the history of comic books was the introduction of Wikipedia and wiki programming to the Web. For comics, manga, and anime fandom in general, Wikipedia has become a site for the collaborative efforts to disseminate information about these popular art forms. This includes not only information about the history of comic books, manga, and anime—and specific artists, publishers, series, and characters—but also about fans, fanzines, conventions, and organizations in comic book and anime-manga culture. There are also other wikis dedicated to more specialized topics like *Comixpedia*, a wiki dedicated to webcomics.

It is clear how the Web has created a new space for comic fandom. The Web also has made comic book culture a more open and accessible fandom. This is most evident in how marginal fans are finding a new social space to intervene in comic book culture. The most successful intervention has been the web-fanzine *Sequential Tart*—a "Web Zine about the comics industry published by an eclectic band of women . . . working towards raising the awareness of women's influence in the comics industry and other realms."[86] *Sequential Tart* since its launch in 1998 has become one of the more popular comics web-fanzines. While maintaining general coverage of comic book culture, this site has promoted greater awareness of women artists and readers in comic book culture.[87] British comic book fans awarded *Sequential Tart* the Eagle Award for "Favourite Fan-organized Comic Related Website" in 2000. This award also points to another important contribution of the Web: the greater links across national borders among fans of English-language comic books. In terms of opening up comic book fandom, one question that remains is whether the Web has expanded this fandom. While *CBR* boasts having two million unique viewers monthly, there is little direct evidence showing the Web has significantly increased comic fandom. But the increased popularity of comic books more generally since 2002 has certainly made the Web the most accessible way for new fans and others to discover the world of comic books. Newsarama.com, for example, found itself in *Entertainment Weekly's* "25 Favorite Entertainment Websites" in 2006.[88]

The Web would have little impact in terms of distribution and sales of printed mainstream comic books mostly because of the threat it posed to comic book shop retailers desperately trying to survive in the direct market. The Big Two and major independent mainstream publishers like Image and Dark Horse, therefore, did little to take advantage of the Web in either online sales of print comic books and graphic novels or online digital versions. Marvel did introduce digital comics in 2002, dotComics, for promotional reasons, or when an issue sold out, but discontinued producing new digital comics in 2003. Now defunct mainstream independent publisher CrossGen also introduced its "Comics on the Web." But major publishers mostly have taken advantage of the Web in promoting their comic books, including providing digital versions of first issues or sneak peaks at upcoming issues.[89] The impact of the Web would be more through the growth of the graphic novel market. Many comic shops, the most successful being Mile High Comics, Lone Star Comics, and Midtown Comics, went online to expand the direct market.[90] But giant online services like Amazon and Barnes and Noble have played a more significant role in the recent graphic novel boom.

With the advent of the Web many rebel artists, independent publishers, and self-publishers saw it as a new social space to promote alternative comic books as well as reaching out to fans and supporting online communities. In 1996 rebel artist Steve Conley began a successful, long-running comics Web site, iComics, which was a site dedicated to independent, alternative comics.

Conley joined rebel artist Rich Veitch in 1998 to create another successful comics Web site Comiccon.com. Veitch in 2001 remembered:

> I'd been meeting with other cartoonists, self-publishers and retailers informally beginning in maybe 1995, trying to figure out a way to make the Web work to cut out the bottlenecks we were experiencing getting our books through the distributors and onto shelves . . . Our main goal was to create a comics community on the Web, and we've accomplished that better than we ever imagined . . . Our big hope was that the community, once it had a place to congregate, would get energized and grapple with the opportunities and difficulties that faced us, especially in shaping the Web to create a new form of comics commerce. That hasn't really happened yet.[91]

Alternative independent publishers and self-publishers certainly took advantage of the Web with their own sites promoting and selling their comic books and graphic novels.[92] But publishers and creators faced the problem that their Web sites alone could not generate more readers beyond the preexisting alternative comics movement. The heady days of the direct market boom did not rematerialize with the advent of the Web.[93]

In 2007, there were signs of a shift in mainstream comic book publishers' attitudes toward the Web.[94] As web-fanzine *Webcomics* noted, "They were finally ready, after eleven years of hemming and hawing, to commit in a big way to placing comics on the Web . . . even with a skeptical eye, the companies' online initiatives look significant."[95] Marvel launched Marvel Digital Comics Unlimited. This service offered twenty-five hundred digital versions of back issues of their titles.[96] Mainstream independent publishers also made new moves onto the Web. Top Cow made digital downloads of some of its popular titles available on Direct2Drive online service. Dark Horse created *MySpace Dark Horse Presents* featuring a digital online version of its popular anthology series. *ComicMix* was launched by mainstream industry veteran Mike Gold, former senior editor at DC. This site offered free online digital comic books supported with advertising.[97] And DC launched Zudacomics. com in 2007 as a site for "amateur" artists to compete to win contracts for their digital webcomics with the publisher.[98]

Since the beginning of the Web, there were alternative comic book artists who viewed it as a new social space for a more revolutionary transformation in comic art. Not surprisingly, alternative comics' spokesperson Scott McCloud was the first to promote the Web's revolutionary potential.[99] In 1996, McCloud told the *Comics Journal*, "Digital *comics* are ultimately about *definitions*. It's about reducing comics down to their simplest possible form, and then allowing them to grow into a new shape. And I think that that shape can be extremely revolutionary."[100] McCloud termed the revolutionary potential of digital comics as an "infinite canvas." His second book, *Reinventing Comics*, presented a creed on the digital revolution in comic art. "The *digital canvas* offers a *malleable world* with limitless opportunities for *revision* and *expansion* . . . In a *digital environment,* comics can take virtually any *size* and *shape* as the temporal map—comics' *conceptual DNA*—grows in its *new dish . . .* No *art form* has lived in a smaller box than *comics* for the last *hundred years.* I say we *blow the lid off!* It's time for comics to finally *grow up.*"[101] McCloud followed his book with an infinite canvas webcomic, *I Can't Stop Thinking* (2000), extolling the virtues of digital technology and the Web for comic art.

Like McCloud, other artists looked at webcomics as a digital extension of alternative comics.[102] But only a few artists pursued McCloud's concept of webcomics as infinite canvases. Those artists who approached comic art as an infinite canvas either created nonpaneled, long, vertical-running comic art scrolls, paneled comic art "branched" in any manner of direction, paneled comic art with interactive features like menus or hypertext links, or the introduction of other media such as animation, sound, or photography.[103] Most alternative comic book artists, however, were more focused on remediating the comic book or graphic novel storytelling tradition in what is referred to as the "long form" webcomic—a story told with traditional comic book pages on the Web.[104] This included both the alt- and pulp-strategies that appeared in the alternative comics movement during the direct market boom.[105]

The biggest success for comic art on the Web, however, has been a webcomics movement that remediated the newspaper comic strip and cartoon onto the Internet. The dominant format for webcomics, therefore, became four-paneled strips or one-paneled cartoons appearing on a regular basis. The movement was made possible with the introduction of host-sites and directories for large numbers of webcomic artists.[106] Search engines and Web directories dedicated to webcomics also appeared, eventually featuring thousands of webcomics.[107] While open host-sites and directories generated the boom in webcomics, smaller collectives of webcomic artists also appeared.[108]

The boom in webcomics was phenomenal, with thousands of artists joining the new comic art movement on the Web.[109] Humor webcomics made up the largest genre. Other major genres were nerdcore, gaming, fantasy, science fiction, and horror. But artists were creating webcomics in genres like high school, college, workplace, crime, romance, media parody, western, anthropomorphic, GLBT, to the various genres found in manga. Special genres included sprite webcomics based on popular electronic game characters or webcomics that feature photographs of posed figurines or other photographed objects. There were twenty-four-hour webcomics where artists sit down and create a webcomic over twenty-four hours without a break. And there are jam webcomics where multiple artists create panels for a webcomic. The webcomic movement also was an overwhelmingly *pulp-centered* movement.

Unfortunately for comic book artists on the Web, there was a general divide between the webcomics movement and the world of comic books. In terms of both artists and fans, there was little crossover.[110] Comics artist Joe Zabel, in *Webcomics Examiner*, addressed this divide between the new webcomics movement and comic book culture. "I don't think a lot of the web-comics artists come from comics fandom. Their main exposure to comics has been from newspapers, and from the commercial art world. Comic books to them mean Spider-man, which doesn't interest them creatively." Comics artist Shaenon Garrity agreed, "A lot of webstrippers seem not very interested in comics in general. The longtime webcartoonists are general-purpose geeks, not comic geeks."[111] Webcomic artists and fans considered themselves rebels, but they were rebelling against what they perceived as a declining field in newspaper comic strips. Alternative comic book artists confronted a new social space occupied by artists and fans more interested in a comic strip rebellion than a comic art rebellion imported from the world of comic books.

It's equally clear that webcomic strip rebels have had little impact in the comic book field. Between 2002 and 2005, the three main comic book awards—Ignatz, Harvey, and Eisner awards—did introduce awards for webcomics. And webcomic artist Derek Kirk Kim's graphic novel adaptation of *Same Difference* won all three awards. Webcomic publishers and artists also have regularly attended comic book conventions. But except for the visibility of Scott McCloud in comic book culture and web-fanzine *Broken Frontiers* coverage of webcomics, the main print and web-fanzines in comic book culture have devoted little attention to the booming webcomic movement. Of course, the webcomic movement is still a relatively young art movement. But comic book fans seem as interested in the digital comic strip form as webcomics fans are in comic books. The future impact of webcomics on the field of comic books remains unclear.

Conclusion

The first years of the twenty-first century have led comic art in new and surprising directions. The century began with a comic book culture struggling with a collapsing market and a sense of irrelevance in relation to official culture. In just seven years, comic book culture was being celebrated as the center of North American popular culture, along with all things geeky.

Graphic novels were being celebrated as the new literary sensation and an essential part of library collections. No longer viewed as a subliterate art form, graphic novels were being held up as literacy builders and wonderful enticements for children and teens to gather in libraries to enjoy the breadth of good literature. And, of course, suddenly sales were moving in a positive direction as a new graphic novel market gained momentum. Alongside these positive developments was a manga revolution that placed comic art even more center stage in North American popular culture while bringing new aesthetics, new content, and new readership to comic books. What had become a medium dominated by teen and adult males was now discovering new audiences among female and young readers. It seemed that a solid bridge certainly had been built beyond comic book culture for both mainstream and alternative comic books.

Two fundamental changes over the last five years point to a possible new era for the English-language comic book. The first is a structural change in the market for comic books. For twenty years a direct market guaranteed the survival of the American comic book. It was crucial in the major aesthetic transformations that occurred in comic books during the Heroic Age. But the direct market in comic book culture also presented major constraints in the evolution of the American comic book and the possibilities of reaching a broader readership beyond the fanboy base of this subculture. The recent growth in the graphic novel market, which includes not only direct sales, but also sales to libraries, indicates a structural change that has the potential to reestablish a mass market for comic books. And in the first years of this new bridge back to a mass market, it is clear that a diversification is occurring in both readership and the type of comic books being sold. These recent changes in the comic book field represent what sociologist Shyon Baumann calls a new "opportunity space"—structural changes that provide an opening to reshape the market, aesthetics, and appreciation of an art form.[112] This new opportunity space for comic books could lead to an even greater comic book revolution. But as Baumann argues, the revolutionary potential of an opportunity space also is dependent on the institutionalization of the changes reshaping an art field.[113] It is hard to predict whether the recent changes in the comic book field will remain in the long term, and even more importantly, whether the new mass market and new readership for graphic novels will continue to grow.

The second major change over the last five years is the transformation in the status of the American comic book, its artists, and its readers. Given the long history in which this art form was considered by official culture as basically a subliterate, if not dangerous, form of popular entertainment, the efforts of comic book culture to transform this misconception seem to have born fruit. What is remarkable is the breadth of this transformation of official culture's view of comic books. It is not just Hollywood that loves comic books, but librarians, teachers, book critics, museum curators, and even some college professors. Just as the rebellion during the Heroic Age included comic books ranging from the most pulp to the most avant-garde, so the impact of this rebellion outside comic book culture has had an equally wide range in gaining "respect" for the American comic book. In many ways, the radical new reception of the American comic book by official culture has been a far greater change than the still relatively small graphic novel market. But official cultures' newfound respect for comic books bodes well for a future mass market in comic books for children, adolescents, adults, males, and females.

As for the alternative rebels who have struggled to make the comic book an art form as legitimate as any other art form, the future certainly looks brighter today than any time in the past. Alternative graphic novels have gained recognition by official culture as serious works of art: more as literature, however, than fine art. And unquestionably the comic book field has more accomplished and committed alternative comics artists than ever before. Given the low status of comic books in the past, and the dominance of superheroes in the comic book field and popular imagination, alternative rebels have accomplished a major transformation in the practice and meaning of an art form. But serious adult graphic novels still remain at the margins of an already small niche market. It remains more a dream than a reality that alternative graphic novels will one day be as regular a reading habit of adults in North America as literary books.

Conclusion

The Development of an Art Form

The comic strip is no longer a comic strip but in reality an illustrated novel. It is new and raw just now, but material for a limitless, intelligent development. And eventually, and inevitably, it will be a legitimate medium for the best of writers and artists.[1]

WILL EISNER, 1942

Will Eisner died on January 3, 2005. No comic book artist was as respected and beloved in the comic book field and comic book fandom than this pioneer of the art form. Eisner had witnessed the history of the modern American comic book from its first beginnings in the comic book shops of the 1930s to its rise as a new literary form in the late twentieth century. And he was there throughout this history as an active artist. Eisner created superhero comic books in the 1930s with characters like Doll Man and Wonder Man. And in 1978 he wrote one of the first literary graphic novels in North America, *A Contract with God and Other Tenement Stories*. And while Eisner believed in the potential of comic books, he was equally aware of the struggle to win respect for this art form. As he told an interviewer in 2002, "Comics has always been regarded as a subhuman art . . . we were a despised art form for years." But in the same interview Eisner remained optimistic about the future of the American comic book. "I believe we've hit a point where we're at the cusp of a growth, and the establishment and the acceptance of this medium."[2] Sixty years since he first dreamed of a bright future for comic books, Will Eisner remained the eternal optimist.

Whether Will Eisner's optimism was warranted is really the crux of my social history of the American comic book. The core of this story is how artists, fans, and publishers transformed the comic book field beginning in the

Late Industrial Age and into the Heroic Age of comic books. But did these transformations radically change the core of the comic book field in the way Eisner dreamed—making the comic book fill its fullest potential as an art form? A superficial glance at the comic book field today might suggest otherwise. The old properties of Marvel and DC from the Industrial Age still dominate the field. They also garner the greatest attention in the newfound love of comic books in the popular entertainment industry. Superman, Batman, Spider-Man, X-Men, Wonder Woman, and other superheroes seem indestructible in their dominance of comic book culture. And the recombinant culture of the old Industrial Age seems to have continually adapted to this field's constantly changing fortunes. Meanwhile, most comic book fans avidly follow the ongoing superhero universes of Marvel and DC. How could one possibly suggest some fundamental change has occurred in the American comic book since the Industrial Age of comic books?

Well certainly old comic book artists who labored under the pulp logic of the Industrial Age might see a fundamental change. Seven-day workweeks, low wages, anonymity, and general disrespect were their lot in life toiling for the old publishing houses. And many artists held no love for the comic books they produced, but simply created assembly-line products to earn a measly paycheck. And they signed all their creative rights away as well. Today, artists are the stars of the comic book field. Fans avidly follow their work, interview them in fan- and webzines, and see them at conventions. Artists move back and forth across the entire field. Sometimes they bring their unique talents to the properties of the old publishing houses for a big paycheck; other times they produce creator-owned properties for special imprints or independent publishers. And while mainstream rebels work for the old publishing houses, the days of signing over their creative rights are over. More importantly, since the early mainstream rebels entered the field, these artists have taken their pulp work seriously as an individual expression of their unique vision. Mainstream rebels unquestionably have pushed the creative pulp boundaries of comic books, whether in the old properties of Marvel and DC or the new properties created for special imprints and independent publishers.

Of course, from the alternative rebels' point of view, maybe not that much has changed. Regardless of their efforts to expand the comic book in "literary" directions, most in comic book culture have shown little interest in these efforts. Some alt rebels have even crossed over to work on the old properties of Marvel and DC with comic book fans celebrating these new artists in the superhero universe. Even mainstream rebels' return to these old properties reflected that their own efforts to expand the pulp universe also faced similar obstacles as the efforts of alt rebels. The truth of the matter is that while the direct market in comic book culture did provide a new social space for mainstream and alternative rebels to create new positions in the comic book field, this new social space relied on the demand of a subculture of comic book fans whose true love, and their financial portfolio, was based on the superhero and other adventure genres of the old publishing houses. In a somewhat ironic twist of fate, while comic book fandom first developed an appreciation of comic books that became the foundation for mainstream and alternative artists to rebel against the artistic limits of the Industrial Age, this fandom was also the greatest obstacle to these rebels' success. It's not that mainstream comic book fans did not acknowledge these rebels and their rebel comic books, but their affection and interests remained the same.

The comic book as an art form survived based on this subculture of comic book fandom by leaving behind a mass market and catering to a direct market with no bridges leading back out. More importantly, both mainstream publishers and underground comix publishers followed this path to survival, bringing together the mainstream and alternative rebellions within one single market and subculture. The structure of the field, to return to the production of culture perspective in sociology introduced at the beginning of the book, both enabled and restricted the new criteria of judgment and claims of autonomy that then emerged in the field during the Heroic Age. While rebellion among artists and readers was possible with the rise of independent publishers and a self-publishing movement within this subculture, the commercial interests of the Big Two and other mainstream publishers, and the preferences of most comic book fans, limited the potential for these rebellions. This was the case for both mainstream rebels and alt rebels, whether they adopted a pulp- or alt-strategy in creating their comic books. And this was certainly the case for women, gay, and minority rebel artists who desperately tried to diversify the comic book field in terms of art, artists, and readers.

While rebel artists and fans did not see as big a market for their pulp and alt comic books as they had hoped, this does not mean they failed in greatly expanding the breadth of expression in this art form: only the rebellion of black and other minority artists to create a more multicultural comic book universe of mainstream and alternative comic books seemed to have failed to create any permanent change. And rebel artists did gain critical recognition for their efforts. While pulp rebels might be more chagrined that the popular fiction they created failed to fundamentally change the balance of genres in the pulp universe of comic books, alt rebels should be less displeased. It is not as if "literary" works in the commercial market of books dominate this market either. The popular aesthetic, pulp fiction, has always been the preferred aesthetic for the majority of consumers of culture in North America. And let us not forget that all comic books, whether superhero, other pulp fiction, or the most avant-garde, existed in a very marginal direct market and comic book culture until only recently. When it came to the actual comic book and the numbers of readers it enjoyed, this art form in general still suffered from the absence of a mass market and the terrible lack of interest it seemed to generate among readers outside comic book culture. Ironically, it took Japanese manga to recapture a mass market for comic books.

The contradictory effects of both enabling, yet limiting, artists' rebellion against the old rules of art of the Industrial Age point again to the mundane "realities" emphasized in the production of culture perspective. But this perspective also suggests what might release the potential of an artistic rebellion, and the full potential of an art form, facing such insurmountable structural obstacles. The recent bridges built to the trade book market and libraries, in this sense, represent a structural change in the opportunity space for transforming the status of comic books. This new opportunity space for comic books could lead to an even greater comic book revolution. But this depends on whether readers unfamiliar with American comic books, and still reticent about the real "seriousness" of comic art, respond to this new market. But the recent manga boom certainly suggests the potential for once again capturing a mass market for American comic books as well. And if such a "revolution" were to occur, while alternative "literary" rebels would find a larger readership, I believe the true beneficiaries would be the mainstream and alternative "pulp" rebels who would find a broad readership interested in a diverse array of popular fiction in sequential art form. As one of the most celebrated mainstream pulp rebels, Alan Moore, exclaimed in 2007, "I hope this signals a general absorption of comic book material into the mainstream culture, which would take it away from these little enclaves that have controlled the destiny of comics for the past . . . goodness, man, can it really be 70 years?"[3]

Whether the ensconced ways of the old publishing houses Marvel and DC will quickly change to take advantage of the broad potential of the new trade book market is questionable. Most likely, if a new artistic revolution comes in the trade book market, it will be driven by independent comics publishers and trade book publishers. But an equally compelling question is what might be the future of superheroes if such a revolution were to take place. The superhero unquestionably has a dedicated fan base that continues to support a direct market of comic book shops. And the mainstream entertainment industry is pushing the superhero tradition for all its worth. But during the comic book boom of the 1940s and 1950s, the superhero genre actually faded away with the onslaught of competing popular genres of comic books. And the dominance of manga in the new trade market strongly suggests that the future of the comic book outside of comic book culture might not be dominated by costumed superheroes. On the other hand, the superhero has been so indelibly marked into the popular imagination over so long a period, if the comic book survives, undoubtedly the superhero will survive as well.

Regardless of the future potential for a mass market of comic books, Will Eisner's optimism certainly makes sense in light of the tremendous change in official culture's view of the once disdained American comic book. Comic book fandom and rebel artists have achieved a significant victory in erasing the stigma attached to comic books and those artists and readers committed to this art form. Of course, Eisner might not be happy that this newfound respect is usually framed as the victory of "geek culture" in the pop culture universe. On the other hand, the call to arms of librarians and teachers to bring graphic novels to libraries and schools across the country would unquestionably put a smile on his face, as would the newfound "literary" jewels covered by *The New York Times*. The Heroic Age was not just about the contentious dancing of positions between fans, artists, and publishers in the field, but also about the struggle all in comic book culture shared against the disdain and misunderstanding that comic books have contended with since the rise of Superman. And the final "respect" that comic books now seem to have attained came about both because of the discourse about comic books developed by comic book fandom and because of the actual changes artists brought to this art form during the Heroic Age of comic books. It also came about through the brilliant marketing strategy of mainstream publishers to bring comic book culture back into the mainstream of popular culture.

One of the difficult aspects of explaining and analyzing the Heroic Age has been the breadth of factors, strategies, points of view, and barriers to be breached in the general rebellion in demanding respect for the American comic book. In the introduction to this book I pointed to the blurring of boundaries between high art and popular art as well as the high art world's loss of cultural authority and status in America since the mid-twentieth century. I also pointed to how sociologists recognized new "omnivorous" tastes among elite and middle-class consumers. Yet we still tend to think in terms of the distinctions between highbrow, middlebrow, and lowbrow art. In part this is because of the institutional and market structures that still retain these distinctions as well as the tendencies for certain audiences to be attracted to certain types of art. As Herbert Gans noted thirty years ago, and Pierre Bourdieu would later articulate in his own theory of cultural tastes and consumption, there is a resonance between the institutional and commercial markets

for art and those who enjoy them.[4] Not surprisingly, there is very little scholarship on artistic movements or artistic subcultures that involve strategies
directed across the boundaries of lowbrow, middlebrow, and highbrow art.
This is most obviously a consequence of how art, artists, and audiences have
been demarcated already by their location in, or against, existing institutional
and market structures.

But as already suggested, the subculture of comic books was the only
place where artists could find a significant market and audience for their
comic books. So the merging of the mainstream and alternative worlds of
comic books, as well as the articulation of identity politics in terms of gender, race, and sexual orientation, within this subculture set the stage for
the wide variety of competing views about comic books and their future.
Certainly other popular art fandoms have had what Derek Johnson calls
"fantagonisms"—conflicts between competing interpretive communities
over the dominant discourse within a particular fandom.[5] And questions
of highbrow art versus lowbrow art, according to Camille Bacon-Smith,
appeared when the old science fiction fandom based on literature looked
down on the emerging science fiction fandom of the television show *Star
Trek* in the 1970s.[6] What is striking, however, about the Heroic Age of comic
books is how competing mainstream and alternative strategies of rebellion
fundamentally structured the comic book field as a whole and how these
strategies reflected competing approaches of both fans and artists. More
importantly, outside of comic book culture the comic book was still perceived for most of the Heroic Age as an art form suitable only for humorous
children's stories or pulp adolescent fantasy. Ironically, even facing the constraints of the dominant tastes and interests in comic book fandom, this was
one place alternative and mainstream rebels could find at least some respect
and interest. And this points to another distinct quality of the comic book
rebellion. Because of the stigma associated with the art form itself, a general
sense of transforming official culture's view of comic books was shared by
artists and fans across the spectrum of different and competing meanings
and practices in comic book culture. Most fanboys might not regularly read
alt-comic books, but they certainly could enjoy a stimulating conversation
about the lack of respect for comic books as an art form.

What is fascinating about the Late Industrial and Heroic Ages is the various ways individuals worked to make the comic book grow up, while working
simultaneously to insure its survival as an art form. The struggles were about
both the low regard held toward comic books and the market forces threatening their existence. One can see how since the 1960s artists, publishers, and
fans have attempted in one way or another to transform the low status of
comic books. This is the case for all genres of comic books and includes both

the efforts of artists, editors, and publishers as well as comic book fans. And in reading the writings coming out of comic book culture, this transformation of comic books is a major part of the collective story of comic books shared by all in this subculture. Certainly different communities would debate about how important particular transformations were in making comic books a more serious art form, or the constraints preventing its further development, but everyone, from fanboys to alt rebels, seemed to be celebrating the evolution of this art form since the Industrial Age.

I began this book by situating the social history of the modern American comic book in the work of the French sociologist Pierre Bourdieu. What I attempted to accomplish was to use this social history to investigate his work on fields of art as well as his work on cultural distinction and status.[7] I first wanted to investigate Bourdieu's conceptualization of industrial (popular) art. I wanted to show how a lowbrow, stigmatized, industrial art form like comic books could generate such a variety of strategies of rebellion. And these strategies were framed not only as a battle against official culture's disdain for this art form, but against the barriers in the comic book field to artistic expression and greater diversity in artists and readers. Bourdieu recognized moments in popular art where demanding greater respect did occur. But Bourdieu focused on moments of pretension to high art, what he called middlebrow art like photography, jazz, and film.[8] He never addressed demanding respect *within* a popular aesthetic or appreciation. But what is striking about the new "social space" opened up during the Heroic Age of comic books is how it allowed individuals to articulate such a variety of rebellions. And the most striking aspect is how the marginal state of the American comic book as an art form led to authentic rebellion spanning the most pulp of fiction to the most avant-garde of sequential art.

Regardless of his view of industrial art, Bourdieu did provide a framework for understanding the distinctions, contradictions, and dilemmas that emerged in the Heroic Age of comic books. In the chaotic positioning of rebel artists during the Heroic Age, for example, I have shown a pattern in which artists tended toward either a pulp-strategy that embraced a popular aesthetic or an alt-strategy that embraced a high art strategy. And in terms of appreciation, I have shown how this pattern reflected a split between a dominant fan pulp art appreciation and a more literary appreciation found in the alternative comics movement. This distinction in comic books in terms of art, artists, and readers is not unlike a similar split in the field of literature noted by Ken Gelder between popular fiction and literary fiction—a split visible in any bookstore between the "literature" section and sections in fictional genres like "science fiction" and "romance." The split in comic books, however, was not in a huge mass market of anonymous readers like in literature, but in a small subculture of comic books. So the tensions between these competing approaches to rebellion in comic books were far more visible and acrimonious. Such status distinction does exist, just barely under the surface, in literature. And it erupts occasionally like when Stephen King received the National Book Award's annual medal for distinguished contribution to American literature. Certain "literati" were flummoxed that a pulp writer could receive such a prestigious award, while King lambasted the literati for their disdain and low regard toward genre writers.[9] So the status hierarchy between popular and high highlighted by Bourdieu obviously remained an important distinction during the Heroic Age of comic books.

I also have shown how the distinction between a popular aesthetic and a high art aesthetic created a strange dilemma in the Heroic Age for those wanting to expand the comic book to encompass more "literary" pretensions. As Bourdieu argues, such "middlebrow" strategies get caught between looking snobbish to those who enjoy the popular aesthetics of a popular art, and looking pretentious to those arbiters of high art who find such claims for a popular art rather unconvincing. Alternative rebels in their attacks against mainstream comic books and their readers also faced the contradiction of reproducing the same stigma found in official culture toward comic books more generally, that is, mainstream comic books as subliterate, childish art. On the other hand, given the loss of status and authority of high art in America, the high art pretensions of alternative rebels might seem incongruous. If the American cultural hierarchy is more "omnivorous" in its tastes, how necessary is a high art claim to make comic books legitimate? It would seem that alternative rebels were reproducing a high–popular dichotomy that long lost significant purchase in America.

The seemingly incongruous and contradictory position of comic books as high art points to the special position of comic books in American culture. While the cultural status between the arts in America have become less pronounced and rigid over the last fifty years, comic books have retained a very low status as a popular art because of the stigma attached to them as subliterate art. What has been stressed in this book is how comic books as an entire art form, or medium, was suspect in the eyes of official culture. One need not defend whether a book can be literary or that popular fiction is suitable for adults. And beginning with the New Hollywood of the late 1960s and early 1970s when auteur directors transformed popular Hollywood film into serious art,[10] popular art like film and television has been taken more seriously by official culture, whether the film *Pulp Fiction* or the television show *Twin Peaks*. But one certainly had to defend comic books having the potential to be serious adult popular fiction, let alone be comparable to a literary work. And the very way in which the high art claims of alternative artists can stand out as pretentious only demonstrates the low status of comic books. Would we so quickly claim literary authors like Toni Morrison or Philip Roth as pretentious? In many ways both the pulp and alternative rebels were making the same claim: comic books are as serious as books! And the eventual recognition in official culture of "literary" comic books such as *Maus* or *Persepolis* helped transform the general perception of comic books in ways that allowed serious pulp comic books like *Sin City* or *History of Violence* to gain recognition as well. And it was this general change in the perception of comic books that made readers more receptive to engaging the "new" American comic book, particularly with the more "omnivorous" tastes found in America today.

But how does one account for the recent change in official culture's view of the American comic book after so many years struggling against the stigma this culture attached to comic books as a subliterate art suitable only for children or fantasy-obsessed adolescents? In part, I would argue that this stigma was based more on a vestigial memory of the comic book's status during the Industrial Age than on contemporary experiences of comic books. For most individuals, the comic book existed more in their imagination than in reality. At the same time, an alternative understanding of comic books developed within comic book culture that legitimated the comic book as popular or fine art. And comic books for over forty years actually did grow up as publishers targeted older readers and pulp and alt rebels expanded the art form. This transformation in comic books actually attracted the attention of official culture as early as the late 1980s. But this first opening occurred when an older generation of cultural gatekeepers, still steeped in the old biases toward comic books, controlled the avenues to legitimating and mass marketing comic books.

By the twenty-first century, a new generation of cultural gatekeepers whose memories were based on the "comics are grown-up" period of the Heroic Age was positioned to advocate more strongly for comic books as serious art. And they had the comic books to prove it. This is most clearly the case in the advocacy for comic books by a new generation of librarians and teachers, but also is evident in every aspect of the new attention, respect, and readership comic books have recently attained. This is why when Japanese manga created a bridge back into a mass market, the American comic book field was better prepared to take advantage of this new opportunity aided by librarians, teachers, trade publishers, book reviewers, and others. The problems faced by the American comic book by the end of the twentieth century were less about official culture's resistance than about the invisibility of comic books and the structural constraints of the direct market. The problem was the Heroic Age of comic books progressed mostly under the radar of official culture. With these new gatekeepers, the changes that evolved in the American comic book during this age could now reach new markets and new readers.

The greatest irony in the social history of comic books is how different the state of affairs has been for comic books in other fields outside the English-language comic book field. Comic book rebels constantly ranted about how in Japan and Europe the comic book was a respected art form unlike its poorer English-language cousin. The diversity and popularity of comic books in Japan and Europe obviously pointed to how the state of the American comic book has never been about the potential of the art form itself, but the particular history of the English-language comic book. In both Japan and Europe, the comic book *slowly* developed a mass market, enjoying a diverse array of comic books and an equally diverse array of readers. Ironically, the unique pulp logic applied to the modern American comic book, based on the pulp fiction tradition already established in pulp magazines, led it in a direction that ultimately instigated an anti–comic book crusade across the major English-speaking markets in the United States, Canada, and Britain. No such crusades occurred in Japan or Europe, because these fields did not adopt a similar pulp logic nor enjoy as booming a mass market as the English-language comic books did in the Early Industrial Age. But the combination of the stigma associated with the English-language comic book since the anti–comic book crusade, the marginalization of this comic book in a direct market, and the survival of this art form based on a comic book culture with a specific love and interest in old Industrial Age superhero and adventure genres, prevented the American comic book from developing in directions similar to comic books in Japan and Europe.

One cannot predict if the recent positive changes in the world of comic books will open the possibility that the American comic book will develop into as popular, diverse, and viable an art form as the comic book has become in Japan and Europe. As fan-journalist Heidi MacDonald wrote in the *Comic Buyer's Guide*, "I wouldn't for a moment suggest that we've *won* the war. But maybe, just maybe, we're winning."[11] The struggle has been long and full of disappointments. But maybe finally the American comic book will actually be taken seriously. One of the early mainstream rebel artists in comic books, Chris Claremont, summed up the frustrations and hopes of comic book rebels during the Heroic Age of comic books. "The problem with comics in America, unlike anywhere else in the world, is that from the beginning they have been viewed as trash/pulp/children's literature. They look like crap, you use 'em and you throw 'em away. But in Europe and Japan, comics are considered another form of literature, as wide-ranging as books. For a long time we squeezed ourselves into a box. We said these are the limits of our lives. We are finding out that we are limited only by our imaginations."[12] Of course, the future of the American comic book really depends on the imagination of readers and others outside comic book culture. Let us hope that their imaginations can embrace comic books as an art form as legitimate and compelling as any other, and not just cultural pabulum for moppets and moppet-minded adults.

Notes

INTRODUCTION

1. This chapter has a few excerpts from Paul Lopes, "Strategies of Rebellion in the Heroic Age of the American Comic Book," *International Journal of the Arts in Society* 2, no. 2 (2007): 127–134. Individuals interested in reproducing this chapter must get permission not only from Temple University Press, but also from Common Ground Publishing, Victoria, Australia.

2. Will Eisner, "Getting the Last Laugh: My Life in Comics," *New York Times,* January 14, 1990, BR1.

3. Paul Lopes, *The Rise of a Jazz Art World* (Cambridge: Cambridge University Press, 2002).

4. John Fiske, "The Cultural Economy of Fandom," in *The Adoring Audience: Fan Culture and Popular Media*, ed. A. Lewis (New York: Routledge, 1992), 30–49.

5. Pierre Bourdieu, *The Rules of Art: Genesis and Structure of the Literary Field* (Stanford, CA: Stanford University Press, 1996).

6. Ibid., 214–277.

7. Ibid., 113.

8. Ken Gelder, *Popular Fiction: The Logics and Practices of a Literary Field* (New York: Routledge, 2004), 9–34, 40–43.

9. Richard A. Peterson and N. Anand, "The Production of Culture Perspective," *Annual Review Sociology* 30 (2004): 313–314; Victoria D. Alexander, *Sociology of Arts* (Malden, MA: Blackwell Publishing, 2003), 67–156.

10. Todd Gitlin, *Inside Primetime* (New York: Pantheon Books, 1983).

11. Richard A. Peterson, "Why 1955? Explaining the Advent of Rock Music," *Popular Music* 9, no. 1 (1990): 98–115.

12. Herman Gray, *Watching Race: Television and the Struggle for "Blackness"* (Minneapolis: University of Minnesota Press, 1995).

13. Henry Jenkins, *Textual Poachers: Television Fans and Participatory Culture* (New York: Routledge, 1992); Joli Jensen, "Fandom as Pathology: The Consequences of Characterization," in *Popular Culture: Production and Consumption*, ed. C. Lee Harrington and Denise D. Bielby (Malden, MA: Blackwell Publishing, 2001), 301–314; Matt Hills, *Fan Cultures* (New York: Routledge, 2002).

14. C. Lee Harrington and Denise Bielby, *Soap Fans: Pursuing Pleasure and Making Meaning in Everyday Life* (Philadelphia: Temple University Press, 1995); Camille Bacon-Smith, *Science Fiction Culture* (Philadelphia: University of Pennsylvania Press, 2000).

15. Matthew Pustz, *Comic Book Culture: Fanboys and True Believers* (Jackson: University Press of Mississippi, 1999).

16. Hills, *Fan Cultures*.

17. Pustz, *Comic Book Culture*.

18. Neal Gabler, *Life the Movie* (New York: Vintage Books, 1998).

19. Lawrence Levine, *Highbrow/Lowbrow: The Emergence of Cultural Hierarchy in America* (Cambridge, MA: Harvard University Press, 1988); Paul DiMaggio, "Cultural Entrepreneurship in Nineteenth-Century Boston," *Media, Culture and Society* 4, no. 1 (1982): 33–50.

20. Bart Beaty, *Fredric Wertham and the Critique of Mass Culture* (Jackson: University Press of Mississippi, 2005); James Gilbert, *A Cycle of Outrage: America's Reaction to the Juvenile Delinquent in the 1950s* (New York: Oxford University Press, 1986).

21. Michael Kammen, *American Culture, American Tastes: Social Change and the 20th Century* (New York: Knopf, 1999).

22. Diana Crane, *The Production of Culture: Media and the Urban Arts* (Newbury Park, CA: Sage Publications, 1992); Paul DiMaggio, "Social Structure, Institutions, and Cultural Goods: The Case of the United States," in *Social Theory for a Changing Society*, ed. P. Bourdieu and J. S. Coleman (San Francisco: Westview Press, 1991), 133–155.

23. Paul DiMaggio, "Classification in Art," *American Sociological Review* 52, no. 4 (1987): 440–455; Richard A. Peterson, "Understanding Audience Segmentation: From Elite and Mass to Omnivore and Univore," *Poetics* 21 (1992): 243–258; Richard A. Peterson and Roger M. Kern, "Changing Highbrow Taste: From Snob to Omnivore," *American Sociological Review* 61, no. 5 (1996): 900–907.

24. Bethany Bryson, "'Anything but Heavy Metal': Symbolic Exclusion and Musical Dislikes," *American Sociological Review* 61, no. 5 (1996): 884–899.

25. Charlotte Brunsdon, *The Feminist, the Housewife, and the Soap Opera* (New York: Oxford University Press, 2000); Joshua Gamson, *Freaks Talk Back: Tabloid Talk Shows and Sexual Nonconformity* (Chicago: University of Chicago Press, 1998); Laura Grindstaff, *The Money Shot: Trash, Class, and the Making of TV Talk Shows* (Chicago: University of Chicago Press, 2002).

26. Stuart Hall, "Notes on Deconstructing the Popular," in *People's History and Socialist Theory,* ed. Raphael Samuel (London: Routledge and Kegan Paul, 1981), 227–240; George Lipsitz, *Time Passages: Collective Memory and American Popular Culture* (Minneapolis: University of Minnesota Press, 1990); Gray, *Watching Race*; Angela McRobbie, *The Uses of Cultural Studies* (Thousand Oaks, CA: Sage Publications, 2005).

27. Stuart Hall, *The Hard Road to Renewal* (London: Verso, 1988); Douglas Kellner, *Media Culture: Cultural Studies, Identity and Politics between the Modern and the Postmodern* (New York: Routledge, 1995); Arlene Dávila, *Latinos Inc.: The Marketing and Making of a People* (Berkeley: University of California Press, 2001); Ron Becker, *Gay TV and Straight America* (New Brunswick, NJ: Rutgers University Press, 2006).

28. Becker, *Gay TV.*

29. Gray, *Watching Race.*

30. M. Thomas Inge, *Comics as Culture* (Jackson: University Press of Mississippi, 1990); William W. Savage, Jr., *Comic Books and America, 1945–1954* (Norman: University of Oklahoma Press, 1990).

31. Roger Sabin, *Adult Comics: An Introduction* (New York: Routledge, 1993); Roger Sabin, *Comics, Comix and Graphic Novels: A History of Comic Art* (London: Phaidon Press, 1996).

32. Amy Kiste Nyberg, *Seal of Approval: The History of the Comics Code* (Jackson: University Press of Mississippi, 1998); Beaty, *Fredric Wertham.*

33. Bradford W. Wright, *Comic Book Nation: The Transformation of Youth Culture in America* (Baltimore: John Hopkins University Press, 2001).

34. Pustz, *Comic Book Culture*; Jeffrey A. Brown, *Black Superheroes, Milestone Comics, and Their Fans* (Jackson: University Press of Mississippi, 2001).

35. Gerald Jones, *Men of Tomorrow: Geeks, Gangsters, and the Birth of the Comic Book* (New York: Basic Books, 2004).

36. "Beyond the Funnies," *Library and Archive of Canada,* http://www.collectionscanada.ca/comics/ (accessed November 7, 2007).

37. Sabin, *Comics, Comix and Graphic Novels.*

CHAPTER 1

1. Bourdieu, *The Rules of Art.*

2. M. Thomas Inge, "Comic Art," in *Handbook of American Popular Culture,* ed. M. Thomas Inge (Westport, CT: Greenwood Press, 1978), 1:78–79.

3. Donald Crafton, "The Silent Film: Tricks and Animation," in *The Oxford History of World Cinema,* ed. Geoffrey Nowell-Smith (Oxford: Oxford University Press, 1996), 72–77.

4. Mike Benton, *Comic Book in America* (Dallas: Taylor, 1989), 30.

5. Bill Blackbeard, "The Pulps," in *Handbook of American Popular* Culture, ed. M. Thomas Inge (Westport, CT: Greenwood Press, 1978), 1:201–208.

6. Ron Goulart, *Great History of Comic Books* (Chicago: Contemporary, 1986), 93–103; Benton, *Comic Book in America,* 90–152; Les Daniels, *Five Fabulous Decades of the World's Greatest Comics* (New York: Harry N. Abrams, 1993), 18; Gerard Jones, *Men of Tomorrow: Geeks, Gangsters, and the Birth of the Comic Book* (New York: Basic, 2004), 187.

7. Benton, *Comic Book in America,* 90.

8. Inge, "Comic Art," 1:77–82.

9. Ibid., 1:79–80.

10. Jules Feiffer, *The Great Comic Book Heroes* (Seattle: Fantagraphics, 2003), 45–49.

11. Blackbeard, "The Pulps," 1:199; Frank M. Robinson and Lawrence Davidson, *Pulp Culture: The Art of Fiction Magazines* (Portland, OR: Collectors Press, 1998), 17–18.

12. Blackbeard, "The Pulps," 1:201–208; Robinson and Davidson, *Pulp Culture*, 2.

13. Ron Goulart, *Cheap Thrills: The Amazing! Thrilling! Astonishing! History of Pulp Fiction* (Neshannock, PA: Hermes), 14–16.

14. Blackbeard, "The Pulps," 1:195–215.

15. Ibid., 1:211.

16. Harold Brainerd Hersey, *Pulpwood Editor: The Fabulous World of the Thriller Magazines Revealed by a Veteran Editor and Publisher* (1937; repr., Westport, CT: Greenwood Press, 1974), 201.

17. Gelder, *Popular Fiction*, 9–34, 40–43.

18. Ibid., 12, 35–38.

19. Ron Goulart, *Great American Comic Books* (Lincolnwood, IL: Publications International, 2001), 61–71.

20. Gitlin, *Inside Primetime*, 63–85.

21. Hersey, *Pulpwood Editor*, 14, 44.

22. "Pulp Writers Find Market Dwindling," *New York Times*, May 13, 1933, 14; Frank Gruber, *The Pulp Jungle* (Los Angeles: Sherbourne Press, 1967), 20–25.

23. "Pulp Magazines," *New York Times*, September 4, 1935, 18.

24. Gruber, *Pulp Jungle*, 24.

25. Gruber, *Pulp Jungle*, 29; Robinson and Davidson, *Pulp Culture*, 179.

26. Hersey, *Pulpwood Editor*, 122.

27. "Pulp Writers," 14.

28. Robinson and Davidson, *Pulp Culture*, 79; Goulart, *Cheap Thrills*, 113.

29. Hersey, *Pulpwood Editor*.

30. Ronald Weber, *Hired Pens: Professional Writers in America's Golden Age of Print* (Athens: Ohio University Press, 1997), 106.

31. Hersey, *Pulpwood Editor*, 135–136.

32. "An Artisan's Defense," *New York Times*, March 18, 1933, 12.

33. Ted White, "The Spawn of M. C. Gaines," in *All in Color for a Dime*, 2nd ed., ed. D. Lupoff and D. Thompson (Iola, WI: Krause Publications, 1997), 23.

34. Jones, *Men of Tomorrow*.

35. Benton, *Comic Book in America*, 90.

36. Ibid.

37. Gary Groth, "Kane: Interview," *Comics Journal* 186 (April 1996), http:www.tcj.com/2_archives/i_kane.html (accessed August 28, 2007).

38. Joe Simon, *The Comic Book Makers* (Lebanon, NJ: Vanguard Productions, 2003), 37.

39. Will Eisner, *Shop Talk* (Milwaukie, OR: Dark Horse Comics, 2001), 232.

40. Jones, *Men of Tomorrow*, 87–108.

41. "Shop System I: Interview with Will Eisner," *Comics Journal* 249 (December 2002): 64.

42. Jon B. Cooke and Christopher Irving, "The Charlton Empire," *Comic Book Artist* 9 (August 2000): 14; Daniels, *Five Fabulous Decades*, 68.

43. U.S. Senate, Subcommittee to Investigate Juvenile Delinquency in the United States, *Comic Books and Juvenile Delinquency*, 84th Congress, 1st Session, 1955, 44–50.

44. Ron Goulart, "The Shop System II: Golden Age Sweatshops," *Comics Journal* 249 (December 2002): 71–81; Benton, *Comic Book in America*, 90. Detailed information on comic shops including artists, owners, clients, and dates can be found in Jerry Bails *The Who's Who of American Comic Books*, http://www.bailsprojects.com.

45. Dick Lupoff and Don Thompson, "Introduction," in *All in Color for a Dime*, 2nd ed., ed. D. Lupoff and D. Thompson (Iola, WI: Krause Publications, 1997), 12.

46. Feiffer, *Great Comic Book Heroes*, 5–6.

47. Robert Arthur, "How the Comics are Made," *Spot*, 1942, in *Fawcett Companion: The Best of FCA* (Raleigh, NC: TwoMorrows, 2001), 20–23; U.S. Senate, *Comic Books and Juvenile Delinquency*, 4–7; P. C. Hamerlinck, "The Jack Binder Shop Days: An Interview with Nat Champlin," *Alter Ego* 3, no. 3 (Winter 1999/2000): 58; Trina Robbins and Catherine Yronwode, *Women and the Comics* (Guerneville, CA: Eclipse Books, 1985), 49; Gary Groth, "Kane: Interview"; Benton, *Comic Book in America*, 90.

48. Benton, *Comic Book in America*, 17–37.

49. "Comics and their Audience," *Publishers Weekly*, April 18, 1942, 1479; "Superman Scores," *BusinessWeek*, April 18, 1942, 54.

50. "Comics and their Audience," 1479.

51. Arthur, "How the Comics are Made," 20.

52. Steve Mitchell, "Slaughter of the Innocents," *Comic Buyer's Guide*, May 17, 1985, 40, 62; Steve Mitchell, "The Red-Hot Thrill: The Comic Book Crisis of 1948, part 2," *Comics Buyer's Guide*, June 28, 1985, 46; Steve Mitchell, "The Best is the Worst," *Comic Buyer's Guide*, July 19, 1985, 30; Steve Mitchell, "Superman in Disguise," *Comics Buyer's Guide*, May 9, 1986, 28.

53. Goulart, *Great American Comic Books*, 137.

54. Benton, *Comic Book in America*, 35–40.

55. Will Lieberson, "Comics is a Funny Business," *Writer's Digest 2*, 1946, in *Fawcett Companion: The Best of FCA* (Raleigh, NC: TwoMorrows, 2001), 16; "540 Million Comics Published During 1946," *Publishers Weekly*, September 6, 1947, 1030.

56. "New York Officials Recommend Code for Comics Publishers," *Publishers Weekly*, February 19, 1949, 977; John R. Vosburgh, "How the Comic Book Started," *Commonweal*, May 20, 1949, 147; "Canada's Comics Ban," *Newsweek*, November 14, 1949, 62.

57. "Horror Comics," *Time*, May 3, 1954, 78; "Horror on the Newsstands," *Time*, September 27, 1954; Benton, *Comic Book in America*, 55. On estimates of annual profits see Frederic Wertham, "Reading for the Innocent," *Wilson Library Journal*, April 1955, 610 (Annual Profit Numbers from Barron's January 17, 1955); T. E. Murphy, "Progress in Cleaning Up the Comics," *Reader's Digest*, February 1956, 105.

58. Arthur, "How the Comics are Made," 22.

59. "Shop System I," 65.

60. Gary Groth,"Infantino," *Comics Journal* 191 (November 1996): 56.

61. Hamerlinck, "Jack Binder Shop Days," 38; Goulart, "The Shop System II," 76.

62. Groth, "Infantino," 60.

63. Groth, "Kane: Interview."

64. Feiffer, *Great Comic Book Heroes*, 66.

65. David Hajdu, *The Ten-Cent Plague: The Great Comic Book Scare and How It Changed America* (New York: Farrar, Straus and Giroux, 2008), 25–28.

66. White, "The Spawn of M. C. Gaines," 23; Eisner, *Shop Talk*, 194–195; "Kurtzman, Kane, and a Career in Comics," *Comics Journal* 157 (March 1993): 13–14.

67. "Future Schlock," *Comics Journal* 146 (November 1991): 87.

68. "I Chose to Be a Genius," (1980) in *Fawcett Companion: The Best of FCA* (Raleigh, NC: TwoMorrows, 2001), 58.

69. Groth, "Infantino," 60.

70. Robbins and Yronwode, *Women and the Comics*, 50, 66.

71. Trina Robbins, *A Century of Women Cartoonists* (Northampton, MA: Kitchen Sink, 1993), 92–109.

72. Simon, *Comic Book Makers*, 53.

73. Feiffer, *Great Comic Book Heroes*, 68.

74. "I Chose to Be a Genius," 58.

75. Benton, *Comic Book in America*, 90.

76. Simon, *Comic Book Makers*, 52–53.

77. "I Chose to Be a Genius," 58.

78. "Up, Up and Aw-a-y: The Rise of Superman, Inc.," *Saturday Evening Post*, June 21, 1941, 14–15, 70–78; Jones, *Men of Tomorrow*, 109–125, 171–186, 242–252; Michael Dean, "An Extraordinary Marketable Man: The Ongoing Struggle for Ownership of Superman and Superboy," *Comics Journal* 263 (October/November 2004): 13–17.

79. Gary Groth and Robert Fiore, *The New Comics: Interviews from the Pages of the Comics Journal* (New York: Berkeley, 1988), 16.

80. "I Admire Craftsmanship," (1980) in *Fawcett Companion: The Best of FCA* (Raleigh, NC: TwoMorrows, 2001), 68; "Shop System I," 65; Eisner, *Shop Talk*, 225; Groth, "Infantino," 54.

81. Eisner, *Shop Talk*, 228.

82. Groth and Fiore, *New Comics*, 16.

83. Marc Swayze, "We Didn't Know It Was the Golden Age!" *Alter Ego* 3 (Summer 1999): 34–35.

84. "C. C. Beck," *Hogan's Alley* 3 (Spring 1996), http://www.cagle.com/hogan/interviews/beck/home.asp (accessed August 29, 2007)

85. Swayze, "We Didn't Know," 35.

86. Eisner, *Shop Talk*, 229.

87. Ibid., 199, 201, 208.

88. Groth, "Infantino," 63.

89. Goulart, *Great History*, 4–5; Jones, *Men of Tomorrow*, 99; Bradford W. Wright, *Comic Book Nation: The Transformation of Youth Culture in America* (Baltimore: John Hopkins University Press, 2001), 3.

90. "Comics and their Audience," 1477; Benton, *Comic Book in America*, 15.

91. In the following section, the date appearing for a comic book title is the year the book was first published. While most dates were originally found in secondary sources on comic book history, all dates were checked in Jackson Miller and others, *The Standard Catalog of Comic Books*, 2nd ed. (Iola, WI: Krause Publications, 2003) and the *Grand Comic Book Database*, http://www.comics.org/index.lasso.

92. Benton, *Comic Book in America*, 21; Goulart, *Great History*, 4–42.

93. Miller, *Standard Catalog*, 21, 474.

94. Goulart, *Great History*, 56–74; Mike Voiles, "Mike's Amazing World of DC Comics," *DC Database*, http://www.dcindexes.com/database (accessed June 26, 2006)

95. Benton, *Comic Book in America*, 188.

96. "Comics and their Audience," 1478; Benton, *Comic Book in America*, 23.

97. "Up, Up and Aw-a-y," 73.

98. Ibid.

99. Daniels, *Five Fabulous Decades*, 26–35.

100. Benton, *Comic Book in America*, 176.

101. "Up, Up and Aw-a-y," 73, 76.

102. Ibid., 14–15.

103. "Comics—Food for Half-Wits?" *Science Digest*, April 1945, 81.

104. P. C. Hamerlinck, "The Fawcetts Could Do It as Well, or Better, than Anybody," (1997) in *Fawcett Companion: The Best of FCA* (Raleigh, NC: TwoMorrows, 2001), 12.

105. Daniels, *Comix*, 49–51; Kristin Thompson and David Bordwell, *Film History: An Introduction*, 2nd ed. (New York: McGraw-Hill, 2003), 164–165.

106. Daniels, *Comix*, 49.

107. Benton, *Comic Book in America*, 30.

108. Goulart, *Great History*, 214.

109. Harvey Zorbaugh, "The Comics—There They Stand! *Journal of Educational Sociology* 18, no. 4 (1944): 197–199.

110. Benton, *Comic Book in America*, 43; Goulart, *Great History*, 241.

111. Benton, *Comic Book in America*, 40, 54.

112. Benton, *Comic Book in America*, 162–164; *Grand Comic Book Database*.

113. Trina Robbins, *From Girls to Grrrlz: A History of Women's Comics from Teens to Zines* (San Francisco: Chronicle Books, 1999), 12.

114. Paul Sassienie, *The Comic Book: The One Essential Guide for Comic Book Fans Everywhere* (Edison NJ: Chartwell Books, 1994), 38–41.

115. Benton, *Comic Book in America*, 181–183.

116. Robbins, *From Girls to Grrrlz*, 38.

117. Benton, *Comic Book in America*, 46.

118. *Grand Comic Book Database Project*.

119. "Love on a Dime," *Time*, August 22, 1949, 41; Benton, *Comic Book in America*, 46; *Grand Comic Book Database*.

120. Simon, *Comic Book Makers*, 112; "Love on a Dime," 41.

121. "Love on a Dime," 41.

122. Benton, *Comic Book in America*, 46; *Grand Comic Book Database*.

123. *Grand Comic Book Database*.

124. Robbins, *From Girls to Grrrlz*, 57–67.

125. Ibid.

126. Benton, *Comic Book in America*, 44.

127. *Grand Comic Book Database*.

128. Ibid.

129. Ibid.

130. "Classic Comics Sell a Hundred Million," *Publishers Weekly*, March 23, 1946, 1736.

131. "Superman Scores," *BusinessWeek*, April 18, 1942, 55.

132. Mitchell, "Slaughter of the Innocents," 52–54.

133. Jay David Bolter and Richard Grusin, *Remediation: Understanding New Media* (Cambridge, MA: MIT Press, 1999).

134. Raymond Williams, *Television, Technology and Cultural Form* (London: Fontana, 1974).

135. U.S. Senate, Subcommittee to Investigate Juvenile Delinquency in the United States, *Comic Books and Juvenile Delinquency*, 84th Congress, 1st Session, 1955, 7.

CHAPTER 2

1. Lovell Thompson, "Not So Comic," *Atlantic Monthly*, January 1941, 105.

2. Nyberg, *Seal of Approval: The History of the Comics Code*, 1–3.

3. Beaty, *Fredric Wertham and the Critique of Mass Culture*.

4. Gilbert, *A Cycle of Outrage*, 3–10.

5. Gerald F. Davis, Doug McAdam, W. Richard Scott, and Mayer N. Zald, *Social Movements and Organizational Theory* (New York: Cambridge University Press, 2005); David A. Snow, Sarah A. Soule, and Hanspeter Kriesi, *The Blackwell Companion to Social Movements* (Malden, MA: Blackwell Publishing, 2004).

6. Margaret Frakes, "Comics Are No Longer Comic," *Christian Century*, November 4, 1942, 1350.

7. Catherine Mackenzie, "The Second Baby vs. the First," *New York Times*, March 2, 1941, SM22.

8. Sterling North, "A National Disgrace: A Challenge to American Parents," *Chicago Daily News*, May 8, 1940; reprinted in *Childhood Education* 17 (October 1940): 56.

9. Sterling North, "The Antidote for Comics," *National Parent-Teacher*, March 1941, 16–17.

10. Thomas Doyle, "What's Wrong with the Comics?" *Catholic World*, February 1943, 553.

11. James Frank Vlamos, "The Sad Case of the Funnies," *American Mercury*, April 1941, 412, 416; for reference to fascism see also "Are Comics Fascist?" *Time*, October 22, 1945, 67.

12. Frakes, "Comics Are No Longer Comic," 1350.

13. "Racketeers of Childhood," *Time*, February 24, 1941, 48–49.

14. North, "The Antidote for Comics," 17.

15. Nyberg, *Seal of Approval*, 5; Beaty, *Fredric Wertham*, 106.

16. Nyberg, *Seal of Approval*, 5–6.

17. S.J.K., "The Comic Menace," *Wilson Library Journal*, June 1941, 846–847.

18. Clara Savage Littledale, "What to Do About the 'Comics,'" *Parents Magazine*, March 1941, 27, 93.

19. Nyberg, *Seal of Approval*, 8.

20. S.J.K. "Librarians, to Arms!" *Wilson Library Bulletin*, April 1941, 670.

21. Steve Mitchell, "Slaughter of the Innocents: Comic Book Controversy before Wertham," *Comic Buyer's Guide*, May 17, 1985, 42.

22. In terms of academic articles, the most important publication was a special issue on comics in the *Journal of Educational Sociology* 18, no. 4 (December 1944). In

terms of press coverage of academic research see "Issues Relating to Comics," *Elementary School Journal,* May 1942, 642–644; Catherine Mackenzie, "Children and the Comics," *New York Times,* July 11, 1943, SM24; "Educators Uphold Children's Comics," *New York Times,* December 2, 1944, 8; "Comics—Food for Half-Wits?" *Science Digest,* April 1945, 79–82.

23. Mackenzie, "The Second Baby," SM22.

24. "Let the Children Read Comics; Science Gives Its Approval," *Science News Letter,* August 23, 1941, 124.

25. William Moulton Marston, "Why 100,000,000 Americans Read Comics," *American Scholar,* April 1944, 35–44.

26. "Issues Relating to Comics," 643.

27. "Not So Comic," 106–107.

28. Lovell Thompson, "How Serious Are the Comics?" *Atlantic Monthly,* September 1942, 127–128.

29. Frakes, "Comics Are No Longer Comic," 1350.

30. Harold C. Field, "On 'Why 100,000,000 Americans Read Comics,'" *American Scholar* (1944): 247.

31. Nyberg, *Seal of Approval,* 17–18.

32. Paul S. Boyer, *Purity in Print: Book Censorship in America from the Gilded Age to the Computer Age* (Madison: University of Wisconsin Press, 2002), 270–316.

33. "Librarians Assail Naming of M'Leish," *New York Times,* June 20, 1939, 27.

34. Judith F. Krug, "Intellectual Freedom and ALA: Historical Overview" in *Encyclopedia of Library and Information Science,* 2nd ed., vol. 2, ed. M. A. Drake (New York: Marcel Dekker, 2003), 1379–1381; Dennis Thomison, *A History of the American Library Association, 1876–1972* (Chicago: American Library Association, 1978), 103–104, 144–146, 187–191.

35. William T. Matchett, "Boston Is Afraid of Books: It Has Yet to Grow Up In Its Approach to Literary Censorship," *Saturday Review of Literature,* July 15, 1944, 6.

36. Paul Blanshard, "The Catholic Church as Censor," *Nation,* May 1, 1948, 459–464.

37. "Burning Next?" *New Republic,* August 30, 1948, 11.

38. Benjamin Fine, "Education in Review: Library Association Asks Support for Fight Against Various Forms of Censorship," *New York Times,* June 20, 1948, E9.

39. Matthew Josephson, "The Battle of the Books," *Nation,* June 28, 1952, 620.

40. Elmer Rice, "New Fashions in Censorship," *Survey,* March 1952, 112–115.

41. Benjamin Fine, "Textbook Censors Alarm Educators," *New York Times,* May 25, 1952, 1.

42. Irene Corbally Kuhn, "Why You Buy Books That Sell Communism," *American Legion Magazine,* January 1951, 19, 53.

43. Paul Blanshard, *The Right to Read* (Boston: Beacon Press, 1955).

44. "Statement on Censorship Activity by Private Organizations and the National Organization for Decent Literature," *American Civil Liberties Union* (1957) in *The First Freedom: Liberty and Justice in the World of Books and Reading,* ed. R. B. Downs (Chicago: American Library Association, 1960), 134–138.

45. John Fischer, "The Harm Good People Do," *Harper's Magazine,* October 1956, 15.

46. Boyer, *Purity in Print*, 99–166; Richard McKeon, Robert K. Merton, and Walter Gellhorn, *Freedom to Read* (New York: R. R. Bowker, 1957).

47. Eric Larrabee, "The Cultural Conflict of Sex Censorship," in *The First Freedom*, 193–201; originally published in *Law and Contemporary Problems* 20 (1955): 272–288.

48. Walter M. Daniels, *The Censorship of Books* (New York: Wilson, 1954), 73.

49. Edward A. Weeks, "The American Public Trusts the Bookseller," *Publishers Weekly* (June 6, 1953) in *Censorship of Books*, 75.

50. Daniels, *Censorship of Books*, 56.

51. J. Alvin Kugelmass, "Smut on Our Newsstands," *Christian Herald*, May 1952, 22.

52. McKeon, Merton, and Gellhorn, *Freedom to Read*, v.

53. John E. Twomey, "The Citizen's Committee and Comic-Book Control: A Study of Extragovernmental Restraint," *Law and Contemporary Problems* 20, no. 4 (Autumn 1955): 621.

54. "Police Fight Comic Books," *New York Times*, August 12, 1947, 20.

55. Judith Crist, "Horror in the Nursery," *Collier's*, March 27, 1948, 22–23, 95–96.

56. Fredric Wertham, "Comics . . . Very Funny!" *Saturday Review of Literature*, May 29, 1948, 6–7, 27–29; *Reader's Digest*, August 1948, 15–18.

57. Nyberg, *Seal of Approval*, 32–34; Beaty, *Fredric Wertham*, 118–119.

58. Wertham, "Comics . . . Very Funny!" 27.

59. Ibid., 27, 29.

60. Ruth Emily Smith, "Publishers Improve Comic Books," *Library Journal*, November 1948, 1649.

61. "The Ubiquitous Comics," *NEA Journal* (December 1948): 570.

62. Jean Gray Harker, "Youth's Librarians Can Defeat Comics," *Library Journal*, December 1, 1948, 1707.

63. Alton M. Motter, "How to Improve the Comics," *Christian Century*, October 12, 1949, 1199–1120.

64. Jesse L. Murrell, "Cincinnati Rates the Comic Books," *Parents Magazine*, February 1950, 38.

65. "Purified Comics," *Newsweek*, July 12, 1948, 56.

66. "Comic Books Censored," *New York Times*, August 3, 1948, 42.

67. U.S. Senate, Subcommittee to Investigate Juvenile Delinquency in the United States, *Comic Books and Juvenile Delinquency*, 84th Congress, 1st Session, 1955, 30.

68. "Not So Funny," *Time*, October 4, 1948, 16.

69. "Modern Comics Hit By Mayors' Report," *New York Times*, November 25, 1948, 50.

70. "Seek Comic Book Censor," *New York Times*, September 17, 1948, 30.

71. "Comic Book Action Set," *New York Times*, November 12, 1948, 29.

72. "Boards to Censor Comic Books," *New York Times*, November 11, 1948, 34.

73. "Sex and Crime Tales Hit: Catholic Students Expand Fight on Magazines Featuring Them," *New York Times*, December 31, 1949, 10.

74. "Pupils Burn Comic Books," *New York Times*, December 23, 1948, 22.

75. Nyberg, *Seal of Approval*, 23.

76. "Statement on Censorship Activity," 134.

77. Murrell, "Cincinnati Rates the Comic Books," 38.

78. Mitchell, "Slaughter of the Innocents," 62–64.

79. "Statement on Censorship Activity," 134–138.

80. "Catholic Students Burn Up Comic Books," *New York Times,* December 11, 1948, 18.

81. "Pupils Burn Comic Books," 22.

82. "Burning of Comic Books Avoided," *New York Times,* January 16, 1949, 59.

83. "The Comics Under Fire," *Publishers Weekly,* December 18, 1948, 2413.

84. Henry E. Schultz, "Censorship or Self-Regulation," *Journal of Educational Sociology* 23, no. 4 (December 1949): 216–217.

85. "Clean-Up Started by Comic Books as Editors Adopt Self-Policing Plan," *New York Times,* July 2, 1948, 23.

86. "Purified Comics," *Newsweek,* July 12, 1948, 56; "Code for the Comics: Comic-Book Publishers' Cleanup Campaign," *Time,* July 12, 1948, 62.

87. Smith, "Publishers Improve Comic Books," 1649–1653.

88. "Modern Comics," 50.

89. U.S. Senate, Subcommittee to Investigate Juvenile Delinquency in the United States, *Juvenile Delinquency (Comic Books),* 83rd Congress, 2nd session, April 21, 22 and June 4, 1954, 69–79.

90. "Outlawed," *Time,* December 19, 1949, 33–34.

91. Steve Mitchell, "The Red-Hot Thrill: The Comic Book Crisis of 1948, part 2," *Comics Buyer's Guide,* June 28, 1985, 32; Edward L. Feder, *Comic Book Regulation, 1955 Legislative Problems No. 2, Bureau of Public Administration* (Berkeley: University of California Press, 1955), 21.

92. Mitchell, "Red-Hot Thrill," 32.

93. Nyberg, *Seal of Approval,* 41; Feder, *Comic Book Regulation,* 19–22.

94. Feder, *Comic Book Regulation,* 23.

95. Walter Gellhorn, "Restraints on Book Reading," in *The First Freedom: Liberty and Justice in the World of Books and Reading,* ed. R. B. Downs (Chicago: American Library Association, 1960), 30.

96. Katherine Clifford, "Common Sense about Comics," *Parents Magazine,* October 1948, 30.

97. Dorothy Barclay, "Comic Books and Television," *New York Times,* March 5, 1950, 180.

98. "Comic Book Censorship," *New York Times,* February 25, 1949, 22.

99. "Personal and Otherwise," *Harper's Magazine,* July 1951, 8.

100. Josette Frank, "Some Questions and Answers for Teachers and Parents," *Journal of Educational Sociology* 24, no. 4 (December 1949): 206–214.

101. Harvey Zorbaugh, "What Adults Think of Comics as Reading for Children," *Journal of Educational Sociology* 24, no. 4 (December 1949): 235.

102. Schultz, "Censorship or Self Regulation," 219.

103. Frederic M. Thrasher, "The Comics and Delinquency: Cause or Scapegoat," *Journal of Educational Sociology* 23, no. 4 (December 1949): 205.

104. "Parents are Warned Not to Blame Comic Books for Juvenile Delinquency," *New York Times,* October 7, 1948, 31.

105. "Comics, as Evils, Called Overrated," *New York Times,* February 20, 1949, 31.

106. "Comic-Book Readers are Just Aping Elders," *New York Times*, December 28, 1949, 31.

107. "Comic Book Bill Assailed," *New York Times*, March 11, 1949, 23.

108. "State Laws to Censor Comics Protested by Publishers," *Publishers Weekly*, March 12, 1949, 1243–1244.

109. Beaty, *Fredric Wertham*, 124.

110. "Walden, N.Y., Dealers Ban Comics on Crime," *New York Times*, December 15, 1952, 27; "Crime Comics Ban Hailed," *New York Times*, December 16, 1952, 15; "2 Youths Arrested in Grocers Death," *New York Times*, November 23, 1952, 49; "Crime of Boy Linked to Lurid Magazines," *New York Times*, December 9, 1952; "Comic Book Ban Fought," *New York Times*, December 28, 1953, 9.

111. "Crime and the Comics," *New York Times*, November 14, 1950, 30.

112. David Park, "The Kefauver Comic Book Hearings as Show Trial: Decency, Authority and the Dominated Expert," *Cultural Studies* 16, no. 2 (2002): 259–288.

113. U.S. Senate, *Juvenile Delinquency (Comic Books)*, 53.

114. Nyberg, *Seal of Approval*, 56–59; U.S. Senate, *Juvenile Delinquency (Comic Books)*, 4–10.

115. Nyberg, *Seal of Approval*, 75.

116. U.S. Senate, *Juvenile Delinquency (Comic Books)*, 75.

117. Ibid., 197, 199.

118. Fredric Wertham, *Seduction of the Innocent* (New York: Rinehart, 1954), 125.

119. Beaty, *Fredric Wertham*, 148–150.

120. "Wertham, Fredric. Seduction of the Innocent," *Book Review Digest* (1954): 940.

121. Ibid., 939.

122. "Scary Comics are Scared," *America*, September 25, 1954, 606.

123. Myrtle H. Gourley, "A Mother's Report on Comic Books," *National Parent-Teacher*, December 1954, 27, 29.

124. Feder, *Comic Book Regulation*, 22–52.

125. Ibid., 12.

126. "Acts on Sale of Comics," *New York Times*, June 4, 1954, 26; "Comic Books Attacked," *New York Times*, August 26, 1954, 25; "Drive on Lewd Books Backed," *New York Times*, August 30, 1954, 6; "Druggists to Curb Comics," *New York Times*, October 1, 1954, 21; "Jersey School Unit Urges 'Comics' Curb," *New York Times*, October 23, 1954, 17; "Women's Clubs Push Battle on Crime Comics," *New York Times*, November 25, 1954, 32.

127. Ward More, "Nietzsche in the Nursery," *Nation*, May 15, 1954, 427.

128. "The Monitor (1954)" in Feder, *Comic Book Regulation*, 11.

129. "Women's Clubs Push," 32.

130. "Magistrate is Made Comics 'Czar,'" *New York Times*, September 17, 1954, 1, 25.

131. "'New' Comic Books to be Out in Week," *New York Times*, December 29, 1954, 8; Office of the Code Authority, "Code for the Comics Magazine Industry," 1954.

132. Nyberg, *Seal of Approval*, 111–112.

133. "Horror on the Newsstands," *Time*, September 27, 1954, 77.

134. Mort Weisinger, "How They're Cleaning Up the Comic Books," *Better Homes and Gardens*, March 1955, 58–61.

135. Fredric Wertham, "Reading for the Innocent," *Wilson Library Bulletin,* April 1955, 613; Fredric Wertham, "It's Still Murder," *Saturday Review of Literature,* April 9, 1955, 48; "Horror Comics (Contd.)," *Time,* May 16, 1955, 50; "Vote at 18 Fought by Women's Club," *New York Times,* May 26, 1955, 21; "Comic Book Curbs Grow," *New York Times,* July 11, 1955, 24; Jesse L. Murrell, "Are Comics Better or Worse," *Parents Magazine,* August 1955, 48; Ruth A. Inglis, "The Comic Book Problem," *American Mercury,* August 1955, 121.

136. T. E. Murphy, "Progress in Cleaning Up the Comics," *Reader's Digest,* February 1956, 105.

137. Charles F. Wheeler, "Annual Rating of Comic Magazines," *Parents Magazine,* July 1956, 48.

138. Margaret Hickey, "Mothers Enforce Cleanup of Comics," *Ladies' Home Journal,* January 1957,122.

139. Nyberg, *Seal of Approval,* 136.

140. Ibid., 132–134.

141. Nyberg, *Seal of Approval,* 125–126; U.S. Senate, *Juvenile Delinquency and Comic Books,* 45; Goulart, *Great American Comic Books,* 219.

142. Benton, *Comic Book in America,* 53–58.

143. Peter Bart, "Advertising: Superman Faces New Hurdles," *New York Times,* September 23, 1962, 166.

144. Goulart, "The Shop System II," 81.

145. "Benefits are Noted in Comic Book Code," *New York Times,* April 19, 1959, W13.

146. U.S. Senate, *Juvenile Delinquency and Comic Books,* 3; Feder, *Comic Book Regulation,* 1.

147. "Infantino," *Comics Journal* 191 (November 1996): 65.

148. Eisner, *Shop Talk,* 12–15.

CHAPTER 3

1. Bourdieu, *Rules of Art.*

2. Bart, "Advertising: Superman Faces New Hurdles," 166.

3. Ibid.

4. Benton, *Comic Book in America,* 109–111.

5. Bart, "Advertising: Superman Faces New Hurdles," 166.

6. Daniels, *Five Fabulous Decades,* 80–81.

7. Saul Braun, "Shazam! Here Comes Captain Relevant," *New York Times,* May 2, 1971, SM41–43.

8. Bradford W. Wright, *Comic Book Nation,* 184–185, 187–199.

9. Frank Miller, "The Price," *Starlog Presents Comics Scene* (May 1982): 37.

10. Bill Schelly, *The Golden Age of Comic Fandom* (Seattle: Hamster Press, 1999), 82.

11. Ronin Ro, *Tales to Astonish: Jack Kirby, Stan Lee, and the American Comic Book Revolution* (New York: Bloomsbury, 2004), 114–116.

12. Ibid.

13. "Turned-On Generation Rejects Adult's Inhibitions," *New York Times,* January 11, 1967, 31.

14. Daniels, *Five Fabulous Decades*, 105.

15. Charlton in particular adopted this strategy wholeheartedly with a stock of superheroes like Mercury Man, Blue Beetle, Captain Atom, Nightshade, Thunderbolt, Peacemaker, Judomaster, and Question.

16. "Look! All Over! It's Esthetic . . . It's Business . . . It's Supersuccess!" *New York Times,* March 29, 1966, 33.

17. Goulart, *Great American Comic Books,* 261.

18. Benton, *Comic Book in America,* 69; John Jackson, "The Sixties," *The Comics Chronicle,* http://www.comichron.com (accessed August 31, 2007).

19. "Look! All Over!" 33.

20. Betty Rollin, "Is it Pop? Is it Camp? Is it Junk?" *Look,* March 22, 1966, 114.

21. "Look! All Over!" 33.

22. Rollin, "Is it Pop?" 114.

23. Braun, "Shazam! Here Comes Captain Relevant," SM32.

24. Benton, *Comic Book in America,* 69–70.

25. Jackson, "The Sixties."

26. Benton, *Comic Book in America,* 74.

27. Daniels, *Five Fabulous Decades,* 139.

28. Braun, "Shazam! Here Comes Captain Relevant," SM36.

29. Wright, *Comic Book Nation,* 229–245.

30. Will Jacobs and Gerard Jones, *The Comic Book Heroes: From the Silver Age to the Present* (New York: Crown, 1985), 157–160.

31. John A. Lent, ed., *Pulp Demons: International Dimensions of the Postwar Anti-Comics Campaign* (Teaneck, NJ: Farleigh Dickinson University Press, 1999), 272–276.

32. Amy Kiste Nyberg, "Cracking the Code: The Liberalization of the Comics Code Authority," *Comic Book Artist* 1 (Spring 1998): 52.

33. Braun, "Shazam! Here Comes Captain Relevant," 32, 36.

34. "The Comics on the Couch," *Time,* December 13, 1971, 70.

35. Jacobs and Jones, *The Comic Book Heroes,* 161.

36. Goulart, *Great American Comic Books,* 291–294.

37. Daniels, *Five Fabulous Decades,* 158.

38. "Lovely and Wise Heroine Summoned to Help the Feminist Cause," *New York Times,* October 19, 1972, 49.

39. "Superwomen Fight Back!" *Newsweek,* March 20, 1978, 75.

40. Old horror titles included *House of Mystery* (1951), *House of Secrets* (1956), *The Witching Hour* (1969), *Ghostly Tales* (1966), and *Ghost Manor* (1968).

41. Other new horror titles included *Chamber of Chills* (1972), *Tomb of Dracula* (1972), *Monster of Frankenstein* (1973), *Vault of Evil* (1973), *Tales of Zombie* (1973), *Forbidden Tales of Dark Mansion* (1972), *Weird Mystery Tales* (1972), *Haunted* (1971), *Midnight Tales* (1972), and *Richie Rich Vaults of Mystery* (1974).

42. Benton, *Comic Book in America,* 77.

43. Ibid., 77–78.

44. "The DC Explosion," *Mediascene* (May/June 1978): 29; Daniels, *Five Fabulous Decades,* 173; John Workman, "The Comic Book Crisis and What Can Be Done," *The Comic Book Crisis, Comics Journal Special* (October 1997): 6.

45. Daniels, *Five Fabulous Decades,* 173.

46. Benton, *Comic Book in America*, 79.

47. "DC Explosion," 29.

48. "DC Explosion," 29; David R. Black, "The DC Implosion," *Fanzing: The DC Comics Fan Site*, http://www.monitorduty.com/mag/fanzing27/feature1 (accessed October 2, 2007); Benton, *Comic Book in America*, 80.

49. "Superheroes' Creators Wrangle," *New York Times*, October 13, 1979, 25.

50. Robert L. Beerbohm, "Secret Origins of the Direct Market: Part One," *Comic Book Artist* 6 (Fall 1999): 85, 87; Workman, "The Comic Book Crisis," 3–4; Michael Dean, "Fine Young Cannibals," *Comics Journal* 277 (July 2006): 49–50.

51. Beerbohm, "Secret Origins of the Direct Market: Part One," 80–88; Workman, "The Comic Book Crisis," 4.

52. Beerbohm, "Secret Origins of the Direct Market: Part One," 82; Dean, "Fine Young Cannibals," 50; "Director Comments," in *Comic Book Artist Collection, Volume 1*, ed. John B. Cooke (Raleigh, NC: TwoMorrows, 2000), 8–16.

53. Dean, "Fine Young Cannibals," 49.

54. Robbins, *From Girls to Grrrlz*, 77.

55. Patrick Parsons, "Batman and his Audience: The Dialectic of Culture," in *The Many Lives of the Batman: Critical Approaches to a Superhero and his Media*, ed. Roberta E. Pearson and William Uricchio (New York: Routledge, 1999), 66–89.

56. Workman, "The Comic Book Crisis," 4.

57. "Superheroes' Creators Wrangle," 26.

58. "The Marketing of Superman and His Paraphernalia," *New York Times*, June 21, 1981, 50.

59. "Turning Superheroes into Super Sales," *New York Times*, January 6, 1985, F6.

60. "Superheroes' Creators Wrangle," 25; Jacobs and Jones, *Comic Book Heroes*, 209–225.

61. Mark James Estren, *A History of Underground Comics*, rev. ed. (1974; repr., Berkeley, CA: Ronin Publishing, 1987), 35; Jay Lynch, "The First Amendment was Easier Then," in *The Official Underground and Newave Comix Price Guide*, ed. Jay Kennedy (Cambridge, MA: Boatner Norton Press, 1982), 17.

62. Lynch, "The First Amendment," 17.

63. Stanley Wiater and Stephen R. Bissette, *Comic Book Rebels: Conversations with the Creators of the New Comics* (New York: Donald I. Fine, 1993), 36.

64. Beerbohm, "Secret Origins of the Direct Market: Part One," 89.

65. Estren, *History of Underground Comics*, 49.

66. Robert J. Glessing, *The Underground Press in America* (Bloomington: Indiana University Press, 1970); Laurence Leamer, *The Paper Revolutionaries* (New York: Simon and Schuster, 1972); David Armstrong, *A Trumpet to Arms: Alternative Media in America* (Boston: Houghton Mifflin, 1981).

67. "Student Activists: Free Form Revolutionaries," *Fortune*, January 1969, 108.

68. Patrick Rosenkranz, *Rebel Visions: The Underground Comix Revolution, 1963–1975* (Seattle: Fantagraphics Books, 2002), 39–65; Dez Skinn, *Comix: The Underground Revolution* (New York: Thunder's Mouth Press, 2004), 19–21.

69. R. C. Harvey, "Zippy and Griffy," *Cartoonist Profiles* 101 (March 1994): 37–38.

70. "Pioneers of Comix Panel," *Comics Journal* 251 (March 2003): 119.

71. Estren, *History of Underground Comics*, 250–256.

72. Gary Arlington, "A Recollection," in *The Official Underground and Newave Comix Price Guide*, ed. Jay Kennedy (Cambridge, MA: Boatner Norton Press, 1982), 35.

73. Wiater and Bissette, *Comic Book Rebels*, 37.

74. Rosenkranz, *Rebel Visions*, 4, 171; "Jay Lynch" in *The New Comics*, ed. Gary Groth and Robert Fiore (New York: Berkeley Books, 1988), 115.

75. Denis Kitchen, "The Formation of Kitchen Sink and Krupp Comics," in *The Official Underground and Newave Comix Price Guide*, ed. Jay Kennedy (Cambridge, MA: Boatner Norton Press, 1982), 23.

76. "The Kitchen Sink," *Comixscene* 2 (January/February 1973): 20–21.

77. Rosenkranz, *Rebel Visions*, 185.

78. Thomas Maremaa, "Who is this Crumb?" *New York Times*, October 1, 1972, SM70.

79. "Lifeboat: Art Spiegelman and Arcade, the Comics Revue," *Comic Book Artist* 2, no. 1 (July 2003): 72.

80. "The Kitchen Sink," 21.

81. Ibid.

82. Patrick Rosenkranz, "Underground Comix Publishers," *Comics Journal* 264 (November/December 2004): 105–124.

83. Estren, *History of Underground Comics*, 249–256.

84. Gary Griffith, "Truckin' Along with R. Crumb, or Something," *Cleveland Magazine* (July 1972) in *R. Crumb Conversations*, ed. D. K. Holm (Jackson: University of Mississippi Press, 2004), 11–12.

85. Maremaa, "Who is this Crumb?" 12–13.

86. Ibid., SM68.

87. "Gilbert Shelton, Fred Todd, and Ron Baumgart" in *The New Comics*, ed. Gary Groth and Robert Fiore (New York: Berkeley Books, 1988), 130.

88. "Manuel 'Spain' Rodriguez," in *The New Comics*, ed. Gary Groth and Robert Fiore (New York: Berkeley Books, 1988), 139.

89. On general politics of comix see Estren, *History of Underground Comics*, 154–205.

90. Estren, *History of Underground Comics*, 154.

91. Ron Turner, "The Art Form that Wouldn't Die," in *The Official Underground and Newave Comix Price Guide*, ed. Jay Kennedy (Cambridge, MA: Boatner Norton Press, 1982), 33.

92. Skinn, *Comix*, 90–100; Estren, *History of Underground Comics*, 206–229.

93. Estren, *History of Underground Comics*, 133–134.

94. Chin Lyvely and Joyce Farmer, "Women's Underground Comix," in *The Official Underground and Newave Comix Price Guide*, ed. Jay Kennedy (Cambridge, MA: Boatner Norton Press, 1982), 28.

95. Wiater and Bissette, *Comic Book Rebels*, 63.

96. Trina Robbins, *A Century of Women Cartoonists* (Northampton, MA: Kitchen Sink Press, 1993), 134–136.

97. Lyvely and Farmer, "Women's Underground Comix," 28.

98. Robbins, *From Girls to Grrrlz*, 89–100; Lyvely and Farmer, "Women's Underground Comix," 29.

99. Diane Noomin, *Twisted Sisters: A Collection of Bad Girl Art* (New York: Penguin Books, 1991), 7.

100. "Pioneers of Comix Panel," 117.

101. "Manuel 'Spain' Rodriguez," in *The New Comics*, ed. Gary Groth and Robert Fiore (New York: Berkeley Books, 1988), 142.

102. Joni Maya Cherbo, "Pop Art: Ugly Duckling to Swan," in *Outsider Art: Contesting Boundaries in Contemporary Culture,* eds. Vera L. Zolberg and Joni Maya Cherbo (Cambridge: Cambridge University Press, 1997), 85–90.

103. Joe Schenkman, "Rat Roots," in *The Official Underground and Newave Comix Price Guide,* ed. Jay Kennedy (Cambridge, MA: Boatner Norton Press, 1982), 25.

104. "Manuel 'Spain' Rodriguez," in *The New Comics*, ed. Gary Groth and Robert Fiore (New York: Berkeley Books, 1988), 143; "Pioneers of Comix Panel," 117.

105. Richard Gilman, "There's a Wave of Pornography, Obscenity, Sexual Expression," *New York Times,* September 8, 1968, SM36.

106. Estren, *History of Underground Comics,* 230–231; "2 Bookstore Clerks Found Guilty in Obscenity Case," *New York Times,* October 29, 1970, 46; "Burger Opinions Say Local Standards on Prurience Apply," *New York Times,* June 22, 1973, 1.

107. Skinn, *Comix,* 145; "Busted: the Story of *Tits and Clits #1,*" in *What Right? Graphic Interpretations Against Censorship,* ed. Robin Fisher (Vancouver, BC: Arsenal Pulp Press, 2002), 16–20.

108. "Comix Book: A Marvel Oddity," *Comic Book Artist* 7 (February/March 2000): 102–103.

109. "Smut, Variously Defined, Is Booming Nationwide," *New York Times,* May 19, 1974, 55.

110. "Comix Book: A Marvel Oddity," 103.

111. Jay Kennedy, "Introduction: Comix, Not Comics," in *The Official Underground and Newave Comix Price Guide,* ed. Jay Kennedy (Cambridge, MA: Boatner Norton Press, 1982), 14, 16; Beerbohm, "Secret Origins of the Direct Market: Part Two," *Comic Book Artist* 7 (March 2000): 120.

112. Beerbohm, "Secret Origins of the Direct Market: Part Two," 120–121; "Comix Book: A Marvel Oddity," 103.

113. Art Spiegelman and Françoise Mouly, "Raw Nerves," in *Read Yourself Raw,* ed. Art Spiegelman and Françoise Mouly (New York: Pantheon Books, 1987), 1.

114. Bourdieu, *Rules of Art.*

CHAPTER 4

1. Bill Schelly, *Golden Age of Comic Fandom* (Seattle: Hamster Press, 1999), 20–25.

2. Schelly, "So You Want to Collect Comics Fanzines?" *Alter Ego* 3, no. 5 (Summer 2000): 39–45.

3. Schelly, *Golden Age of Comic Fandom,* 130–132, 137–142.

4. David Zinman, "Comicdom's Cult of Collectors," *Newsday* (November 4, 1965) in Schelly, *Golden Age of Comic Fandom,* 92.

5. "Comic Books Get Star Billing at Convention Here," *New York Times,* July 6, 1968, 18.

6. Schelly, *Golden Age of Comic Fandom,* 116–128.

7. "Comic Mania," *Newsweek,* September 4, 1972, 75.

8. "Old Comic Books Soar in Value," *New York Times,* December 6, 1964, 141.

9. "Shazam! Vintage Comics Prices Up, Up and Away," *New York Times,* January 30, 1965, 31.

10. Zinman, "Comicdom's Cult of Collectors," 92.

11. "Comicon," *The New Yorker,* August 21, 1965, 23.

12. Zinman, "Comicdom's Cult of Collectors," 92.

13. "Superfans and Batmaniacs," *Newsweek,* February 15, 1965, 89.

14. "Comic Mania," 75.

15. "Comic Books Can Prove Super Investment," *New York Times,* January 1, 1973, 22.

16. "Comic Mania," 75.

17. Shel Dorf, "The Detroit Triple Fan Fair," *Alter Ego* 3, no. 31 (December 2003): 44.

18. Schelly, "What's So Great about Comic Art?" *Alter Ego* 3, no. 10 (September 2001): 44.

19. "The Golden Age of Comic Fandom Panel," *Alter Ego* 3, no. 9 (July 2001): 48.

20. "Readers Write," *Alter Ego* 5 (1962) in *Alter Ego: The Best of the Legendary Comics Fanzine,* ed. Roy Thomas and Bill Schelly (Seattle: Hamster Press, 1997), 67.

21. Frank Miller, "The Price," *Comics Scene* 3 (May 1982): 37.

22. Schelly, *Golden Age of Comic Fandom,* 158.

23. Don Thompson and Maggie Thompson, *Comic Book Superstars* (Iola, WI: Krause Publications, 1993). The shift to more comic book artists attending college is evident in this book's long list of short biographies of comic book artists active in the comic book field.

24. Jon B. Cooke,"Rich Buckler Breaks Out!" *Comic Book Artist* 7 (March 2000): 85.

25. Jon B. Cooke, "The Blue-Jean Generation," *Comic Book Artist* 7 (February/ March 2000): 97.

26. "The Golden Age of Comic Fandom Panel," 47; Schelly, *Golden Age of Comic Fandom,* 105.

27. Beerbohm, "Secret Origins of the Direct Market, Part One," 84.

28. Schelly, *Golden Age of Comic Fandom,* 145–146.

29. Beerbohm, "Secret Origins of the Direct Market: Part One," 84–85.

30. Ibid.

31. Dean, "Fine Young Cannibals," 50–51.

32. Beerbohm, "Secret Origins of the Direct Market: Part Two," *Comic Book Artist* 7 (February/March 2000): 119; Dean, "Fine Young Cannibals," 51.

33. "The Direct Sales Boom," *Comics Journal* 64 (July 1981): 7.

34. Dean, "Fine Young Cannibals," 54.

35. Goulart, *Great American Comic Books,* 297–298; Daniels, *Five Fabulous Decades,* 187; Dean, "Fine Young Cannibals," 57.

36. Marc Patten, "It's a Four-Color World, We Just Read It, Part 2," *Comics Buyer's Guide* 1642 (June 2008): 94–98.

37. Goulart, *Great American Comic Books,* 300–301; Benton, *Comic Book in America,* 81–84.

38. Ken Jones, "This Business of Comics: An Interview with Mark Evanier," *Comics Journal* 112 (October 1986): 64–65.

39. Ken Bruzenak, "Guilding the Comics," *Mediascene* 31 (May/June 1978): 14–15.

40. Michael Dean, "Collective Inaction: The Comics Community Tries and Tries Again to Get it Together," *Comics Journal* 262 (August/September 2004): 17–19.

41. Bruzenak, "Guilding the Comics," 14.

42. Dean, "Collective Inaction," 19–21; Gary Groth, "The Comics Guild," *Comics Journal* 42 (October 1978): 15–17.

43. Dean, "Fine Young Cannibals," 57.

44. Miller, "The Price," 40.

45. "Comics Contracts: What the Various Companies Offer," *Comics Journal* 113 (December 1986): 19–23.

46. Pustz, *Comic Book Culture*.

47. "The Comics Industry: 1989," *Comics Buyer's Guide*, March 31, 1989, 58; "Seriously, We're No Weirdos," *Arkansas Democrat-Gazette*, September 5, 1995, 1D.

48. "Comics Industry: 1989," 58.

49. Julie Stuempfig, "State of the Industry," in *Comics Buyer's Guide 1994 Annual*, eds. Don Thompson and Maggie Thompson (Iola, WI: Krause Publications, 1993), 35.

50. Parsons, "Batman and his Audience: The Dialectic of Culture," 77.

51. "Drawing on History," *Esquire*, May 1985, 25; Gary Groth, "Comics: The New Culture of Illiteracy," *Comics Journal* 152 (August 1992): 4.

52. "Whoosh! New Superheroes Liberate the Old-Boy Network," *New York Times*, August 4, 1993, C1.

53. "Comic Book Wizard," *Inside Media*, January 20, 1993, 43; "Pow! How Comic Magazines are Riding High," *Advertising Age*, March 8, 1993, 33.

54. *Comic Reader* (1963) and *Interlac* (1976) were fanzines from early fandom lasting into the 1980s. Other small fanzines included *Comix World* (1973), *Kraft's Comics Interviews* (1983), *Comic Culture* (1993), *Comic Effect* (1993), *Destroy All Comics* (1994), *Crash the Quarterly Comic Book Review* (1994), *Jack Kirby Collector* (1994), *Juxtabox* (1994), and *Subliminal Tattoos* (1994).

55. Other book histories include *The Comic Book Heroes: From the Silver Age to the Present* (1985), *Great History of Comic Books* (1986), *Great Comic Book Artists* (1986), *The Comic Book Makers* (1990), *A Century of Women Cartoonists* (1993), and *The Comic Book* (1994).

56. Other books on the comics business and the craft of mainstream comic art include *How to Draw Comic Book Women* (1991), *How to Draw Your Own Comic Book* (1994), *How to Draw Comic Book Heroes and Villains* (1995), *A Writer's Guide to the Business of Comics* (1995), *A Guide to the Comic Book Business* (1997), *How to Self-Publish Your Own Comic Book* (1997), and *The Business of Comics* (1998).

57. Pustz, *Comic Book Culture*, 188–198; Jeffrey A. Brown, *Black Superheroes, Milestone Comics, and Their Fans* (Jackson: University of Mississippi Press, 2001), 85–86.

58. Mariane S. Hopkins, ed., *Fandom Directory #12* (Springfield, VA: Fandata Publications, 1990); Mariane S. Hopkins, ed., *Fandom Directory #19* (Springfield, VA: Fandata Publications, 2000).

59. *30 Anniversary Program Book*, San Diego Comic-Con, 1999.

60. Advertisement, *Wizard* 15 (November 1992), 66.

61. Hopkins, *Fandom Directory #12*, 76–105; Hopkins, *Fandom Directory #19*, 85–137.

62. "Seriously, We're No Weirdos," 1D.

63. "Zowie! 50,000 Comic Book Fans Gather," *Boston Globe*, July 22, 2001, A6.

64. Jenkins, *Textual Poachers*, 9–24.

65. "Dear Wizard," *Wizard* 36 (August 1994): 12.

66. "Biff! Pow! Comic Books Make a Comeback," *BusinessWeek*, September 2, 1985, 59.

67. "Comics Aren't Just for Kids," *St. Petersburg Times*, July 7, 1987, 1D.

68. "Grown-ups Gather at the Comic Book Stand," *New York Times*, September 30, 1987, A1.

69. Joe Queenan, "Drawing on the Dark Side," *New York Times*, April 30, 1989, 79.

70. Sabin, *Comics, Comix and Graphic Novels*, 160.

71. Gelder, *Popular Fiction*, 11–17.

72. Benjamin DeMott, "Darkness in the Mall," *Psychology Today* (February 1984): 48.

73. Mark A. Perigard, "Death of the Superheroes," *Newsweek*, November 11, 1985, 15.

74. "Novel Comics: The American Comic Book is Growing Up," *St. Petersburg Times*, January 7, 1987, 3D.

75. "What's New in the Comic Book Business," *New York Times*, January 31, 1988, A1.

76. "DC Launches Vertigo Line," *Comics Journal* 152 (August 1992): 13.

77. "Violent Comics Draw Unfavorable Media Spotlight," *Comics Journal* 130 (July 1989): 5–10.

78. "Drawing on the Dark Side," 86.

79. "Out of the Ghetto, Into the Mainstream," *New York Times*, January 31, 1988, A1.

80. Gary Groth, "Mainstream Comics Have, At Best, Tenuous Virtues," *Comics Journal* 152 (August 1992): 92.

81. Kim Thompson, "All They Have to Lose is a Cog in a Wheel," *Comics Journal* 152 (August 1992): 74.

82. Wiater and Bissette, *Comic Book Rebels*, 183.

83. Nick Hasted, "I'd Rather Write Broadway Musicals: Neil Gaiman and Comics, 1996," *Comics Journal* 188 (July 1996): 120–122.

84. "Childhood Heroes are Big Business for Comic Collectors," *Globe and Mail*, June 7, 1986, D22.

85. "Professor Finds Comic Books Culturally Significant," *Oregonian*, December 29, 1990, E10; "From Archie to Spider to Anne," *New York Times*, February 17, 1991, F5; "Racking Up Sales," *Washington Post*, August 12, 1991, F8; "Comic Book Convention No Laughing Matter," *Boston Globe*, November 4, 1991, 30; "Superman Sells Faster Than . . ." *USA Today*, November 20, 1992; "D.C. Comics: KRAANG! KRAANG . . ." *Washington Post*, June 11, 1993, N7; "For Comic Heroes, the Past Mutates," *New York Times*, July 24, 1994, 41.

86. M. Clark Humphrey, "Records for Marvel and Dark Horse," *Comics Journal* 137 (September 1990): 20; "Kaboom! Dark Horse Vanquishes Foes," *Business Journal-*

Portland, September 23, 1991, 1; "Comic Publisher Marvels over New Talent," *Los Angeles Business Journal,* February 24, 1992, 10; Valerie Potter, "Malibu Moves Ahead of DC in Comics Market," *Comics Journal* 152 (August 1992): 7; "Fast Movers: Comic Book Merger Makes Malibu Comics a Video Superhero," *California Business,* October 1992, 12.

87. William Christensen and Mark Seifert, "The Wizard's Crystal Ball," *Wizard* 15 (November 1992): 79.

88. Rob Samsel, "The Future of the Comic Book Market Place," *Wizard* 29 (January 1994): 105.

89. "D.C. Comics: KRAANG! KRAANG," N7.

90. "Comics Retailers Survive by Diversifying," *Arkansas Democrat-Gazette* (Knight Ridder Byline), October 26, 1998, D6.

91. Annie Gowen, "Frustrated Fans Zap Comics Sales," *Business and Industry* 4, no. 3 (April 1996): 4.

92. "Fans, Publishers Fear Death of an Icon," *Denver Post,* December 8, 1996, 1; "Dark Horse Rising," *Oregonian,* February 2, 1997, E01; "Comics Retailers Survive by Diversifying," *Arkansas Democrat Gazette,* October 26, 1998, D6; "Rescuing the Heroes," *New York Times,* April 16, 2001, 18; "Comics Still Flying High," *Washington Times,* February 6, 2002, A02.

93. "Bam! Kapow! Blasting the Code," *Newsweek,* May 28, 2001, 10.

94. Bourdieu, *The Rules of Art.*

CHAPTER 5

1. Bourdieu, *Rules of Art.*

2. Kennedy, "Introduction: Comix, Not Comics," 14–15.

3. G. Erling, "Alternative Comix," in *The Official Underground and Newave Comix Price Guide,* ed. Jay Kennedy (Cambridge, MA: Boatner Norton Press, 1982), 36–38.

4. Dale Luciano, "Newave Comics Survey," *Comics Journal* 96 (March 1985): 52–53.

5. Dave Sim, "A Declaration of Independence," *Comics Journal* 105 (February 1986): 90.

6. Tom Spurgeon, "You Have No Power. You Just Don't Have Any Power: The State of Self-Publishing—1996," *Comics Journal* 188 (July 1996): 50.

7. "Turning Teenage Mutant Ninja Turtles into a Monster Hit," *New York Times,* December 25, 1988, F6; "TMNT Origin Story," *Official Teenage Mutant Ninja Turtle Web Site,* http://www.ninjaturtles.com/origin/origin.htm (accessed October 31, 2007).

8. Dave Sim, "Notes From the President," *Cerebus* 170 (May 1993): 1.

9. "Gary Reed's Guide to Self-Publishing (1993) in *Cerebus* 171 (June 1993), Artist's Info: Notes from the President Archive," *Cerebus Fangirlcom,* http://www.cerebusfangirl.com (accessed October 14, 2007).

10. "You Have No Power," 48; "History," *A Distant Soil,* http://www.adistantsoil.com (accessed November 2, 2007).

11. "Comic Book Onslaught," *Ottawa Citizen,* June 5, 1993, F1.

12. Gary Groth, "Can Alternatives Sell? And If So, How?" *Comics Journal* 141 (April 1991): 8.

13. M. Clark Humphrey, "Sexual Comics Increase; So Do Challenges," *Comics Journal* 137 (September 1990): 12–13.

14. Greg Stump,"The State of the Industry, 1996," *Comic Journal* 188 (July 1996): 34.

15. Gelder, *Popular Fiction,* 11–17.

16. Randy Reynaldo, "Reassessing Comics," *Comics Journal* 101 (August 1985): 89.

17. Gary Groth, "What the Direct Sales Market has Wrought Part Two," *Comics Journal* 85 (October 1983): 8.

18. Reynaldo, "Reassessing Comics," 89.

19. Pustz, *Comic Book Culture,* 66–109.

20. Groth, "Can Alternatives Sell," 7.

21. Wiater and Bissette, *Comic Book Rebels,* 107.

22. Susan Pierce, "Seriously, We're Not Weirdos," *Arkansas Democrat-Gazette,* September 5, 1995, 1D.

23. Will Eisner, *Comics and Sequential Art* (Tamarac, FL: Poorhouse Press, 1986), 5.

24. Scott McCloud, *Understanding Comics* (New York: Paradox Press, 1993), 211.

25. McCloud, *Reinventing Comics* (New York: Paradox Press, 2000), 3.

26. "The Maus that Roared," *Toronto Star,* October 11, 1986, G1.

27. Gary Groth, "Art Spiegelman," *Comics Journal* 180 (September 1995): 71, 62.

28. Kent Worcester, "Fireworks Display," *Comics Journal* 188 (July 1996): 118.

29. Ray Mescallado, "Drawing Distinctions," *Comics Journal* 188 (July 1996): 107.

30. Charles Hatfield, "The Current State of the Art?" *Comics Journal* 188 (July 1996): 105–106.

31. "The Comic Book Grows Up," *Christian Science Monitor,* December 28, 1988, 14.

32. Beth Levine, "Graphic Novels: The Latest Word in Illustrated Books," *Publishers Weekly,* May 22, 1987, 45, 47.

33. "Comic Books for Grown-Ups," *Adweek,* November 7, 1988, HP12.

34. Bart Bull, "Comics," *Spin,* August 1988, 41, 42–43.

35. Will Eisner, "Getting the Last Laugh: My Life in Comics," *New York Times,* January 14, 1990, BR1.

36. Gary Groth, "So Far, So Bad: The Schlockification of the Comics Market," *Comics Journal* 140 (February 1991): 7–8.

37. Paul Bennett, "Trading on Comics: The Art of Selling Comics and Graphic Novels," *Publishers Weekly,* August 17, 1998, 32–40.

38. "The 'Funnies' Have Grown Up. But are They Art? Comics Books are Winning New Respect," *U.S. News and World Report,* September 21, 1987, 69.

39. Ibid.

40. "What's New in the Comic Book Business," *New York Times,* January 31, 1988, A1; M. Clark Humphrey, "Sexual Comics Increase; So Do Challenges," *Comic Journal* 137 (September 1990): 13.

41. M. Clark Humphrey, "Police Crackdown in Toronto," *Comics Journal* 141 (April 1991): 18; "Censorship, Seizures, and Auctions," *Comics Journal* 157 (March 1993): 30–31.

42. Humphrey, "Sexual Comics Increase"; "Censorship, Seizures, and Auctions."

43. Mark Macdonald, "Introduction," in *What Right? Graphic Interpretations Against Censorship*, ed. Robin Fisher (Vancouver, BC: Arsenal Pulp Press, 2002), 3.

44. Tom De Haven, "Comics," *New York Times Book Review,* May 31, 1998, 9, 16.

45. Robbins, *From Girls to Grrrlz,* 125.

46. Trina Robbins, *The Great Women Cartoonists* (New York: Watson-Guptill Publications, 2001), 130.

47. Jordan Raphael, "We Never Had Any Illusions: Young Cartoonists Roundtable, Seattle," *Comics Journal* 188 (July 1996): 130.

48. T. M. Lowe, "Women Drawing the Deed, or: Another Unturned Stone," *Comics Journal* 237 (September 2001): 55.

49. Ibid., 52–53.

50. Robbins, *The Great Women Cartoonists,* 116–117.

51. Sherrie A. Inness, *Tough Girls: Women Warriors and Wonder Women in Popular Culture* (Philadelphia: University of Pennsylvania Press, 1999), 138–159.

52. Robbins, *The Great Women Cartoonists,* 102–105.

53. Raphael, "We Never Had Any Illusions," 129.

54. Deni Loubert, *How to Get Girls (Into Your Store): A Friends of Lulu Retailer Handbook* (Pasadena, CA: Friends of Lulu, 1997).

55. Ibid., 32.

56. "Dear Wizard," *Wizard* 39 (November 1994): 8.

57. The history of gay comics was especially helped by the "LGBT Comics Timeline," *The Gay League: The FAN Site for Gay Comic Readers and Creators!* http://www.gayleague.com/gay/timeline/index (accessed November 10, 2007).

58. "Homosexuality in Comics, Part III," *Comic Book Resources,* July 18, 2007, http://www.comicbookresources.com/news/newsitem.cgi?id=11190 (accessed July 19, 2007).

59. "Queer Eye for the Comics Gal and Guy," *Sequential Tart,* August 2004, http:www.sequentialtart.com/archive/aug04/rthigpen (accessed November 11, 2007).

60. Joe Palmer, "Looking Back at *Gay Comix #1,*" *The Gay League,* http://www.gay-league.com/forums/display.php?id=266 (accessed November 11, 2007).

61. Andy Mangels, "Out of the Closet and into the Comics—Gays in Comics: The Creations and the Creators, Part II," *Amazing Heroes* 144 (July 1, 1988): 62; Andy Mangels, "Out of the Closet and into the Comics—Gays in Comics: The Creations and the Creators, Part I," *Amazing Heroes* 143 (June 15, 1988): 39–54.

62. "Queer Eye for the Comics Gal and Guy."

63. Paige Alexis and Kevin Alexis, "Queer Year in Review," *Prism Comics* 5 (February 2007): 8–19; Andy Mangels, "A Brief History of Marvel's 2006 Gay Policies—In and Out," *The Gay League,* September 29, 2006, http://www.gayleague.com/forums/display.php?id=458 (accessed November 11, 2007); Joe Palmer, "The State of Gay," *The Gay League,* July 6, 2008, http://www.gayleague.com/forums/display.php?id=541 (accessed November 26, 2008).

64. Brown, *Black Superheroes, Milestone Comics,* 43–53.

65. Jeffrey Winbush, "The New Black Age of Comics," *Comics Journal* 160 (July 1993): 80.

66. Gary Groth, "Nabile Hage 'I Will Always Speak Out,'" *Comics Journal* 160 (July 1993): 41.

67. Tony Norman, "Sims Brothers," *Comics Journal* 160 (July 1993): 96.

68. Groth, "Nabile Hage," 42.

69. Brown, *Black Superheroes, Milestone Comics,* 53–54.

70. Veronica Byrd, "The Men Behind the Superheroes," *New York Times,* September 13, 1992, F8.

71. Tony Norman, "Milestone: 'This is a Beginning, Not a Fad,'" *Comics Journal* 160 (July 1993): 72.

72. Carolyn M. Brown, "Marketing a New Universe of Heroes," *Black Enterprise,* November 1994, 80.

73. Brown, *Black Superheroes, Milestone Comics,* 56.

74. "If It Ain't Broke . . . Fix It!" *Wizard* 38 (October 1994): 81.

75. "Straight (and Not) Out of the Comics," *New York Times,* May 28, 2006, 2/25.

76. Brad Mackay, "Hero Deficit: Comic Books in Decline," *Toronto Star,* March 18, 2007, http://www.thestar.com/printarticle/193167 (accessed November 10, 2007).

77. Mackay, "Hero Deficit."

78. Carole Sobocinski, "Building the Issue," *Comics Journal* 160 (July 1993): 5.

79. Gray, *Watching Race.*

80. Becker, *Gay TV.*

81. Pierre Bourdieu, *Photography: A Middle-brow Art* (Stanford, CA: Stanford University Press, 1990), 95–98.

CHAPTER 6

1. On the history of manga in Japan see Frederik Schodt, *Manga! Manga!* (Tokyo: Kodansha International, 1983) and Paul Gravett, *Manga: Sixty Years of Japanese Comics* (New York: HarperCollins, 2004).

2. Gravett, *Manga,* 14.

3. "Manga Sells Anime—And Vice Versa," *Publishers Weekly,* October 18, 2004, 30.

4. "Japan, a Superpower among Superheroes," *New York Times,* September 17, 1995, H32.

5. "Convention Schedule," *AnimeCons.com,* http:/www.animecons.com/events/calendar.shtml (accessed November 28, 2007).

6. "New Largest Event in North America," *Anime News Network* (December 22, 2003), http://www.animenewsnetwork.com/news/2003–12–22/new-largest-event-in-north-america (accessed November 30, 2007).

7. Calvin Reid, "Manga: Comics Japanese Style," *Publishers Weekly,* June 30, 1997, 50.

8. Douglas Wolk, "Manga, Anime Invade the U.S." *Publishers Weekly,* March 12, 2001, 35–36.

9. "How Manga Conquered the U.S." *Wired* 15.11 (November 2007) http://www.wired.com/images/pdf/wired_1511_magnaamerica.pdf (accessed November 28, 2007); Wolk, "Manga, Anime Invade the U.S."

10. Calvin Reid, "Asian Comics Delight U.S. Readers," *Publishers Weekly,* December 23, 2002, 26.

11. "U.S. Manga Sales Pegged at $100 Million," *Publishers Weekly,* February 9, 2004, 16.

12. Michael Dean, "2004—A Good Year to Get Out of the Manga Business?" *Comics Journal* 259 (April 2004): 5.

13. "Manga Bonanza," *Publishers Weekly,* December 6, 2004, 38–39.

14. Kai-Ming Cha, "Fans Mob Anime Expo 2007," *PW Comics Week* (July 3, 2007), http://www.publishersweekly.com/article/CA6457071.html (accessed December 4, 2007).

15. "Manga Releases Up 16% in 2007," *ICv2*, http:/www.icv2.com/articles/news/10034.html (accessed November 29, 2007); "Graphic Novels by the Numbers," *Publishers Weekly*, March 5, 2007, 9.

16. "American Association of Publishers 2006 S1 Report," *American Association of Publishers*, http:/www.publishers.org/main/PressCenter/documents/S12006FINAL.pdf (accessed November 30, 2007).

17. Dirk Deppey, "Opening Shot: She's Got Her Own Thing Now," *Comics Journal* 269 (July 2005): 10–13; "Manga for Girls," *New York Times*, September 18, 2006, 16L.

18. "Young Women Speak Manga-nese," *Edmonton Journal*, July 13, 2002, H3.

19. "Girl Power Fuels Manga Boom in U.S." *New York Times*, December 28, 2004, E1.

20. Gravett, *Manga*, 74–95.

21. "Four Mothers of Manga Gain American Fans with Expertise in a Variety of Visual Styles," *New York Times*, November 28, 2006, E5.

22. "The Year in Books 2003: Comics," *Publishers Weekly*, November 17, 2003, 27.

23. Calvin Reid, "Manga Is Here to Stay," *Publishers Weekly*, October 20, 2003, S6.

24. Reid, "Manga Is Here to Stay," S6.

25. Pustz, *Comic Book Culture*, 110–156.

26. "A Cause for Marvel: Rise of Films Based on Comic Books," *Los Angeles Times*, July 10, 2001, Calendar, 5/1.

27. "Are You on the List?" *License* (April 2005): 17–18.

28. "Wanted: Superheroes," *Forbes*, November 12, 2001, 120.

29. "Sin City Trades Take Off," *ICv2* (March 24, 2005), http://www.icv2.com/articles/news/6624.html (accessed October 15, 2007); "'V for Vendetta' Tops in Bookstores," *ICv2* (March 30, 2006), http://www.icv2.com/articles/news/8442.html (accessed November 30, 2007); "'300' Dominates Q1 Graphic Novel Sales," *ICv2* (June 1, 2007), http://www.icv2.com/articles/news/10676.html (accessed November 30, 2007).

30. Misha Davenport, "Pop Culture on Tap at Convention," *Chicago Sun-Times*, July 5, 2002, 16.

31. A. O. Scott, "Revenge of the Nerds," *New York Times*, May 8, 2005, 2A/1.

32. "Geek Revival," *Entertainment Weekly*, July 27, 2007, 9–10; "In a Packed San Diego, Entertainment Worlds Collide," *New York Times*, July 28, 2007, B7.

33. "Around Here, the Geeks Decide What's Cool," *San Diego Union-Tribune*, July 19, 2006, A1.

34. "Geek Revival," 10.

35. "Comic-Con: Where 'Nerd has Become Normal,'" *San Diego Union-Tribune*, July 30, 2007, 1D.

36. Manohla Dargis, "We're All Geeks Here," *New York Times*, August 1, 2007, http://www.nytimes.com/2007/08/01/movies/05dargis.html (accessed August 8, 2007).

37. Henry Jenkins, *Convergence Culture: Where Old and New Media Collide* (New York: New York University Press, 2006).

38. Heidi MacDonald, "Comics Publishers Look Ahead," *Publishers Weekly*, October 18, 2004, 24.

39. "U.S. Graphic Novel Market Hits $200M," *Publishers Weekly,* April 18, 2005, 15.

40. Douglas Wolk, "The Road to Fruition," *Publishers Weekly,* August 22, 2005, 30.

41. "With Help from Hollywood, Graphic Novels Gain Popularity," Associated Press, July 19, 2002.

42. "Graphic Novels Come of Age," *Sacramento Bee,* April 10, 2003, E1.

43. "From Pulp to Pulitzer: How the Underground Comic Found It's Way to the Mainstream," *Houston Chronicle,* August 29, 2004, Z6.

44. Charles McGrath, "Not Funnies," *New York Times Magazine,* July 11, 2004, 24–26.

45. Ann Elizabeth Moore, "Preface," in *The Best American Comics 2006,* ed. Harvey Pekar (New York: Houghton Mifflin, 2006), x.

46. "Top Selling Graphic Novels of 2004," *Publishers Weekly,* October 18, 2004, 24.

47. James Sturm, "Comics in the Classroom," *Chronicle of Higher Education,* April 5, 2002, B15.

48. "Schools Offering Comics Art Curriculum," *NACAE,* http://www.teaching-comics.org/curriculum.php (accessed November 20, 2007).

49. Douglas Wolk, "Comics: Not Just for Specialty Stores Anymore," *Publishers Weekly,* October 16, 2000, 38; Greg Cwiklik, "Chris Ware at the Museum of Contemporary Art in Chicago," *Comics Journal* 278 (Oct 2006): 186.

50. Ann Philbin and Jeremy Strick, "Director's Forward," in *Masters of American Comics,* eds. John Carlin, Paul Karasik and Brian Walker (New Haven, CT: Yale University Press, 2005), 10.

51. R. C. Harvey, "Masters of Comic Art," *Christian Science Monitor,* December 2, 2005, 11; "Masters of American Comics," *Comics Journal* 282 (April 2007): 178–185.

52. "Yale University Press Looks at Comics," *PW Comics Weekly* (March 20, 2006), http://www.publishersweekly.com/eNewsletter/CA6317276/2789.html (accessed November 30, 2007).

53. Tom Spurgeon, "An Interview with Todd Hignite," *The Comics Reporter* (July 23, 2006), http://www.comicsreporter.com/index.php/resources/interviews/5349 (accessed October 15, 2007).

54. Michael Dean, "New York Conjures a New Comic Art Museum," *Comics Journal* 242 (April 2002): 18–20.

55. "About MoCCA," *MoCCA,* http://www.moccany.org/about.html (accessed October 20, 2007).

56. "Dollar Revenue for Graphic Novels Now Higher than that of Comics," *Comics Journal* 282 (April 2007): 32; "Graphic Novel Sales Hit $330 Million in 2006," *PW Comics Week* (February 23, 2007), http://www.publishersweekly.com/article/CA6418995.html?nid=2789 (accessed December 10, 2007); "Graphic Novels by the Numbers."

57. "Trade Book Comics in Demand at Comic-Con," *Publishers Weekly,* August 12, 2002, 142.

58. James L. Thomas, *Cartoons and Comics in the Classroom* (Littleton, CO: Libraries Unlimited, 1983).

59. Keith R. A. DeCandido, "Picture This: Graphic Novels in Libraries," *Library Journal,* March 15, 1990, 50, 52; Gale W. Sherman and Bette D. Ammon, "Beyond Superman: The Boom in Trade Comics," *School Library Journal* (May 1993): 343.

60. DeCandido, "Picture This: Graphic Novels in Libraries," 51–52.

61. Michele Gorman, "What Teens Want," *School Library Journal* (August 2002): 42.

62. Stephen Weiner, "Beyond Superheroes: Comics Get Serious," *Library Journal,* February 1, 2002, 55.

63. Heidi McDonald, "The Year of the Graphic Novel," *Publishers Weekly,* December 23, 2002, 22.

64. "Libraries Become New Spot for Comics," *Chicago Daily Herald,* August 12, 2002, 1.

65. "Back to the Drawing Board," *Washington Post,* May 17, 2002, B01.

66. Judith Rosen, "Selling Graphic Novels to Retailers," *Publishers Weekly,* October 20, 2003, S2.

67. "Graphic Novels for (Really) Young Readers," *Library Journal,* March 2006, 56–61.

68. Philip Crawford and Stephen Weiner, *Using Graphic Novels in the Classroom: A Guide for Teachers and Librarians* (New York: Scholastic, 2005), 4.

69. Heidi MacDonald, "Graphic Novels Sales Hit $330 Million in 2006," *PW Comics Week* (February 23, 2007), http://www.publishersweekly.com/article/CA6418995.html (accessed December 10, 2007).

70. Other books on library collections and comic books in the classroom include *The 101 Best Graphic Novels* (2001), *Graphic Novels in Your Media Center: A Definitive Guide* (2004), *Graphic Novels: Everything You Need to Know* (2005), *Graphic Novels Now: Building, Managing and Marketing a Dynamic Collection* (2005), *Going Graphic: Comics at Work in the Multilingual Classroom* (2004), and *Getting Graphic: Using Graphic Novels to Promote Literacy with Preteens and Teens* (2004).

71. "Schools Turn to Comics as Trial Balloon," *Washington Post,* December 13, 2004, B01; Carol Simpson, "The Debate Over Graphic Books," *Library Media Connection* (February 2007): 6.

72. Crawford and Weiner, *Using Graphic Novels in the Classroom,* 5.

73. Gorman, "What Teens Want," 44.

74. "Libraries Developing Guidelines for Graphic Novels," *Publishers Weekly,* November 22, 2004, 12.

75. "Library Patrons Object to Some Graphic Novels," *Washington Post,* December 18, 2006, C03.

76. "Manga Tackled at NY Comic-Con," *Library Journal,* April 1, 2006, 20.

77. Calvin Reid, "Tokyopop Bows New Ratings," *Publishers Weekly,* February 19, 2007, 8.

78. "Librarians Out Front at Comic Con," *Library Journal,* April 1, 2007, 15.

79. "Where the Girls Are," *Publishers Weekly,* April 23, 2007, 25.

80. Bolter and Grusin, *Remediation.*

81. Martin Lister, Jon Dovey, Seth Giddings, Iain Grant, and Kieran Kelly, *New Media: A Critical Introduction* (New York: Routledge, 2003), 13–37.

82. John B Horrigan, *Online Communities: Networks that Nurture Long-Distant Relationships and Local Ties* (Washington, DC: Pew Internet and American Life Project, 2001).

83. Jonah Weiland, "Hot Seat," *Comic Book Resources* (2001), http://www.comicbookresources.com/columns/index.cgi?column=thehotseat&article=1242 (accessed

December 5, 2007); John Weiland, "CBR Celebrates 10 Years in Operation Today," *Comic Book Resources* (May 8, 2006), http://www.comicbookresources.com/news/newsitem.cgi?id=7278 (accessed December 5, 2007).

84. "About Newsarama," *Newsarama*, http://www.newsarama.com/NRamaHistory.html (accessed December 6, 2007).

85. *Grand Comic-Book Database*, http://www.comics.org/index.lasso (accessed December 6, 2007).

86. *Sequential Tart*, http://www.sequentialtart.com/archive/sept98/ (accessed November 21, 2001).

87. Kimberly M. De Vries, "A Tart Point of View: Building a Community of Resistance Online," presented at Media in Transition 2: Globalization and Convergence, MIT, Cambridge, MA (May 10–12, 2002).

88. "About Newsarama.com; 100 Sites to Bookmark Now: Our 25 Fave Online Entertainment Sites," *Entertainment Weekly*, June 23, 2006, 38.

89. Todd Allen, *The Economics of Web Comics* (Chicago: Indignant Media, 2007), 33–41.

90. "Selling Comics Online," *Publishers Weekly*, June 25, 2001, 32.

91. Michael Dean, "Hear Him Roar: Rick Veitch on Toon Culture, Living Ideas and Immersive Interactive Virtual Reality," *Comics Journal* 232 (April 2001), http://tcj.com/232/i_veitch.html (accessed April 4, 2002).

92. "About Mars Import," *Mars Import*, http://www.marsimport.com/about.php (accessed May 2, 2008).

93. Steve Grant, "The Enemy of the Better," *Comics Journal* 275 (April 2006): 170.

94. "Comics Publishers Cautiously Going Online," *Associated Press*, November 14, 2007.

95. "The Year's Top Stories, #1: The Sleeping Giants," *Webcomics* (December 7, 2007), http://webcomics.com/full_blog_story.php?id=92 (accessed December 10, 2007).

96. "Comics Shows Marvelous Colors in Online Archive," *USA Today*, November 13, 2007, L1.

97. "Web Comics with Ads on ComicMix," *Publishers Weekly*, October 1, 2007, 9.

98. *Zudacomic.com*, http://www.zudacomics.com/rights_agreement (accessed December 9, 2007).

99. T. Campbell, *A History of Webcomics* (San Antonio, TX: Antarctic Press, 2006), 29–35.

100. Gary Groth, "The Change Has Already Begun: Scott McCloud on the Digital Future of Comics," *Comics Journal* 188 (July 1996): 82.

101. McCloud, *Reinventing Comics*, 149, 223, 235–236.

102. Joe Zabel, "The Future of Webcomics: A Webcomic Examiner Roundtable," *Webcomics Examiner* (December 13, 2004), http://webcomicsreview.com/examiner/issue041213/future.html (accessed December 7, 2007).

103. Campbell, *A History of Webcomics*, 115–117.

104. Zabel, "The Future of Webcomics."

105. A large number of these artists became part of the "Modern Tales Family"—a set of Web sites created by Joey Manley to support artists in this movement. He first started with the alternative host-site *Modern Tales* in 2002. Manley later spun off other host-sites for more pulp long-form webcomics. *Girlamatic* (2003) focused on webcomics

for a female readership; while *Graphic Smash* (2005) focused on bringing action-comics to the long-form webcomic.

106. The first successful long-running open host-site was *Keenspace*, which launched in 2000. The successful host-site *Webcomics Nation* launched in 2005.

107. See *onlinecomics.net* (2001) and *thewebcomiclist* (2005).

108. Webcomic collectives include *Altbrand Studios* (2000), *The Nice* (2001), *Dayfree Press* (2001), *PV Comics* (2005), and *Dumbella* (2005). Campbell, *A History of Webcomics*, 61–75.

109. At the end of 2007, for example, *Webcomics Nation* had around fifty-four hundred webcomics, *onlinecomics.net* had around sixty-nine hundred, *Drunk Duck* had around seven thousand, *Comics Genesis* had around ninety-four hundred, and *thewebcomiclist* had around 10,200.

110. Heidi MacDonald, "Web Comics: Page Clickers to Page Turners," *Publishers Weekly*, December 19, 2005, 24–28.

111. Zabel, "The Future of Webcomics."

112. Shyon Baumann, *Hollywood Highbrow: From Entertainment to Art* (Princeton, NJ: Princeton University Press, 2007), 1–20.

113. Ibid.

CONCLUSION

1. Jon B. Cooke, "Blithe Spirit," *Comic Book Artist* 2, no. 6 (November 2005): 5.

2. Jon B. Cooke, "Will Eisner: The Creative Life of a Master," *Comic Book Artists* 2, no. 6 (November 2005): 46–47.

3. "Alan Moore," *Wizard* 195 (January 2008): 20.

4. Herbert Gans, *Popular Culture and High Culture: An Evaluation of Taste* (New York: Basic Books, 1974); Pierre Bourdieu, *Distinction: A Social Critique of the Judgement of Taste* (Cambridge: Harvard University Press, 1984).

5. Derek Johnson, "Fantagonism: Factions, Institutions, and Constitutive Hegemonies of Fandom" in *Fandom: Identities and Communities in a Mediated World*, ed. J. Gray, C. Sandvoss, and C. L. Harrington (New York: New York University Press, 2007), 285–300.

6. Bacon-Smith, *Science Fiction Culture*.

7. Pierre Bourdieu, *The Field of Cultural Production* (New York: Columbia University Press, 1993); Bourdieu, *Distinction;* Bourdieu, *The Rules of Art.*

8. Bourdieu, *Photography*, 95–98.

9. "A Literary Award for Stephen King," *New York Times*, September 15, 2003, E1; "At Book Awards, Culture High and Low," *Washington Post*, November 20, 2003, C01; "King Gets Award, Issues a Challenge to Literary Elitism," *USA Today,* November 20, 2003, 8A.

10. Shyon Baumann, *Hollywood Highbrow.*

11. Heidi MacDonald, "Are We Winning the War? Comics Hit the Big Time," *Comics Buyer's Guide* 1599 (December 2004): 46.

12. "Pow! Move Over Superheroes! Comic Book Readers Want Something New, and They're Getting It," *St. Louis Post-Dispatch*, May 26, 1994, 1G.

Index